ETHNIC REALITIES

BY THE SAME AUTHOR
The Bridges of God
How Churches Grow
Understanding Church Growth
The Clash of Christianity and Cultures

DONALD A. McGAVRAN

ETHNIC REALITIES

and the Church

Lessons From India

William Carey Library

533 HERMOSA STREET • SOUTH PASADENA, CALIFORNIA 91030

International Standard Book Number 0-87808-168-2
Library of Congress Catalog Card Number 78-11517

Published by William Carey Library
1705 N. Sierra Bonita Avenue
Pasadena, CA 91104, USA
Telephone (626)798-0819
Print On Demand Edition 2000
PRINTED IN THE UNITED STATES OF AMERICA

This book is dedicated to
Mary Elizabeth McGavran,
comrade and consolation
in the gathering gloom and the brightening day,
fellow missionary of the Gospel and
fellow pilgrim to Zion,
whose goodness has enfolded so many —
including me.

ABOUT THE AUTHOR

Donald McGavran has served as a missionary to India for thirty-six years under the United Christian Missionary Society. He has taught missions in the United States since 1957 and was the founding dean of the School of World Mission and Institute of Church Growth of Fuller Theological Seminary in Pasadena, California. Dr. McGavran has a B.D. from Yale Divinity School and a Ph.D. from Teachers College, Columbia University. He is the father of the Church Growth Movement.

His teaching, amassing evidence from every continent, that world evangelization stands at midday, not sunset, has been influential in many circles. He insists that, since at least three billion have yet to believe, Christian Mission must continue strong and vigorous, a duty and privilege of every denomination and congregation in every land. *Bridges of God, How Churches Grow, Understanding Church Growth, The Clash of Christianity and Cultures,* and regional books on the growth of churches in the Philippines, Mexico, Jamaica, North America and other lands have widely affected missiological thinking.

Perhaps more than anyone else he has explored and stated the case for encouraging ethnic diversity within the over-arching theological unity of the Christian Church. This present volume is an extended argument that ethnic realities have always conditioned particular Churches and rightly continue to do so — provided only that the biblical and theological foundations of brotherhood are maintained intact. This means that Christians openly accept that all men are sons of Adam and hence brothers; and that all Christians are equally sinners redeemed by grace through faith in Jesus Christ and hence have equal status before the Throne.

CONTENTS

Table, Maps and Charts

The normal man is not an isolated unit, but part of a whole which makes him what he is . . . Society either determines or strongly influences every aspect of what he says, thinks, and does. Consequently when we comprehend the social structure of a particular segment of the total population, we know better how churches are likely to increase and ramify through it.

Understanding Church Growth, page 183

PREFACE

ON ALL SIX continents and in every country of the earth, ecclesiastical and theological understandings have dominated the church scene. Churches are described by their denominational character. This one is Baptist, that Roman Catholic. Or the Church is declared to be the Body of Christ, a society of the redeemed, a pilgrim congregation, or a sacramental fellowship. Such conceptions are, of course, true and express legitimate ways of thinking about the Church in any land. It certainly is all these things.

However, it also involves other elements which are most important for understanding its spread on new ground. Ethnic realities are concerned. The Church is made up of persons who are invariably part of some social order. They speak particular languages. They belong to certain races, castes, tribes, and other segments of society. They have distinctive cultures. Their part of the human race practices subsistence agriculture, slash-and-burn, or mechanized farming. When new congregations are being formed in a dominantly non-Christian population, members have particular and often widely differing relationships with those who have not become Christian. Christians may be fiercely persecuted or effectively ostracized. Frequently converts to the Christian faith come one by one into the Church, severing their relation to the social matrix from which they have sprung. Sometimes they come maintaining their former relationships intact; perhaps they are cordially regarded as showing others a better way of life.

Sociological/anthropological situations are exceedingly important if we are to comprehend the ability of congregations and denominations to flourish on new ground, reproduce themselves, communicate the Christian faith, and influence their nation. *It is desirable therefore to understand the Church as it advances into new areas along the lines also of these sociological/anthropological characteristics.* They add a depth of comprehension which remains hidden if we employ only ecclesiastical or theological frames of reference.

This book attempts to see the Church in the light of the relation of its members, its congregations and denominations, to the social structures of the country. But, while the Church on the vast Indian subcontinent is being thus described and categorized, I hope the reader may be observing the method and applying it to Churches on his own continent and in his own land. The Church in India will be seen to exist in nine clearly discernible types. Every congregation in India belongs to one of them. Each denomination is made up of so many congregations of — say — Type 2, Type 5, and Type 9. Some are made up entirely of Type 3 congregations, others entirely of Type 1.

We shall see also that each type — depending on its relation to the unconverted segments of society, and especially to the unconverted in the particular segment from which those Christians have come — has its own growth potential, encounters its peculiar obstacles, and faces its particular opportunities. Thus we must not imagine that Type 1 congregations can grow in the same way as Type 3 and Type 4. Type 1 *can* spread the faith, but in ways which suit it. If it attempts to follow methods suited only to other types, it will fail, no matter how ardently it tries.

Similarly, *Churches in every land may be described in terms of the socioeconomic realities in which they are immersed and of which they are parts.* For example, Assemblies of God congregations in São Paulo, Brazil, composed of northeasterners who have migrated to the south in search of work, grow enormously from the repeated waves of immigration from the northeast. But Methodist congregations made up of educated third- and fourth-generation Christians who hold good jobs are not and probably cannot be greatly increased by northeasterners flooding into southern cities. To use a different illustration, Quechua Indians in Ecuador who join Protestant congregations made up of mestizos and rapidly become, so to speak, mestizoized, are ineffective in spreading the Gospel to solidly Quechua villages. But Protestant congregations *made up wholly of Quechua Indians,* who worship and pray and read the Bible in Quechua and maintain cordial relationships with their yet unconverted fellow villagers, have high ability to communicate the Gospel. They are rooted in purely Quechua villages and spread the biblical faith there with great effectiveness. The Protestant Quechua congregations in Chimborazo Province grew from a few hundred members to over 15,000 in less than ten years.

In every land we have congregations not only of different denominations, but of different social structure and differing degrees of tolerance or ostracism — different relationships *to* and degrees of acceptance *by* the "yet to believe." In the present volume we shall explore this new perspective in understanding the Church. I trust it may be useful to Christians both in India and in other countries of the world.

Hundreds of authors have described the ecclesiological and theological factors that help to produce growth. Their usefulness and power are beyond question. Since, however, growth is frequently slowed or stopped in the midst of great opportunity because of ethnicity and other sociological factors, I have thought it important to concentrate some attention on these, in a setting where they can be both broadly and coherently examined in relation to the society and also to each other. *Ethnic Realities and The Church: Lessons From India* will, therefore consider the 16-million-member Indian Church, noting its spread in the various provinces and its relation to the tribes and castes from which it has derived, as well as to those with which it has had no connection. I hope that readers may thereby obtain a vivid sense of the social reality we call the Church, paying particular attention to the delicate and subtle relationship of new Christians to their non-Christian relatives, which is of such great importance for the spread of the faith.

As men and women from other lands and from India too read this book, they will, I trust, find their understanding of the social structures surrounding their particular congregations deepened, and will themselves discover the ways in which they really can or cannot multiply churches. No one wants to try to propagate the Gospel through means not blessed by God. We all want to use ways which God has blessed to the growth of His Church and apparently wants us to use.

Donald Anderson McGavran

School of Missions
Pasadena, California, U.S.A.
September, 1978

Terminology and References

IN THE INTERESTS of clarity rather than in defense of any one ecclesiology, in this book I shall use the following four words to describe the flesh-and-blood companies of Christians.

Church with a capital *C:* the Church Universal, or a particular denomination, or the Church in general or in a given district.

church with a small *c:* a local congregation, or as an adjective as in "church union."

congregation: a local church, a worshiping group of Christians.

denomination: a cluster of congregations, generally with an agreed body of doctrine, polity, or an ethnic unity. They act together and regard themselves as one branch of the Church. Denomination is a synonym for Church. The Church of North India, for example, may be called a denomination. So may the Council of Baptist Churches in North East India.

These four words are used in an attempt to treat all Churches (or denominations) fairly. In Chapter 8, "The Great Conglomerates," I shall be speaking of eight great denominations in India. It would be highly prejudicial to call some of them "Churches" and others "denominations," so the two words are

5

used interchangeably. The Evangelical Lutheran Church of Andhra is both a Church and a denomination. The Mar Thoma Church may with equal propriety be called the Mar Thoma Denomination. "Ten urban churches" may also be referred to as "ten urban congregations." The sentence, "Every Christian feels a sense of denominational loyalty," can be equally well rendered with the term "church loyalty."

In similar fashion I have accepted the fact that various denominations call their constituent parts by different names, not assuming that any one set of names is more correct than others. A bishop in one denomination may be called an executive secretary in another and a ruling elder in a third. A small administrative committee may be called a presbytery or the executive council. The terminology of the Syrian Orthodox is right for it, and that of the Federation of Lutheran Churches right for it. Conventions, synods, districts, assemblies, presbyteries, annual conferences — all are equally acceptable forms.

In regard to terminology, however, two qualifications must be borne in mind:

1. Biblical terms have great value for unity and universality. The Bible is not a European book. It was written mostly in western Asia, and Christians believe that it was given by God for all mankind. Its terms have value for Churches in all cultures.

2. Some current names are merely European and reflect, not the Bible, but European culture. They are an inheritance from one continent. Such names are therefore transitional. In the region we are exploring, they will in time surely be replaced by the truly Indian names which the rich cultural heritage of this continent is abundantly able to provide. Robin Boyd has written a provocative book called *India and the Latin Captivity of the Church,* in which he argues that the philosophical terms common in Hindu thought ought to be used in Christian theology. Whatever one may think of this idea, it is high time that Greek/Latin organizational words such as *synod* be replaced in North India by Sanskrit/Hindi terms such as *mahasabha.* Till such indigenization takes place, it would appear to be the part of wisdom to accept

whatever European terms are in use at present. The Indian
words will gradually take their place.

Sociological terms also require some explanation. One cannot
talk about society in any country without explicit mention of the
sociological components of its population. In the United States,
for example, out of a population of 220 million, 25 million are
African Americans and an equal number Americans of Spanish
name. Indeed, there are over fifty blocks of ethnic Americans, a
few larger, most smaller than these. America is not a melting pot
in which all metals are speedily reduced to a single
comprehensive alloy. Rather, what used to be called the New
World is a curry in which potatoes are still potatoes and chunks of
meat are still meat. Ethnic, linguistic, economic, and occupational
homogeneous units in every land are what make up the total
population. India is no exception to the rule.

People from many races and ethnic groups have poured into
India: Dravidian, Aryan, Mongolian, Arab, Persian, Portuguese,
English, and others. There are over three thousand ethnic units
of various kinds. Each is very largely endogamous: that is, marries
within itself and thus holds itself separate from all the others, or
tries to. Each has a high consciousness of being itself. Narmadiya
Brahmans know they are not Kankubj Brahmans, and vice versa.
Nadars know they are not Nairs, Khasis never imagine that they
are Jamatias.

Each major division of Hindu society — Brahman, Kshatriya,
Vaishya, Shudra, and Scheduled Castes — is in fact composed of
many castes and subcastes.

The Church grows among these more than three thousand
ethnic units: *jatiyan* in Hindi. But how is one to refer to these
social realities? In modern India, particularly among Christians,
the word *caste* for instance is distasteful. The government plays
down caste, which smacks of racism and introduces various
complications. In popular usage it has been largely replaced by
"community." In polite society one never asks "What is his caste?"
but rather "What is his community?" — or better, "What is his
background?" Caste is a dirty word.

In view of that stigma, I have at times substituted for caste such terms as "community," "natural social grouping," or "background." However, speaking in the unavoidable language of anthropologists, sociologists, and census takers, I generally use the word caste, but without any pejorative meaning. It simply denotes a common reality, which in all the great languages of India (Hindi, Tamil, Telegu, Marathi, and others) is openly referred to: a common cultural component of the Indian scene.

The reader will note that in this book figures are substituted for the term *billion* referring to population, because of the discrepancy between American and English usage, the United Kingdom meaning of the word being what Americans would call a *trillion*. And those familiar with my earlier writings will recognize the condensed coinage of such terms as *Eurican* and *Latfricasian*. Their meaning seems clear, and it is hoped that the reader will regard sympathetically the verbal dilemma that gave rise to them, to avoid cumbersome, sometimes repetitious locutions for which no single word exists.

Extract and other references are keyed by author, title, and date in text to the brief Bibliography following the Appendices, where the usual publishing date will be found.

INTRODUCTION

INTRODUCTION

The Church in India, its Matrix, Denominations, Distribution, Particularities, and Types

CHURCH GROWTH begins in and is required by Christian *theology*. God wants the Church to grow. He wants His lost children found. But the structures of the Church and its modes of growth are heavily conditioned by *sociology*. Sociological factors affect it. The Church always grows in a society. Its denominations and congregations, forms of worship and learning, its opportunities to grow, and the obstacles to its growth are conditioned by the innumerable soils in which it develops. Society is a vast mosaic with many languages, many races, many classes, many cultures. The Church takes on a different form, is established and matures in a different way, in each of the numerous pieces of the mosaic. The ethnicity of each piece affects the structure and spread of the Church.

This book illustrates this universal principle from India. India clearly sets forth how congregations and denominations — arising in different segments of the general population — came to be very different organisms with different structures and growth potentials. India demonstrates the principle in many different ways. The reader from Nigeria, it may be, or Taiwan, or Roumania — the principle applies in all lands though in varying degrees — will discover in the structure and growth of churches in India clues concerning churches in his own land.

I turn to an exposition of the Church in India, trusting that readers outside and inside India will both profit. Those outside will find fruitful keys to the types and structures, growth patterns and potentials of the congregations and denominations of their own lands. Those inside India will recognize how the tremendous complexity of society in the federations of nations, languages, customs and cultures which is Great India affects the growth of the churches there.

I shall describe and discuss the Church in India — understanding the Church in India is my theme; but every now and then I shall throw in a phrase or a sentence to remind readers that I am setting forth a global principle: how ethnicity affects the structure and spread of congregations and denominations in every land.

A great Church of more than 16 million Christians in 1976, which will be at least 18 million by 1981, has grown up in India very largely during the last hundred and fifty years. Almost every Indian state now has thousands of Christians in it. Some have hundreds of thousands. Christians play a part in the government of this mighty nation. Christian ideals are openly espoused by many of its leaders, and indeed often set forth as those which India herself has stood for throughout the ages. The Constitution of India declares that country to be a secular state defending equally all its various religions and guaranteeing to each the right to profess, practise and propagate its own faith. Christianity has entered into the warp and woof of Indian thinking, regarded sometimes cordially, sometimes critically by non-Christians. This is the great Church we now seek to understand at closer range. Such understanding will help us be more effective advocates of the Gospel — no matter in what land we work.

RELATION TO TIGHTLY
STRUCTURED ETHNIC SOCIETIES

The relation of individual Christians and the congregations they form to the society in which they live is a factor of considerable weight in the growth of the Church and the spread of the saving Gospel of God. How does the society perceive the Christian? How does the Christian perceive the society? What does it mean to "become a Christian" vis-a-vis the social structure of the general public, and especially the homogeneous unit from which men and women are being invited to join the Christian faith? Contextualization is much talked about these days, as indigenization was a few years ago. The temptation is to think about contextualization or indigenization a) in superficial exterior ways (contextualization means using drums in worship, entering the church barefoot, or dancing in the church) and b) in merely theological ways (contextualization means avoiding Greek concepts like omniscience and speaking of God in ways to which converts have long been accustomed). There is, to be sure, something in each of these ideas of contextualization; but the powerful meaning of contextualization is that which has to do with the new Christians's relationship to his people, his tribe, his caste, his *ethnos*. *That* is his life. His society very largely formed him, and gave him the language he speaks and the value system he holds, and the customs which feel good to him.

The new Christian society — the congregation — flourishes best when it thinks of itself as still a part of the old society. The converted Christian Jews at Pentecost thought of themselves as fulfilled *Jews:* Jews who had found the Messiah, Jews who still went to the temple, Jews who still married Jews. And the non-Christian Jews still thought of them as *our people.* Paul repeatedly claimed that he was still a Jew, "a Hebrew born of Hebrews, as to the law a Pharisee, as to zeal a persecutor of the church, as to righteousness under the law blameless" (Phil. 3:5).

Yet, of course, in regard to certain matters, the Christian and the congregation must think of itself as a new creation, which has repented of its sins and walks in the light. It must do this while speaking the old language, living in ancestral houses, earning its living in accustomed ways, and being thoroughly a part of its culture and its ethnic linkage. Christians must not betray and abandon their ethnic units in becoming Christian. They must not *think of themselves* as doing this, and they *must not seem to others to have done this.*

At its deepest and most powerful level, contextualization means that Christians continue to be part of their social context, while at the same time being part of the new creation. This is not impossible, but it is difficult. A tremendous amount of slow church growth is caused by the move to Christian Faith being viewed *by convert and his people alike* as a traitorous abandonment of family and people. Whether that is what it is or not is not important. If it even looks that way, the Church will grow only slowly.

The *structure* out of which conversion to Christ takes place is of enormous importance. Does the convert leave it altogether, or remain — in some measure at least — a part of it? Are Christians those who renounce their own hereditary societies? Or do they stay in their own societies and there walk the path of discipleship to the Lord? Is each society a loose, atomistic crowd like that in a Western city, or a tight organism in which everyone has a place and no one moves unless all move? Is there freedom of religion, or is the whole weight of the state arrayed against any departure from the presently existing faith, whether that be animism, Hinduism, Marxism, or Roman Catholicism?

Any understanding of the Church in India, where the caste system is still influential and all congregations and denominations must speak to a public heavily conditioned by caste, requires careful attention to *the relation of Christians to caste society.* Other factors, of course, must be taken into account; but we are here concerned to develop a typology of the Church in India which focuses on this one vital and greatly neglected aspect of the spread of the Gospel and the health of the Church.

S. Vasantha Kumar of Bangalore, in the January, 1976, issue of the *International Review of Missions,* says,

In our diocese in Bangalore we conducted a survey on the growth of the Christian community. We found out that the growth is entirely due to children born to Christian parents and to the influx of Christians coming to the city from other places. This is so in spite of the fact that the diocese is involved in evangelistic work and many voluntary organizations are committed to the spreading of the Gospel. This example should motivate us to think about where exactly we are at fault. We must reconsider the methods we use. This also means listening to people of other faiths and to unbelievers. *We need training to see the image we create in the eyes of others.* . . . [italics supplied] (p. 112)

One can only agree and point out that the relationship of the Christian to tightly structured ethnic societies is a fact of enormous importance, and that ethnic societies are found in many, if not most, lands.

LEADERS, INSTITUTIONS, AND BUILDINGS
OF THE CHURCH IN INDIA

The Church in India has hundreds of executive secretaries of various regions (called bishops, district superintendents, moderators, regional evangelists, and chairmen), and more than a hundred thousand pastors, elders, village leaders, workers, catechists, and the like. If to these are added the lay leaders of the churches — elders, deacons, Sunday-school teachers, business managers, and the like — and it is realized that all leaders, lay and ordained, are educated, able men and women, it will readily be seen that the Church in India is indeed a great Church.

Largely by virtue of its founding missions, it is distinguished by a considerable body of institutions: schools, hospitals, dispensaries, colleges, medical training schools, vocational schools, leprosy homes, business offices, printing presses, magazines; organizations for preparing radio broadcasts in India for transmission to stations outside the country, whence they are beamed back to India; theological training schools and seminaries, institutes of social and religious research, provincial and national Christian councils, and denominational headquarters of all varieties. The land and properties involved run into hundreds of millions of rupees, dollars, and pounds.

In the seventies one of the most crucial issues is the scaling down of the institutional presence to one which the Church in India itself can maintain. Should such reductions be carried out or not? Is there danger that India will ban all monies from abroad, or is this a baseless fear? Do the institutions furnish a service to India as well as to the Christian community? Is such service one of the most valuable gifts the world Church can give? Or is it essential for the Church in India to strip down rapidly to the institutional burden she can carry unassisted? However these questions may be answered, they bear testimony to a tremendous institutional presence which is part of the Church in India.

This Church is marked by its buildings. During the last hundred years (and with the Syrian and Roman Churches, for centuries before that) the Church in India has erected numerous places of worship. Some have been cathedrals; some, imposing buildings used by the British regiments stationed in India; many have been humble sanctuaries. All urban churches were constructed of brick or stone, laid in lime and intended to last for decades if not centuries. As one travels through Kerala and sees the permanent buildings of the Roman Catholic and Syrian Churches, he realizes that church buildings are an ineradicable part of India. In practically all district headquarters and cities, and many major towns, well-built churches on public thoroughfares, surrounded by spacious grounds, often walled, are a common sight.

In village India, churches are of two kinds. The first buildings erected are usually of temporary materials — mud brick or wattle with light roofs, sometimes of thatch, sometimes country tile. Second generation buildings are of brick or perhaps stone, with permanent roofs and well-made doors and windows. Those few sections of the land through which a people movement to Christ has run have little churches in most of the villages. In by far the greater part of the country, however, once out of the towns and cities, one finds very few if any church buildings.

Added to the places of worship and their adjacent parsonages are the numerous and often impressive buildings in which Christian institutions are housed, and the bungalows in which the missionaries used to live. These are less and less occupied by missionaries and have become residences of noted leaders of the Indian Church, district headquarters, denominational offices, and the like.

The burden of keeping up the buildings and paying taxes on the land on which they stand is heavy. As a result, in places in India where the Church is small and weak, buildings are often in poor condition. Whether the Church in these areas will be able to keep them all is an open question. Quite likely some will be sold, and gradually the amount of building which the Church in a given place can keep up will be established by trial and error. How to maintain the physical presence and the base which an actively evangelizing Church needs, while the actual Church there is small and weak, is one of the perplexing questions facing the Christian enterprise in India today. The cordial cooperation between the Indian Church and the missions from abroad, which would easily make such a base possible, often meets with opposition, deriving from national aspiration which regards any dependence on foreign resources as demeaning and is apparently willing not to evangelize unless it can be done on 100 percent Indian resources.

In parts of North East and South India the Church is strong. The last thirty years have seen considerable additional building and an added number of new institutions. Much of this has been done through Indian resources. However, even in these two areas, evangelism among non-Christians is weak and sparse.

THE MATRIX — THE CASTE SYSTEM

The Church in India is rising in a thousand places in intensely caste conscious societies and is colored by caste. Yet we read that in Christ "there is neither Jew nor Greek, there is neither slave

nor free, there is neither male nor female, for you are all one in
Christ Jesus" (Galatians 3:28). How greatly ought caste conscious
society to influence the true Church as it expands? How greatly
can the Church influence society? What impact on society does
the Church have and ought it to have? A small part of its impact is
exerted by avant guarde thinkers who seek Christian solutions to
the complex problems facing society heavily influenced by caste.
The battles against caste and for brotherhood, against economic
imbalance and for equal opportunity for all, are fierce. Many
modern thinkers appear to favor some form of socialism,
including Marxism; but the fluid situation changes so rapidly that
the outcome is hard to predict. With the shift in many developing
nations to tighter political controls, it is not clear what Christian
action is possible. It is easy enough to fulminate against racism in
South Africa or in the United States, but much more difficult to
know what should be done with the caste system which is the
matrix out of which the Church grows. For example, what should
Christians do in regard to the rising economic power of the upper
castes — the real rulers of India — often exercised in subtle ways?
It is by no means certain that a government directed by privileged
men and women, whether socialist or other, will insure enonomic
justice. Or again, what should Christians do in regard to
discriminations based on caste, which harass the victims of the
social order?

Though men and women of the many castes now work, study,
and travel — and on occasion even eat — together, caste is still a
major factor in India. There are more than 3000 endogamous
ethnic units in India — castes and tribes. Each has a high
consciousness of being a separate people. Since castes far
outnumber tribes, the word 'caste' is often used to denote ethnic
consciousness or ethnicity — whether of caste or tribe.

The eminent Indian anthropologist, M.N. Shrinivas, says in his
Caste in Modern India (1962)

> Caste is even today an institution of great strength and, as
> marriage and dining are forbidden with members of other

castes, the members of a caste living in a village have many important ties with fellow caste men living in neighbouring villages. These ties are so powerful that a few anthropologists have been led into asserting that the unity of the village is a myth and the only thing which counts is caste. . . . Caste is an institution of prodigious strength and is pervasive. . . . In many spheres the strength of caste has increased in the last few decades and bitterness between castes is a prominent feature of our urban life. (pp. 6,9)

Others, affirming the values of caste, say it should be "reformed, not rooted out" (Majundar and Madan, *Introduction to Social Anthropology*, 1976:238).

For the most part, the Church in India takes the position that caste is an evil and the Church lives above it, combatting it on every hand, looking forward to a casteless nation. Whether this is the correct and only Christian position is one of the crucial issues facing the Church.

It is essential to recognize that caste is perceived differently by Christians in different parts of India. (So are ethnic and class differences in all continents and all nations.) In North India those who read this book will feel that India is not nearly as caste conscious as I have portrayed her. They will insist that the Church is almost free of caste prejudice. They will be irritated at my "misrepresentation" of the situation. Some have written me saying, "We Christians have very little caste feeling, and while the Hindus do have some, it too is rapidly diminishing. You are describing the India that existed a hundred years ago — not today." In short, *North India readers will blame me for overplaying caste.*

In South India, however, through the ages caste has assumed a much more cruel aspect. It was not modified by centuries of Moslem rule and the reform movements of Kabir, the Sikhs, and others. Furthermore, the great movements into Christianity from the oppressed castes took place largely in the South. The Syrian Christians, who are still very caste conscious (see Appendix B), influenced what Christians thought was proper to do. It was in

South India that — until the early 1800s — upper caste Christians in Protestant congregations were seated separately from Christians of the masses and served communion first.

Even today caste feeling among Christians is vivid — often much too vivid. Bishop Stephen Neill writes in 1978,

> While Christians will eat together at large gatherings, especially if the food has been prepared by a Brahman, it is the rarest thing for a higher caste Christian to invite a lower caste brother to his house or to eat with him individually at a family gathering.
> The attitude of Hindu society has to be taken into account. If a Nadar Christian working as a teacher in a mainly Hindu village is known to have invited a low caste Christian into his house to eat, or even has eaten food prepared by a low caste Christian, he will at once be excommunicated by the village; his wife will not be able to draw water from the village well, the barber and the washerman will not come to his house, and he will not be able to buy in the village shop.

South Indian readers are likely to feel that there is much more caste in the Church than I have indicated. Since many South Indian leaders and missionaries burn with desire to bring more brotherhood into the Church, *South Indian readers will probably blame me for underplaying caste.*

Having lived for seventeen years in villages and towns where, because Mrs. McGavran and I ate in the homes of our Christian friends of the Satnami caste and they ate in ours, the town *dhobi* (washerman) and the town *nai* (barber) would not serve us, I hear clearly what Bishop Neill is saying. Yet because I am writing of the Church in all India, I must paint the big picture; and because India is changing rapidly, I must paint the contemporary picture. What then do I say to these friends in North and South India?

To those in North India I say, "Caste is really much more powerful in almost all parts of India than you like to think. You are probably influenced more by it than you realize. You experience the very weak ethnicity of your multiethnic churches, which Chapter 2 will describe; but remember that India has many monoethnic congregations and clusters of congregations. In *them* caste feeling is powerful."

To those in South India I say, "The intense consciousness of caste for which South India is famous has affected, is affecting, and will affect Christian communities in your land. It will be particularly potent in those congregations which have moved to Christian faith in a people movement. This is true. Yet you must remember that there are tens of thousands of multiethnic congregations in other parts of India in which caste feeling is slight. Indeed, it is regarded as the great enemy. In addition to which the tide in modern India sets away from caste. The World Church constantly works for brotherhood and against considering any race or caste inferior or subordinate. Above all, the Christian Faith and the Bible remind all races and tribes and castes that all are sons of Adam, all alike sinners needing forgiveness, all equally children of God. In short, in the modern world the swing to brotherhood is irreversable. It may take time to achieve what we long for, but its coming is as certain as the sunrise. Be patient. Trust the Holy Spirit."

The theme of this book is that Christianity ought to flow into every ethnic unit. Christ has commanded us to disciple *ta ethne* — the ethnic units of the world. As Christianity flows into each unit in all six continents, it takes on much of its color. It becomes indigenous to that unit — that class, or caste, or tribe. After it has flowed in and a substantial part of the unit has been churched, the Christians, led by Christ their Lord and guided by the Bible which they have accepted as their sole Scripture, purify, and beautify and transform such elements of that culture as they themselves perceive need to be transformed.

In the beginning, of course, those who lead them to Christ accept them on condition that they renounce such cruelties, immoralities, and idolatries as are clearly forbidden by the Bible. Fijian cannibals when they turned in great numbers to the Lord, did *not* become man-eating Christians, and then as they perceived cannibalism wrong, renounce it. Rather, they repented of eating human flesh and *then* were baptized. To insist on this was the plain duty of the missionaries who brought the message of salvation to them. The task is to disciple the castes and tribes. In Hindi, Matthew 28:19 reads, *"Sab jatiyon ko chela karo." Jati* is the Hindi word for caste.

Chapter by chapter this theme will unfold. Just because the issues are grave, I beg readers to be patient and follow the argument to the end. Both North India and South India might remember that conditions do differ in different parts of Great India. Let both read the whole book, including Appendix B before rendering judgment. I have studied caste consciousness carefully in many parts of India in order to portray the exact situation. Many India leaders from all over this great nation have helped gather the data on which this volume is based. If the picture of the whole seems unreal to those who live in one part of the land, let them remember that there *are* other parts of India. Christians hold varying convictions about caste. The degree to which Christian practice is forced into sub-Christian molds by the powerful pressures of the caste system differs from city to village and from state to state. Tolerance, as well as action, is demanded.

Readers from other lands must not imagine that caste and class distinctions are found only in India. Ethnicity in its broadest sense is the way in which different groups act. Ethnic realities affect church growth everywhere.

Many Denominations*

The Church of Christ is essentially, intentionally, and constitutionally One. The Bible vigorously warns against the error of Christians considering themselves of Apollos, of Cephas, or of Paul. Nevertheless, the Church as it actually appears in the various countries of the world takes the guise of large or small

---

*Appendix A, setting forth the ecclesiological point of view from which this book is written, will be of interest to some readers.

clusters of congregations which bear distinctive names and hold
distinctive doctrines, as: the Lutheran Church, the Mennonite,
the Methodist, the Presbyterian, the Anglican, the Roman
Catholic, and many others. India is no exception to this general
rule. The Church in India appears as a company of Christian
denominations. Nagaland is substantially Baptist; Goa is
substantially Roman Catholic. Mizoram is Presbyterian in the
north and Baptist in the south. Andhra Pradesh's main Churches
in 1945 were Anglican, Methodist, Baptist, Lutheran,
Mennonite, and Roman Catholic.

Missions from many countries have naturally established their
own kind of Church, and thus congregations have arisen with
Swedish, Australian, German, Portuguese, Syrian, English, or
North American ways of doing things. It was the only thing that
could happen. While it is the current fashion to bewail this
multiplicity of denominations, it would seem the better part of
wisdom to thank God that bands of warmhearted Christians from
many denominations did in fact carry on the Christian mission
for decades and did establish devout and liberated congregations
and denominations.

These have substantial unity in their diversity. By
non-Christians, they are all called "Christians": Isai, Masihi,
Krishtyan in the Hindi language. Since most of them interdine,
intermarry, and attend each other's funerals, they appear as one
people despite their denominational differences. Unity in India
consists in *roti, beti, mati* (bread, daughter, earth). In the things
that really matter — interdining, intermarriage, and common
sorrow at the time of death — Christians in India of most
denominations act like *one* community. Furthermore, all
Christians have the same sacred book, observe the same day of
worship, trust in the same Lord for salvation, and appear very
much like each other. The differences of ritual, polity, and creed
can easily be exaggerated.

Visible unity is, however, desirable and is being enhanced by
two movements. First, a spirit of mutual respect and cooperation
between the various denominations marks the current scene. The

unity of the Spirit is notable. Few if any denominations are attacking others. Second, denominations are regrouping themselves into Federations and United Churches. Much of Chapter 8 will be devoted to these.

Since their various denominational differences are not the most prominent division in the Church in India, and these differences have been already more than amply discussed by others, I shall say little in this volume about them. Village churches in Andhra Pradesh or the Sialkot Pasrur districts of Pakistan look very much alike whether Baptist, Lutheran, Methodist, Anglican, or Presbyterian. Conglomerate churches of any denomination in towns are so similar that if an observer does not already know, he has to inquire what denomination they belong to. But people movement congregations in the villages (of any denomination) look, and are, very *unlike* conglomerate congregations (of whatever denomination) in towns and cities.

Moreover, denominational distinctions are not a significant factor in the spread of the faith. Baptist Churches do not propagate the Gospel more effectively than the Roman Catholic or the Anglican. The Mar Thoma denomination is not evangelistically more potent than the Mennonite. The way in which these denominations and congregations have arisen, their sociological and economic standing, the subtle but strong bonds between their members, the degree to which the various ones do or do not enforce endogamy,* the sense of peoplehood within a congregation or denomination, linguistic ties, and cultural patterns — these are significant factors in both the understanding of the Church as it really is and in the spread of the Gospel. Our attention will therefore be focused upon them.

The ordinary typology which arranges denominations by doctrine, polity, founding mission, and ecclesiology is useful. These differences are real. A Roman Catholic congregation is distinguishable from the Friends, and a liturgical denomination

---

*See "Terminology and References," paragraph dealing with caste and endogamy, p. 7.

from a nonliturgical. The doctrines believed, the view taken of the Bible or of apostolic succession, the kind of baptism practised, all are held by great Churches to be matters of substance. Biblical Christians maintain vigorously that certain beliefs are necessary to salvation. While cordially granting the existence and even the weight of these variations, what I wish to affirm here is that the ethnicity of congregations and denominations is a matter of such importance that really to understand the Churches in every land it must be taken fully into account. The typology here proposed sees the Churches in the perspective of their varying degrees of ethnicity. Such a view is essential to effective contextualization.

THE DISTRIBUTION OF THE CHURCH IN INDIA

A Few Dominantly Christian Districts

In North East India, in the hills surrounding the Brahmaputra valley of Assam, several states now have a majority of Christian citizens. Mizoram counts more than 90 percent of its population as Christian; practically all Mizo tribesmen have become Christians. In Nagaland, most of the fourteen Naga tribes have become substantially Christian — 80 percent, 75 percent, 60 percent, 55 percent. In Meghalaya, more than half the Khasis and the Garos are now Christian. In Manipur, the hill tribes — Thankul Nagas, Kukis, Mizos, and others (surrounding the Meitei plain which is still almost entirely animistic Hindu) — are solidly Christian.

In Chhota Nagpur, two hundred miles northwest of Calcutta, the Uraon and Munda tribesmen have become Christian almost to a man, so that the central districts are heavily Christian. The outlying districts where the tribals form a much smaller percentage of the population are still dominantly non-Christian. In both Chhota Nagpur and North East India the Christian faith ran through various tribal populations, winning their adherence to Christ. Since tribals composed the majority of the population, the whole population became dominantly Christian.

In Kerala and the southern tier of Tamil Nadu, some districts are heavily Christian: some 50, some 40, and some 30 percent. But in 1971 Kerala as a whole was only 21 percent Christian and Tamil Nadu only 6 percent.

Some Districts Are 5 to 10 Percent Christian

Here one of two things has happened: (1) A people movement to the Christian faith has occurred in one or two castes. In them, and in them alone, are found Christians in any considerable numbers, comprising a substantial part of the total membership of that caste. For example, Tinnevelly Diocese in the southeast corner of Tamil Nadu is about 11 percent Christian. In Andhra Pradesh, several districts are between 5 and 10 percent Christian. As one journeys through the land he finds church buildings in most *palems* (the Harijan or Untouchable ward just outside the village proper). Christian cemeteries with stone markers bearing crosses and other Christian inscriptions are common. In addition, of course, the central towns, sites of mission stations, have their usual complement of schools, missionary residences, hospitals, and big permanent church buildings.

Or (2) rural Christians have flocked to the cities for work, and coming from far and near, now compose more than 5 percent of a city's population. Bombay, for instance, though not the scene of the discipling of any caste, is almost 7 percent Christian. These are mostly Roman Catholics from Goa who have come up the coast a few hundred miles to live and work in Bombay.

Many Districts Are 1 or 2 Percent Christian

In these typical districts, Christians exist either as urban renters, employed people, laborers, carpenters, teachers, a few lawyers, a few businessmen, and factory workers; or as scattered village groups of one to ten houses of Christians, the remains of an arrested people movement to Christ. The present Christians are the descendants of those few who turned from "the world" to Christ perhaps fifty or a hundred years ago. These small communities tend to be made up of the elderly, since young people migrate to the cities in search of work. The Mahar Christians of east Maharashtra and the Namashudra Christians of Barisal and Jessore districts in Bangladesh are examples.

Where only 1 or 2 percent of the population is Christian, a typical mind-set is observable. In the towns the Christians are confident, unoppressed. Several members of their community have good positions. Christians feel themselves a respectable community, small but distinct and in many ways superior to the general run of non-Christians. In villages, however, where they are still regarded as Harijans, the Christians are subdued. Theirs is, to say the least, not a high position. But compared to the Harijans who did not become Christians years ago, they consider themselves slightly better off. If the church is vigorous and the shepherding good, their morale is high. If not, they tend to be depressed Christians.

In both cases, where the Church is composed of only one or two out of every hundred, it is weak and knows it. Flaming evangelism is not a part of its psychology.

Most Districts in India Have Less Than 0.5 Percent of Christians

Where Christians are only five in a thousand or one in a thousand, or indeed perhaps one in four thousand, the Church is very weak. In central towns where the mission stations were, and a hundred years of missionary labor created a small, solid Christian community, there may be two in a hundred; but out in the district one can easily find populations where not one in ten thousand is Christian. Where outlying Christians are found, they are likely to be in the police force, or teachers in village schools, or health workers, or forest rangers, or part of some other government force. The impact of "the Church" on its environment under such circumstances cannot be great, though occasionally some strong character in a small town has notable influence.

Were a map to be prepared showing every district in India, each being colored according to the following code, one could see the distribution of Christians at a glance.

Percent	Map Color
50 — 80	White
10 — 50	Yellow
5 — 10	Light gray
1 — 2	Dark gray
Less than 1	Black

Most of the map would be black or dark gray; perhaps one percent of the land area would be yellow or white. The map would be more accurate if the population of each subdivision (*tahsil* or *taluq*) could be shown.

The evangelization of India should cease to be glibly talked about, as if it were a task which the Church in India could accomplish without any aid from the world Church. The great Indian Christian Church I have been describing, of more than 16 million souls, containing some of the most articulate and able Christians on earth, would then be seen to be still only 2.6 percent of the total population and *confined to a few castes and tribes*. Among the more than three thousand castes and tribes, only twenty-one have had major movements to Christ. Minor movements in about fifty others have left tiny sealed-off congregations which have very little effect either on their own ethnic communities or the general population.

Distribution Not Only Geographical but Social

Thus — to sum up — in only twenty-one of the more than three thousand ethnic groups of India (castes and tribes) do Christians form any considerable proportion of the total population. In perhaps fifty more, small arrested people movements to Christ have taken place, leaving tiny sealed-off congregations here and there. *In more than 2900 castes and tribes there are practically no Christians at all.* What few converts there have been from any one of these have been forced out of their families and communities and the door locked and barred against normal intercourse. The evangelization of India poses a *missionary* problem in at least 2900 castes, tribes, and subcastes. Near-neighbor evangelism — E-One as I have called it later — cannot establish churches in them. It will take special emissaries of the Cross — *missionaries* — largely Indian, but also Korean, Japanese, European, or American, to establish congregations among them. Contextually sound conversion is required. No conceivable amount of conversion by extraction will liberate these castes. Any converts from them will simply be purged out of the caste fabric, forming their tiny part of the existing conglomerate churches and leaving the 2900 peoples more adamant than ever against the Christian faith.

Census Data

The table on the following page gives some of the census figures on which the foregoing conclusions have been based. As the eye runs down column 5, of percentages, it is immediately apparent that many large populations in India are only very slightly Christian. Uttar Pradesh in 1971 had fifteen Christians to every ten thousand of the population. In Rajasthan there were only twelve in ten thousand. Hariana and Himachal Pradesh had only ten in ten thousand.

Then come states which have ten, eleven, twelve, or fourteen in a thousand: Tripura, Bihar, Punjab, Maharashtra. Bihar divides sharply into the Gangetic plain, in which are less than two in a thousand, and the Chhota Nagpur hills in which some *tahsils* are dominantly Christian.

Third, we note Andhra Pradesh, Assam, and Tamil Nadu with 4 to 6 percent Christian. Here again some districts are heavily Christian and some very slightly. This is especially true in Assam and Tamil Nadu.

Finally come those small parts of India — Goa, Kerala, Meghalaya, Nagaland, and Manipur — which are Christian in numbers running from 21 to over 66 percent. Mizoram, which may be the most Christian of all states, is omitted from this 1971 list, because in 1971 it was still included as a district in Assam. Now it is a separate state.

It is worth noting that the all-India figures at the end show that the percentage of Christians has increased from 2.44 in 1961 to 2.60 in 1971. This general finding is borne out by the percentages

State	Year	Total Population	Percentage Increase in Population	Christian Population	Chinese as Percentage of Total	Percentage of Increase in Chinese Population
Andhra Pradesh	1971	45,932,708	20.00	1,823,434	4.19	27.65
	1961	35,983,447	15.65	1,428,729	3.97	15.91
	1951	31,115,289		1,263,621		
Assam (including Nefa)	1971	14,957,542	34.71	667,151	4.46	35.15
	1961	11,871,772	34.45	764,585	6.44	56.89
	1951	8,830,732		487,331		
Bihar	1971	56,353,369	21.31	658,710	1.17	31.17
	1961	46,455,610	19.77	502,195	1.08	20.85
	1951	38,786,184		415,948		
Gujarat	1971	26,697,475	29.39	109,233	0.41	20.12
	1961	20,633,350	26.88	91,028	0.44	16.61
	1951	16,262,657		78,061	0.43	
Hariana	1971	10,036,808	32.71	9,802	0.10	32.85
Himachal Pradesh	1971	3,460,434	23.04	3,556	0.10	8.61
	1961	2,812,463		3,274	0.12	
Jammu and Kashmir	1971	4,616,632	29.65	7,180	0.16	152.18
	1961	3,560,976	9.44	2,848	0.08	
	1951	3,293,852		(Not available)		
Kerala	1971	21,347,375	26.29	4,494,091	21.05	25.23
	1961	16,903,715	24.76	3,587,365	21.22	26.95
	1951	13,549,118		2,825,720	20.85	
Madhya Pradesh	1971	41,654,119	28.67	286,272	0.69	51.91
	1961	32,372,408	24.17	188,314	0.58	
	1951	26,071,637		81,004	0.51	
Maharashtra	1971	50,412,235	27.45	717,176	1.42	27.93
	1961	39,553,718	23.60	560,594	1.42	29.39
	1951	32,002,564		433,255	1.35	
Meghalaya	1971	1,011,699	31.50	475,267	46.98	75.43
	1961	769,390		270,912	35.21	
Mysore	1971	29,299,014	24.22	613,040	2.09	25.73
	1961	23,586,772	21.57	487,587	3.07	16.52
	1951	19,401,956		418,453	2.16	
Nagaland	1971	516,449	39.88	344,793	66.76	76.29
	1961	369,200	14.97	195,538	52.98	99.44
	1951	212,975		98,068	46.05	
Orissa	1971	21,944,615	25.05	378,888	1.73	88.18
	1961	17,548,846	10.82	201,017	1.15	41.63
	1951	14,645,946		141,934	0.97	
Punjab	1971	13,551,060	21.70	162,202	1.20	
Punjab and Hariana	1961	20,306,812	25.86	149,834	0.74	51.56
	1951	16,134,890		98,853	0.62	
Rajasthan	1971	25,765,806	27.83	30,202	0.12	32.09
	1961	20,153,602	26.20	22,864	0.11	100.19
	1951	15,970,774		11,421	0.07	
Tamil Nadu	1971	41,199,168	22.30	2,367,749	5.75	34.31
	1961	33,616,953	11.85	1,062,954	5.23	23.51
	1951	30,119,047		1,427,382	4.74	
Uttar Pradesh	1971	88,341,144	19.76	131,810	0.15	29.63
	1961	73,746,401	16.66	101,641	0.14	-17.95
	1951	63,219,742		123,896	0.20	
West Bengal	1971	44,312,011	26.87	252,752	0.57	23.09
	1961	34,936,279	32.80	204,530		12.50
	1951	26,299,930		181,779	0.69	
SELECTED UNION TERRITORIES						
Delhi	1971	4,067,698	52.93	43,720	1.03	49.73
	1961	2,653,012	52.44	29,269	1.10	56.64
	1951	1,744,072		18,685	1.09	
Goa, Daman and Diu	1971	857,771	36.88	272,509	31.77	19.94
	1960	626,667	5.14	227,202	30.25	-2.66
	1950	596,055		235,403	39.16	
Manipur	1971	1,072,753	37.53	279,243	26.03	83.66
	1961	780,037	35.14	152,043	19.49	122.30
	1951	577,635		63,394	11.84	
Tripura	1971	1,556,342	36.28	15,713	1.01	56.52
	1961	1,142,215	73.71	10,039	0.88	90.71
	1951	638,839		5,262	0.82	
All India *	1971	547,949,809	24.80	14,223,382	2.60	32.69
	1961	439,301,771	21.51	10,730,086	2.44	27.53
	1951	351,980,860		3,385,958	2.55	

Source: World Vision International Unreached Population Survey

*But note that, according to the 1976 World Population and Data Sheet, published by the Population Reference Bureau Inc., Washington, D.C., the population of India in 1976 was 620 million and rising at 2 percent per annum.

of specific states. Most show a slight increase. Eight show a slight decrease. However, in several cases the decrease comes about (as in Assam) by the separation out into other states of largely Christian sections. The Christian population is holding its own, when the whole of India is considered. In a few localities it is growing vigorously. In a few it is diminishing.

Christian Leaders Often Think of the Church in Inadequate Terms

Much writing and speaking about the Church down the centuries has been done in theological terms. The Church is the Body of Christ, the Household of God, and the Temple of the Holy Spirit. The Church of Jesus Christ is One: in the Church there is neither Jew nor Greek, slave nor free, laborer nor lawyer nor bishop nor commoner. All these affirmations are biblical and true. They tell us what the Church is in God's sight. The ideal Church is like this.

However, the empirical Church, the actual Church, is made up of men and women, sinners on their way to Zion, people who speak Hindi, Tamil, Khasi, English, or other languages. It is made up of flesh-and-blood human beings. The Church has a theological dimension, to be sure; but it also has a sociological structure. Members of one congregation average an annual income of six thousand a year; of another six hundred. The two are equally households of God, but they act in very different ways, dress differently, and support their pastors at quite different levels.

Again, much of the writing and speaking about the Church in India has been along Western lines. The battles fought in the West against racism are imported into India and the same slogans and goals set up there. Cultural carry-over is most noticeable in this regard. Generally speaking, Indian leaders trained in the West who have attended the great councils of the Church held first in one country and then another are particularly subject to

simplistic thinking along Western lines. They conceive of the
Church by means of thought forms they have learned in
European or American seminaries. They speak as if it were
sociologically one, not seeing the enormous complexity that arises
with the different types of Church that really exist in India. The
point of view this volume seeks to set forth, describing the actual
congregations and denominations that have arisen in that land
and indicating the types of action which are both valid and
possible for each, stands in vivid contrast to some of the
inadequate thinking that currently characterizes much of what is
said and written about the Church in India. This same
inadequacy, arising from failure to allow for the high degree to
which ethnicity affects the structure and spread of churches,
marks much thinking about the Church in every land.

The error arises quite naturally. This or that speaker is an
educated man. He associates with educated Christians. He sits
with them in church. The sermons are geared to his mind. He is a
city man. Almost all his associates are city people. Rural Christians
live far away and are not part of his immediate concerns —
though he prays for the whole Church. His teachers in college
and seminary were also urbanites, educated, and out of touch
with the rural churches. He reads Western-oriented books and
magazines and talks continually about the One Church, the
brotherhood of man. If occasionally a picture of other kinds of
churches flashes across his mind, he represses it with some sense
of guilt. The Church ought not to be that way. He states
emphatically that there is no caste in the Church in India. Yet
when he chooses a daughter-in-law he will get one from the right
segment of the Church, and when Christians in his state vote, he
knows that they will vote mainly along caste lines: Nadars for
Nadars and Vellalas for Vellalas. These uncomfortable thoughts,
however, are in the main shoved down below the threshold of
consciousness and denied. As a result, in all six continents
missionaries and nationals alike often harbor and project, a
simplistic picture of the Church as if it were living above caste and

class and pioneering a path to the classless social order of universal brotherhood.

This is a rather false notion, however, of the present-day Churches anywhere. In India churches are of at least nine distinct types, and very complex. What is true of one may be definitely not true of another, since they reflect the enormous variety India presents to the anthropologist and sociologist. For this is not a single homogeneous country, but rather something like what the United States of Europe will be when it finally takes form. India is a vast federation of peoples, speaking fifteen major and over three hundred minor languages and dialects. The greatness of the country is not in its homogeneity but in its diversity, all bound together in one strong nation.

The Churches in each state, and indeed each district, in each of the twenty one castes and tribes where Christianity has become the religion of a substantial part of the population, reflect that diversity and present very different faces to the world. Conglomerate (multiethnic) congregations and denominations are very different from people movement (monoethnic) congregations and denominations. Understanding the Church in India means seeing these variations and working for the welfare of existing Churches, and extending the Church of God within the hundreds of real but differing situations facing Christians on the subcontinent.

Understanding the Church of Christ in India will not come by strictly theological definitions, or by regarding all variations from these as error and heresy; but by realizing that *Churches* in general and of this land in particular *have many different faces, and each is a true face.* It has often been said, for example, that the Church in India is a defeated Church, sitting quietly, not attracting attention to itself, not vigorously evangelizing non-Christians, but quarreling over properties and splitting into numerous factions. *Parti bazi* — to use an Urdu term meaning factional fighting — is said to prevail generally. In some types of Church that affirmation is entirely correct. The phrase describes them well.

The congregations that exist as tiny enclaves of weak Christians — one in a thousand or less — are for the most part sitting quietly. Some have just cause to fear calling attention to themselves, and so withdraw from active evangelization.

But other parts of the Church in India are vigorous, aggressive, spreading the Gospel faithfully, fearlessly talking back to the great in the land, and serving the nation in a splendid way. Both are equally the Church in India, but until they are seen as two distinct types, conversation about the Indian Church will be hopelessly confused. Each constitutes a special problem in nurture and offers a special opportunity for evangelism. Each can serve India, but in very different ways.

Return for a moment to the common assertion that there is no caste among Christians in India. The statement is almost true of the conglomerate denominations and congregations. But of the monoethnic denominations such as the Mar Thoma or the Naga it is quite false. Both of these Churches have a well-developed sense of racial identity (the essence of caste feeling) and mean to keep it.* They do not intend to intermarry with outsiders, and — to use a Eurican euphemism† — they penalize those who do marry "beneath their status." One of my best students here at the School of Missions, a national of great ability who had held high position in his Church in India and who went back to a still higher one, took violent exception to my statement in class that the Church in India was heavily infected with caste feeling. But on his return to India, he suddenly realized that in great stretches of the Church there — to be exact, in four out of the nine types we shall presently explore, and among eight out of ten Christians — caste plays a great part in the thinking of both leaders and followers.

The key to understanding is to recognize the types of Church. Much of the strategy planned for the Church in India, and much of what one hears at international gatherings, sounds as if that

---

*As a Christian leader from India wryly remarked to me, "Race, you know, is what Europeans practice against us. Caste is what we practice against other Indian communities."
†See "Terminology and References," p. 7.

Church were largely urban. The city is where almost all bishops live, where all seminary professors live, where all editors of Christian magazines live, where all great gatherings are held, where conference, synod, and presbytery headquarters are found. The churches are lighted with electricity and cooled with ceiling fans. Well-dressed men and women come to them on bicycles or in rickshaws or cars. Yet probably less than one-fourth of all Christians in India (perhaps 4 million of them) live in towns and cities, while three-quarters live in villages where no seminaries, no colleges, and no hospitals exist, and where the Word of God is still read in the evening by lantern light. The congregations gather on foot and return to homes less than a hundred yards from the church building. Here again the key to understanding is to distinguish the urban from the rural Church; the frequently multiethnic congregations and denominations of the cities from the often monoethnic congregations and denominations of the villages.

THE PARTICULARITY OF EACH CHURCH

As a result of this thinking of the Churches, as if they were all of one stamp, proposals for the good of the Church and the liberation of the lost into Christ often miss the mark. Leaders will suggest what is good for the initial stages of a people movement but not for a mature one. They will advocate what is good for a small conglomerate congregation, but not what a strong conglomerate denomination should be doing. They see action which is desirable for a cluster of small congregations in towns of 50,000, but not what ought to be done by the Christian movement and Christian missions in the huge industrial cities rising in every state.

Leaders are prone to recommend what in their own experience, given a certain set of conditions, has proved practicable and effective. What is advocated is good for a particular unit of the Church — yet not for the whole. For many other units it is not feasible. The suggested action may in fact be a past goal of the Church during the days of British power, or a future goal — something that "ought to" prove effective in the midst of Hindu culture but is so far untried. Under these conditions, therefore, what is advocated may not actually communicate the Gospel in most types of Church. Let us look at four examples.

1. Very large numbers in the Church in India are illiterate; but most programs are developed for literates and indeed for the well educated. Few denominations have yet built the teaching of illiterates to read into their essential activities. Elsewhere *(Understanding Church Growth,* 1970) I have said,

> The open Bible should be made available as an essential part of redemption. Since so many of the masses are illiterate — as they were in Europe and America in 1700 and earlier — this involves teaching Christians to read the Bible as a religious duty, an inalienable part of church life. Making provision for the Lord's Supper is no more sacred a part of Christian activity than making provision for believers to partake of the Lord's Word. Ordinary Christians should teach other Christians to read the Bible. . . . Literacy classes should be in church buildings, closely tied to church programs and built around a sharply worded doctrine which demands Bible reading as a normal Christian duty. (p. 266)

When leaders of the Church in India see clearly the nine types of Church involved and devise a strategy for the health *of each,* they will build teaching illiterates to read the Bible *into the worship services* of at least three of these types.

2. Nine-tenths of all future conversion growth of the Church in India will come by people movements to Christ; but since the congregations and denominations of most *leaders* of the Indian Church are conglomerate and not people movement by nature, these leaders neither know nor teach the monoethnic way of becoming Christian. Indeed, in most seminaries and Bible schools in India people movements are seldom mentioned. The very concept is often disapproved. The one thing that most

conservative evangelical theological training schools stress vigorously is personal holiness and dedication. These are, beyond doubt, excellent qualities. They are necessary in all branches of the Church. Nevertheless, so long as personal holiness and dedication are linked to the one-by-one-against-the-current mode of church growth, the Church in India will continue to limp forward where it could be running. True, the people movement to Christ is not possible in all types of Church. In some, only the one-by-one-against-the-current mode of increase is likely to happen; but the people movement should be taught in all training schools and all literature campaigns, so that when God gives His Church anywhere the precious beginning of such a movement, His obedient servants will recognize it and nurture it in the proper way.

3. Another example may be taken from the urban church field. The great cities south of Nagpur, and some sections of cities in most parts of India, are wide open to evangelism which multiplies congregations in responsive ethnic and linguistic units. But with our limited understanding of the Church in India and our mistaken conviction that it should never plant one-caste congregations, little church multiplication is actually going on. What is occurring is a limited growth of small conglomerate churches which gather existing Christians into new congregations.

4. Finally, one may consider the common impression that Christians are those who have turned to Christ for the material benefits of medicine, education, famine relief, and other rich services which missions have made available during the past hundred and fifty years. The record of Churches and missions in India is one of which they can be proud. They have served India well. They have given largely and generously of knowledge, health, welfare, and development. But the marginal learning which has accompanied this continuous program of "social justice and the alleviation of all that depresses mankind" is a strange distortion of the Gospel. Millions of Indians believe that it is a good thing to become Christian *if* by so doing their children

receive free education, their sick receive free medical attention, and their status in the world is enhanced. If these social benefits are not forthcoming, if all they get is the naked Gospel, then they say, "Why become Christian for nothing?"

This distortion afflicts some types of Church more than others. In some it would be unknown. In others, evangelization must go forward in this climate, in the face of this marginal learning. It is a counsel of desperation to overreact and say, "No more evangelization at all, until the general public has learned that we are not buying Christians." After all, many of the multitudes who followed the Lord Jesus hoped to partake of the loaves and fishes. They expected the Messiah to drive the Romans out. Yet He called them His own. In many homogeneous units, evangelization must go forward trying to counter the distortion and building up congregations whose materialistic expectations are not likely to be fulfilled. In other homogeneous units, evangelization and nurture can go forward in a climate free from that particular kind of smog.

Nine Main Types of Indian Church

I shall present nine types of Church found today in India.* In constructing any such typology there is danger of oversimplification. The reality is far too complex to be fully described in even nine categories. The Church as it arises in the multitudinous homogeneous units of this tremendous subcontinent is conditioned by the characteristics of each. It is dressed in many different costumes. Contextualization is different in each. Each has its own particular economic, social, theological, and ecclesiological life. The Church in Meghalaya or Mizoram, where a true cross section of the entire society has

*Readers from outside India will at once realize that the types of congregations and denominations in many countries have yet to be described. How ethnicity affects the structure and spread of Protestant churches in Chile, for example, has been insufficiently explored and stated.

become Christian, is a very different organism from the Church
in Andhra Pradesh, where 98 persent of its members have come
from cruelly oppressed victims of the Hindu social order.
Conglomerate congregations in Shillong are not like
conglomerates in Ludhiana, and these again differ markedly
from those in Ballia District. Nevertheless, conglomerates have
remarkable similarities. So do the congregations and
denominations belonging to each type. The linguistic,
sociological, and economic characteristics of each are much the
same in every part of India. It is helpful to see that the One
Church is composed of many different kinds of congregations
and denominations. In them one may see clearly the nine types
described below.

These, arising in many different situations, may not provide us
with a wholly adequate typology of the Indian Church, but they
do at least enable us to think fruitfully about the real Churches —
empirical organisms made up of different kinds of men and
women. Each shades off into other kinds. The dividing lines may
be drawn at this or that point. Pundits may debate whether a
given congregation or denomination is of this or that type.
Nevertheless, I believe Christians will find the classification
useful: a key to understanding the Church in India and a clue to
strategies and policies which will be pleasing to God in the coming
evangelization of India's 620 million recorded in 1976. (World
Population and Data Sheet, Population Reference Bureau,
Washington, D.C.)*

This typology was first begun in 1964, when I identified five
basic types of Indian Church. In the early 1970s George Samuel
of Bombay, Amirtharaj Nelson of Madras, and T.C. George of
Bangalore studied with me, identifying the forms of Church they
found in those cities. It became apparent that while the five basic

---

*The basic population figures used in this book are deductions from the fact that
in 1976 India had a population of 620 million. Since 16 million of these were then
Christians, there are about 600 million yet to be evangelized. Since about 100
million are tribal animists or Muslims lightly influenced by Hindu social structure,
there are about 500 million whose culture is heavily conditioned by caste.

types did describe the Church as it arose by conversion of
non-Christians in various parts of India, secondary types were
needed to describe those formed by existing Christians as they
moved to great industrial cities. I have therefore, profiting by the
insights of these Indian scholars, added four secondary types,
making a total of nine types of Indian Church.

Dr. Samuel rightly points out *(Growth Potential of Urban
Churches,* 1973) that congregations and denominations

> are usually known by their denominational titles; but
> sociological similarities are much more significant than
> denominational differences. In visiting congregations, in
> certain cases, due to structural similarities, one has to read
> the title most carefully if he is to identify the denomination.
> Christians as they come to the city, join congregations in
> which they feel at home. Similarly, new converts are
> attracted to the particular congregations in which they can
> share cultural values. They do not see them as Type One or
> Type Five. They look for a church which is linguistically,
> culturally, and ethnically theirs. Since Bombay is a mosaic of
> many cultural, linguistic and ethnic units, churches to serve
> mankind there, and to propagate the Gospel of Christ to the
> urbanites, must see themselves as a great diversity within the
> one great unity — His Body. (p. 76)

I hope future students will use the names that Drs. Samuel,
Nelson, George and I have given to these types. No good purpose
will be served by dreaming up new sets of names. These nine are
adequate.

We may expect, however, that additional types of Indian
Church will be discovered. The types required in the northeast
will be somewhat different from those required in Andhra
Pradesh. This typology is offered, therefore, in the hope that it
will provide a working basis for further and more exact
understanding of the great Church which God is calling forth on
the subcontinent of India. In this volume a chapter giving
definitions and descriptions will be devoted to each of the nine
types. Here they are simply listed for clarity in discussion.

The Five Basic Types

Type 1. *Fully Monoethnic Syrian Churches.* Four large Syrian denominations exist in India: the Orthodox Syrian Church, the Syrian Rite Roman Catholic Church, the Reformed Syrian Church (Mar Thoma), and the St. Thomas Evangelical Church of India.

Type 2. *Fully Conglomerate or Multiethnic Churches*

Type 3. *People Movement or Monoethnic Churches from Caste*

Type 4. *People Movement or Monoethnic Churches from Tribe*

Type 5. *Modified Conglomerate or Multiethnic Churches*

The Four Secondary Types

Type 6. *Urban Conglomerates or Multiethnic Churches*

Type 7. *Urban Monoethnic Churches*

Type 8. *The Great Conglomerates*

Type 9. *The Indigenous Churches*

The first five — three monoethnic and two multiethnic types — are the basic building blocks for the Church in India. It will be seen that our four secondary types can all be listed under one or another of the basic five, being composed of different combinations of them. For instance, "urban English-speaking multiethnic Churches" (a form of Type 6) are essentially either fully conglomerate or modified conglomerate Churches. They are made up of Christians who have moved to the cities from various districts of India. To classify them as Type 6 is simply to emphasize that multiethnics which regroup in cities are somewhat different from multiethnics formed out of non-Christian faiths in small towns. They could be listed as Type 2, but it clarifies our understanding to give them a separate category of their own.

Dr. Samuel points out that Syrian Christians on coming to the great city of Bombay sometimes join Pentecostal or other Malayalam-speaking congregations. These are largely Syrian in makeup but include members from other ethnic units. Intermarriage takes place, and the resulting congregations cannot be classified as fully monoethnic Syrian. They have become modified monoethnic Syrian congregations. As more and more members from other ethnic units join, these city congregations gradually become multiethnic, Malayalam-speaking urban congregations. Theoretically, one might have a Pentecostal congregation made up entirely of Syrian Christians. It could then be classified as fully monoethnic Syrian (Type 1), but since actually Pentecostals do not enforce endogamy within the Syrian community, such congregations tend to become urban multiethnic churches (Type 6).

The United Churches (Type 8) when viewed as single organisms are obviously superconglomerates or multiethnics. They are composed of Christians from many linguistic and ethnic units of society. They are federations of various kinds of monoethnic and multiethnic congregations and denominations. In enhanced size and variety they are so different from the fully conglomerate small-town congregations and denominations which arose at mission stations, that I have not called them Type 2, or Type 6 or 7, but list them here as Type 8, to encourage exact thinking.

The reader, on facing the complexities of five basic and four secondary types of Indian Church may well exclaim that he much prefers to think simply of "Indian Churches." In this, however, he would be making a serious error. A modified monoethnic Syrian congregation in Bombay, which functions in Malayalam, is a unique organism. It is very unlike a fully monoethnic Syrian congregation, and even more unlike a modified multiethnic congregation in Bombay which speaks Marathi. Granting that the student will at first find it difficult to keep clearly in mind these different types, nevertheless, doing just that is essential to accurate and fruitful thinking.

The physician has continually in mind many different kinds of medicine. Only so can he be professionally competent. He would be no physician at all were he to prescribe indiscriminately merely "medicine". We should not be aghast, I think, at the much less complicated and elusive, though complex, task that faces us here as Christians. Particularly when it comes to the kind of evangelism each type of Church can best carry on, in order to expose the vital riches of the Gospel to its neighbors and across barriers to other homogeneous units, it is absolutely essential to have a real understanding of the various types.

This is not a classifying for the sake of classification, but in the belief that each main type of Church should have an effective strategy. In India, we distinguish nine kinds of Church — and in other lands other kinds — in order to be good stewards of the grace of God. Just as different children require different kinds of care — this one a college education, that one more mother's milk — so do different types of Church require varieties of nurture.

Two groups of Christian leaders are deeply concerned about the Church in India:

First come the Indian leaders of the various denominations — Roman Catholic and Protestant, mission-connected and truly indigenous, large and small, wealthy and poor. These leaders are seminary professors, bishops, district superintendents, regional pastors, evangelists at large, principals of Christian colleges, moderators of assemblies, thinkers and authors, and others on whose hearts God has laid the burden of the denominations of this great land.

Second come the executive secretaries of missionary societies in Korea, Japan, the Philippine Islands, India itself, Europe, and the United States and Canada. *These executives and the career missionaries they send out* are deeply concerned with the Church in India. They are giving their lives to planting the Gospel among the 600 million Indians who have yet to believe. The task is enormous. Even when the Churches in India have done all they can, there will still be left hundreds of thousands of villages — and some towns — in which there is no Christian, no Bible, no church, and no opportunity to partake of Holy Communion. Large numbers of missionaries must continue to be sent.

Womack's great book, *Breaking the Stained Glass Barrier* (1973:4) has a passage which will startle both groups of leaders. It reads as follows: "Many Churches and mission boards appear to be satisfied with and willing to settle for a token presence in each country rather than a serious attempt to fulfill the commands of Christ. They rejoice over a few sheaves of gathered grain, while ignoring the massive harvest still standing in the fields." To use a modern metaphor, they are proposing that the Church everywhere is *pars pro toto,* a small part of the whole which in some vague way represents the whole and influences it.

The *pars pro toto* theory of mission intends to settle for a token presence in each country. This mistaken approach cannot prepare the Church to carry out its biblical task. It condemns most of our brothers and sisters to life without Christ, both in this world and in that to come. It must be rejected. The biblical mandate to disciple *ta ethne (sab jatiyon ko chela karo* in Hindi) must be inscribed over the doorway of every church and written on the heart of every Christian.

It is my firm belief, expressed in this volume, that God is going to use the Church in India — all nine types — to bring in a tremendous harvest of souls. The greatest service the Churches can render to India, and every other land, is to make available to more and more people that knowledge of Christ and that faith in Him which will lift individuals, families, castes, classes, minorities and whole states to the plane on which God intends them to operate to His glory and to the welfare of the nation.

PART I
THE FIVE BASIC TYPES

((In the rest of this book I shall not repeatedly call to the attention of the Western reader that each type of Indian Church will help missiologists, ministers and missionaries working in other nations to understand their own types.

Precisely the types found in India will not be found in other countries and other social orders. Yet monoethnic and multi-ethnic congregations and denominations of various kinds will certainly be found. Seeing them clearly in India will help distinguish them in other lands. Seeing the evangelistic potential of each type in India will help the readers discern the evangelistic potential of the types he faces in his own experience.

As I am writing, a Chinese Christian from Hong Kong has spent two hours with me describing a current open door there not being entered. Factory workers, who are somewhat responsive to the Gospel, are not becoming Christians in large numbers, partly because the existing congregations and denominations are led by middle class educated men and women, and factory workers feel out of place in most such congregations, even in the "lower class congregations." The concept of types of churches would greatly help the situation. The congregations led by educated people, with educated deacons and elders, and many students and ex-students constitute one Type. Those composed of and led by factory workers constitute another. The evangelistic potential of each is quite different. The ways in which the 750,000 factory workers in Hong Kong *perceive* the Church and those of their number who become Christians are quite different.

I trust that outside India *Ethnic Realities* will be read as a vivid illustration of contextualization, rather than as a means for understanding the Church in India.))

1

SYRIAN CHURCHES

TYPE 1 denominations are called Syrian, not because these Christians are Syrian by race or have emigrated from Syria, but because over the centuries their Bible and liturgy have always been in Syriac. The Syrian Churches (denominations), which together now number about 3 million souls, rightfully form Type 1 for two reasons. First, they are unquestionably the first Christian Churches founded in India. They believe that the Apostle Thomas came to India during the first century, made many converts on the southwest and southeast coasts, and was killed near Madras City. There is nothing inherently improbable in this. Jewish trading settlements existed in some ports of the Asian coasts fringing the Indian Ocean. It was not much more difficult for Thomas to go to India than it would have been for Paul to go to Spain.

The synagogue communities in India had cores of racial Jews and, like those in the Mediterranean world, may have had concentric circles of proselytes, devout persons, and interested Gentiles. The Christian churches arose partly from converted Jewish traders, partly from converts from the Brahman and other upper castes, and as the years rolled by, partly from Christians from "Syria" who emigrated to India at various times for various reasons. No one can now say certainly what part came in from each source. The Christian community was influential. The rajahs granted it substantial rights. It took its place in the Hindu social order as one of the upper castes. Its bishops were consecrated by the Patriarch in Babylon.* The language of worship — for Christians — was and, for most of the community, still is Syriac, though Syrians operated in daily life in the language of the people, now known as Malayalam.

The Syrian Churches were and are strong chiefly in what is now central Kerala, from Calicut to Quilon.† Today (see map 1) that is still their heartland,‡ but tens of thousands of them have settled in the towns and cities of all the states of India. They are well known in other lands as well. There were 16,000 communicants in thirteen Mar Thoma and Orthodox congregations in Bombay in 1970. A Syrian community of hundreds is found in Kuwait in the Persian Gulf. Four Syrian families have settled in Amarkantak, a remote mining town recently established by the

---

*Bishops were in certain periods ordained by the Monophysite Patriarch at Antioch and at other times by the Nestorian Patriarch at Babylon, but the connection was loose. The full story is very involved. Keay in his *History of the Syrian Church in India* has long sections recounting the moves.
†Pothen *(Syrian Christians of Kerala)* says they numbered 200,000 in the sixteenth century.
‡The 1931 census states that in the following *takluqs* the Hindu/Christian percentages were as follows:

Muvatupuzha	39/53
Thodupuzha	39/52
Meenachad	37/61
Kottayam	45/53
Changanassery	41/55

In other districts Hindus heavily outnumbered Christians, as in Trivandrum, where the percentages were 75/15 and Quilon, where they were 70/18.

MAP 1 — SOUTH INDIA

Madhya Pradesh government. Thousands of Syrians now live in the United States. Paul Verghese, before he became Mar Gregorius, Bishop of the Orthodox Church, was an executive of the World Council of Churches in Geneva, and M.M. Thomas (of the Mar Thoma Church) was for years chairman of its Central Committee. In short, Syrians are about 3 million able, intelligent, well-to-do, and immovably Christian people. They are not becoming Hindus or Muslims — though a few profess Marxism as a political creed and many are only nominally Christian.

Second, I classify them as Type 1 because during the long centuries when they were the only Christians in India and had scant connection with the rest of the Christian world, they became thoroughly Indian. If one wants to see what a truly indigenous Church is, he should look at the Syrian Churches before the nineteenth century. Type 1 is well worth the scrutiny of anyone interested in the indigenous Church. What ought to be done by way of becoming indigenous, and what ought not to be done, are both clearly seen. The matter is so important that I quote some illustrations from S.G. Pothen of the Orthodox Syrian Church, who says (in his *Syrian Christians of Kerala*, 1963),

> The Syrian Christians were Christians in faith only, but in all else they were assimilated to the society and environment in which they lived. They had a rightful place in the society and shared common interests and took pride with the rest of the citizens of Kerala that they were all Malayalees, speaking the same Malayalam language, wearing the same dress, and observing the same customs. . . .]They] had necessarily to develop an almost identical culture. . . . (p. 91)

> [At birth] care is taken to note the exact time so that the horoscope of the newborn baby may be cast. This is a practice copied from the Hindus and reliance is placed on the events of life predicted in the horoscope of the child. . . . (p. 61)

> The dowry was given with a specific ceremony, always in an odd number of rupees, because an even number would bring bad luck. . . .
> The bride's mother stood apart, watched the proceedings with a lighted lamp in her hand, and made the remark that fire or *Agni* was a permanent witness to this transaction. (p. 99)

> The Syrians made no attempt to evangelize. . . . Their primary concern was to live in harmony and requite the hospitality and toleration shown them by the Hindu kings and princes. This could only be done by respecting the faith and customs of their rulers. . . . Since they desired to occupy an important place in society, they had necessarily to conform to the pattern and practices of a caste society . . . conformity was essential to survival. In this they succeeded completely . . . by adopting the language, dress, and habits of their Hindu brethren. (pp. 54-55)

That some modern Syrians say, "Pothen's remarks are no longer true," reveals the many pieces in the Syrian mosaic. Pothen describes some; his critics are thinking of others.

How the Syrian Churches Came to Be

The history of the Syrian Christians from the earliest times till the latter half of the sixteenth century is that of a single denomination, with loose ties to the Nestorian and/or Monophysite Churches of Babylon and Syria. Then Vasco da Gama, coming around the Cape of Good Hope, landed at Calicut in 1498 — six years after Columbus crossed the Atlantic. He opened India to Portuguese and Roman Catholic power. Francis Xavier arrived in Goa in 1542. The Church of Rome began to make strenuous efforts to bring the erring Syrian Christians back to the "true Church." By 1599 a combination of persuasion, coercion, Portuguese military power, and the impact of the great world to the west swung the entire Syrian community (rather unwillingly) into Rome's orbit.

But by 1653 the seething discontent at domination by Rome was provoked into open revolt at the news that Bishop Ahatalla, sent by the Patriarch of Babylon, had been burned at the stake in Goa. See. F.E. Keay's *History of the Syrian Church in India* (1960:54). At the Coonen Cross in front of the church in Mattancheri, thousands took an oath that they were done with Portuguese bishops. They linked themselves to the cross with long ropes so that the "current of virtue" might flow into them and sustain them in their brave stand for freedom and their own Church. Thus the Syrian Church, which for fifteen centuries had been a single Monophysite denomination and for fifty years a single Roman Catholic denomination, became two: about half defected to Rome, about half remaining Orthodox Syrians.

In the hundred and fifty years before 1653 the Roman Catholics in that part of India had won from two fishing castes — the Mukkuvas and Paravas — considerable numbers to the

Christian faith. These converts from Hinduism had come in typical people movement fashion with 20,000 coming in 1534. Their mass was conducted in Latin. They are called Latin Rite Roman Catholics. The Syrians, however, who would have rejected Roman Catholicism if required to change to Latin, were granted the privilege of worshiping in their own liturgical language: Syriac. Of much higher social status than the humble fishermen, they therefore retained their own sacred language and are known as Syrian Rite Roman Catholics.

Early in the nineteenth century, as English power waxed in India, the Church Missionary Society sent missionaries to Cochin and Travancore. These, with Colonel Munro, the British resident in Travancore, proposed to the Orthodox Metran (Archbishop) that the Bible be translated into Malayalam and a college opened to train Syrian priests, who would not be subverted to Anglicanism but would continue as Orthodox Syrians. This arrangement continued from about 1816 to 1835. By that time the new wine of the Bible in the language of the people, and the example of Anglican and other Western Churches which had been through their own Reformation only three hundred years before, were producing such a ferment in the Orthodox Church that its leaders held a council at Mavelikara in 1835 and took an oath as desired by the Metran that they would have "no further intercourse whatever with the Church missionaries." The Anglicans severed connections with the Orthodox, taking with them several small groups who chose to become Anglicans. However, the movement toward reformation had really begun in several Orthodox families. In 1837 for the first time in history the liturgy was read in Malayalam. The reformation continued underground till 1875 and then burst out into the Reformed Syrian Church — known today as the Mar Thoma Church. The process here so briefly described was in fact most complex. Keay tells the story well in his *History*. Recently a further division has taken place in the Orthodox Church.

Dr. J. Canjanam Gamaliel of Concordia Seminary in Nagercoil, Kerala, in 1967 drew up the chart on the following page, which is

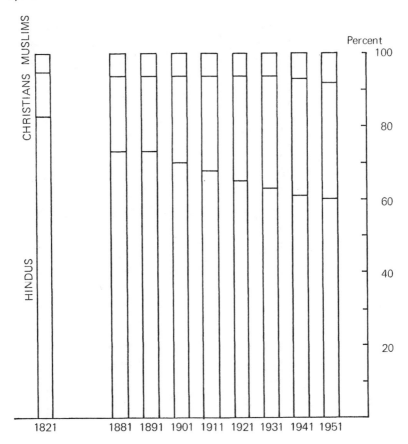

SOURCE: Census of India, 1931, 1941, 1951

Fig. 1 Rate of religious change in Travancore: 1821-1951. Showing the
percentage of Hindus, Christians, and Muslims in the total population of
Travancore in the years cited. (Adapted from J.C. Gamaliel's "The Church
in Travancore: A People Movement Study." Dr. J. Canjanam Gamaliel's
master's thesis, School of Missions, Fuller Theological Seminary, 1967.)

of considerable interest as one studies the Syrian Churches in
Kerala. The figures are taken from the censuses of Travancore,
most of which was merged into Kerala when that state was
formed. Consequently the chart cannot be taken as reflecting
Kerala as a whole today. However, it does cast a revealing
sidelight on the southwestern tip of India. Since part of
Travancore (Kanniyakumari) has been added to Tamil Nadu and
Cochin added to the rest of Travencore to form, with Malabar,

Kerala, it would be difficult to calculate the 1977 figures for comparison with those of 1951. But one may hazard a guess that the percentage of Christians has increased only slightly since then.

In 1977 there were about 1,400,000 Orthodox, 1,400,000 Catholic, and 400,000 Mar Thoma Christians.* These comprised the chief Syrian denominations. Several small denominations of Syrians are also found. In 1961, from the ranks of the Mar Thoma Syrians, a Church which in 1974 claimed 50,000 members broke away to form the St Thomas Evangelical Church. We therefore mention four Syrian denominations, one much smaller than the others.

The Church of South India has many Syrian congregations and so do the Pentecostals. Endogamy in these congregations follows somewhat different patterns. Syrians in the Mar Thoma or Orthodox may marry Syrians in the CSI or vice versa. However, Mar Thoma and Orthodox will not ordinarily marry Syrian Pentecostals. In general, one may say that while most Syrians marry within the Syrian community, some outside marriages occur. More, one imagines, in the educated upper ranks than in the rest of the community.

Characteristics of Syrian Denominations

Syrian Christians are often men and women of ability. With one minor exception they have never admitted to their Church converts from the oppressed and depressed castes of India. They are propertied people in Kerala — merchants, editors of papers, landowning families for twenty generations, industrialists, bankers, teachers, and government officials. They send their sons and daughters to college.

*The Orthodox and the Syrian Rite Catholics both claim somewhat higher numbers (1,600,000 and 1,700,000 respectively). The difficulty is that when the claims of all the denominations are added up they come to more than the census totals!

In competition with other Indians all over the subcontinent they do well. Many rise to the top and become headmasters, managers, directors, foremen, executives, head clerks, and the like. They achieve this by merit, not by favor. Indeed, Christian Indians in general fear the Syrian community. Let one of them in, it is said, and soon he will rise to the top and will thereafter appoint his friends and relatives. Local men will find it difficult to get a job. While Syrian Rite Roman Catholics number 1,400,000 out of 8,500,000 Catholics in India, more than half of all Indian Roman Catholic priests and brothers and more than three-fourths of all sisters are Syrians by race.

Not all Syrians are able and wealthy. Large numbers are poor and little educated, but the community as a whole is noted for its ability.

Syrian Christians are immovable Christians. One almost never hears of Syrians becoming Muslims or Hindus. The Syrian community does not gradually decrease as members quietly move into other castes. Indeed, in caste-conscious India, no caste can decrease in that way. First, each (particularly each upper caste) is fiercely proud of being itself. Second, no other caste will take in renegades from outside. However, "immovable Christians" does *not* mean "personally convinced Christians who live in an ardent relationship to the Lord Jesus Christ." Syrian Christians — like all denominations whose members are born into the Church — have their fair share of nominals. They may have no consciousness of their need for a Saviour, no intention of considering the Bible their rule of faith and practice; but will still maintain that they are good Christians! Certainly not Buddhists or Hindus. Thus it comes about that the leadership of the Communist party in Kerala contains quite a number of Syrian Christians — exactly as in Italy most Communist leaders have been as infants baptized into the Roman Catholic Church.

The Syrian Catholic and Orthodox Churches would be considered by most Protestants doctrinally corrupt. They have borrowed many customs and beliefs from the Nambudri Brahmans, Nairs, and other Hindus, to say nothing of European and Near Eastern corruptions. Calvin and Luther would have banned many of their ways of worship and life. Indeed, the Bible in Malayalam by itself sparked a tremendous reformation. Between 1880 and 1920 tens of thousands of Orthodox converted to the Mar Thoma Church, which intended to be both truly Syrian and truly Reformed. Despite the good example set by the Mar Thoma Church, the Orthodox and Catholic branches have a long way to go before they include any sizable number of biblical Christians.

In understanding the four main Type 1 Churches, an important point to remember is that they are all, with very rare exceptions, *strictly endogamous, in a Hindu society dedicated to the caste system.* The Syrian Churches intend that all their members be of the Syrian "caste." I put the word in quotes to indicate that Syrian leaders wince at it. In civil discourse they maintain that they do not think of the Syrians as a caste. But despite the denial, what Pothen says is substantially true. Syrians have conformed "in the pattern and practices governing a caste society." As to marriage inside the Syrian community, they prefer it and mean to continue it. Like European communities in India, like the Mennonite denominations in Russia and North America, they intend to marry women of their own sort — there are none better. As we shall see regarding other types of Church in India, Type 1 is not alone in this preference and intention. The caste structure of India means that clusters of congregations commonly have an intense consciousness of being distinct units of society. All men on all continents have this feeling to some extent. Consequently this study of how ethnicity affects the spread of the Church in India is of interest all over the world. Upper class Brazilians have a distinct consciousness of being different from poverty stricken Northeasterners. University professors in England know they are not factory workers. Christians in India, immersed in a society conditioned and controlled by caste, have class consciousness to a high degree and thus illustrate well the general condition of mankind.

When a small number of Syrians live in some city in India, they

will worship with some of the congregations already there of
any denomination; but they will not marry with them, and as soon
as sufficient Syrians gain employment in that town or city, the
Syrians will organize a church of their own. The Syrian principal
of a college or seminary is a Christian gentleman, and with his
wife will worship in the same congregation as the teachers and
students, but he seldom becomes fully a part of it. If a Mar Thoma
or Orthodox congregation is established nearby, he is likely to
join it. He wants to be sure that his children marry within the
Syrian fold. This is quite natural. It is what a Japanese, Scottish, or
American principal will do. Syrian Christians are Indian
Christians, but they intend to maintain their ethnic purity.

This ethnicity of the Syrian Churches has tremendous meaning
for the other eight types. The reader will remember the
illustrations from S.G. Pothen regarding adoption of Hindu
cultural elements. Let me quote a further one.

> . . . immediately the newborn child is bathed, a priest
> repeats in the child's ear "Moron Yesu Masiha" [Jesus Christ
> is Lord]. The baby is also given a few drops of honey in
> which some gold is mixed. This is done by the grandmother
> or presiding lady, rubbing a ring or other gold ornament on
> a stone on which some drops of honey have been smeared.
> This custom, shared with the Nambudri Brahmans, is
> claimed to insure prosperity. (pp. 61-62)

Many customs borrowed from the Hindus, like this one or that
of the bride standing to the right of the groom (instead of to the
left as in Western weddings), are clearly innocuous. Either they
never did have any idolatrous significance or they have been
"baptized into Christ" by the use of suitable Scripture. They can
be followed freely by Christians. But is the adoption of the caste
system equally innocuous? For example, in the Reformed Syrian
Church (the Mar Thoma) in the late nineteenth and early
twentieth century a small number of Harijans — then
Untouchables — were baptized and formed into Mar Thoma
congregations. But till 1968 no Harijan Christian had been
elevated to the priesthood — to say nothing of the episcopate.

Most Harijan Mar Thoma Christians (about 15,000 of them) live in congregations led by Harijan Christian catechists and local laymen. Is this desirable in a world where racism is severely castigated?

The argument is not one-sided. Syrian Christians might well reply that in India, which is still largely committed to the caste system, some way must be found for believers from each caste to become Christian within their castes while maintaining their endogamous restrictions — while keeping the blood "pure." Syrians might very well say to Hindu friends: "This is what we are doing. You can do the same. We were upper-caste Hindus; we have become Christians while still remaining very much ourselves as far as purity of blood is concerned." The issue is intensely relevant in India and to a lesser degree in most countries. We shall return to it again and again in this volume. Here it is sufficient to say that the characteristics of the Syrian Churches that most sets them apart from other Indian Christians, and that makes it essential for us to identify the Syrian as a separate type, is not doctrine, but is precisely the Syrian intention, steadily maintained, of being Christian *at the same time as keeping marriage to non-Syrians to an absolute minimum,* if not barring it entirely.

As Christianity everywhere adapts to various components of culture, it is essential for missiologists to see the complexity of each. We must not be guilty of oversimplification. The Syrian Church has not only maintained the ethnic purity of the Syrian community, not only practiced endogamy; but it has also failed or even refused to evangelize non-Christians. Oversimplifying, Pothen says this "was essential for survival." It is true that the practice of rigid endogamy was a help to survival. It created a tight community in which social cohesion fortified Christian conviction and maintained the community flame, when conviction burned low. It is also true that, had the Christians converted individuals from other communities and added them to their own, they would have angered those other groups. To have converted a member of the ruling rajah's family, married him to a Syrian girl, and incorporated him fully in the Syrian community, would no doubt have greatly displeased the king. But there was another option.

The Syrian community, while maintaining rigid endogamy itself, could have evangelized other castes, *expecting the congregations formed in them to practice the same rigid endogamy, and thus, while becoming Christian, to remain ethnically pure.* To say the same thing in other words, it was *right* for the Syrians while making adaptations to Indian culture to maintain rigid endogamy; but it was wrong — and unnecessary — for them to cease from all evangelism. For nineteen hundred years, because they did not want to mix their blood with that of other ethnic units, they ceased to propagate the Christian faith. That was wrong. Even today, ardent Syrian Christians who proclaim Christ to non-Christians, on obtaining converts say to them, "You will not feel comfortable in the Syrian Church. Why don't you join the Methodists, the Baptists, or the Church of South India?" This is particularly true outside Kerala in other states where all converts speak Tamil, Hindi, or other Indian languages, while the Syrian congregations worship in Malayalam.

Ethnicity is crucially important for the spread of the Christian faith in all lands and especially in India. In Type 1 Churches we can see it with startling clarity. As Christians propagate the Gospel they must of necessity decide what to do with those who, on coming under its power, decide to become followers of Jesus Christ and members of His Body. Shall they say to such would-be Christians something like this: "Leave your own ethnic unit (caste) and join ours. Worship with us. Eat with us. Intermarry with us. Join this segment of the Indian people. Become one with us in *roti, beti, mati.* That is what it means to become a Christian."

Or shall they say something like the following. "You should become a baptized member of the Universal Church of Christ. This exists as thousands of separate congregations and clusters of congregations, divided by language, economic condition, education, occupation, and place of residence. You can join our congregation if you wish; but since you belong to a certain section of the Indian people you may want to spread the Good News to others of your comrades and caste fellows and create a new congregation of *your own kind of people*. You will still be part of us. In Christ we are all one.

"But to keep the door of salvation open to your relatives, the degree of actual physical fellowship with us may remain small for years or even for decades. We Syrians do not intermarry with other kinds of Christians, whether European or Indian, Japanese or African, and there is no need for you to do so. The Jewish Christians in Jerusalem and Judea during the first century continued to be racially and culturally Jews. You can continue to be racially and culturally of your own caste. The only things you must renounce are idolatry and allegiance to other gods and other scriptures. We encourage you to cultivate warm and friendly relationships with your caste fellows and to follow all those customs and components of your culture which are not expressly prohibited by the Christian scriptures. We do not want you to change your ethnic heritage. We want you, within the rich cultural heritage you possess, to know the glorious new life in Christ. Do not change your language. Do not change your dress. Do not change your eating habits. Do not change any of the beautiful and useful aspects of your culture. But do be assured that as you come to know Christ more and more intimately, He will so enrich your heritage that, while it remains recognizably of your caste, it is elevated, purified, and beautified."

This last characteristic of Type 1 denominations — their endogamy — is most important and has many bearings on the whole future of the Christian faith in India and in other lands. As will be seen in the following section, it closely conditions the potential of churches for evangelism.

EVANGELISTIC POTENTIAL
OF THE SYRIAN CHURCHES

We now come to the most important question regarding the Syrian Churches: *What is their evangelistic potential?*

We see that for perhaps eighteen hundred years they have been very largely nonevangelistic. They have coexisted with Hindus, neither attempting nor desiring to win them to faith in the Saviour. However, that policy was followed when the Syrian Church was a tiny minority with a Syriac liturgy, a largely illiterate membership, no knowledge of the Bible, and practically no fellowship with the world Church. What took place in those very different, far-off times may be assumed to be all that *could* then happen.

Today conditions are very different. All branches of the Syrian Church are in contact with the world Church. Syrian leaders flit from continent to continent in jet planes and confer in great ecumenical meetings of ardent Christians from Asia, Africa, Europe, and North and South America. Today India has in its Constitution declared itself a secular state, giving equal protection to all religions and guaranteeing to all Indians the right to worship and believe as they please, and to propagate their religions — within the limits of public order.* Today, the Syrian Churches look out on sister denominations in many parts of India who have won hundreds of thousands to Christian faith and have cheerfully endured whatever degree of harrassment such action brought upon them. Surely the wealthy, educated Syrians need not flinch at harrassment which poor denominations arising from animistic tribes and humble castes have patiently endured.

What is the evangelistic potential of Type 1 Churches *today?* Several comments should be made.

Each Syrian denomination varies in evangelistic potency. *(a)* The Orthodox Syrians and *(b)* the Syrian Rite Catholics are stolidly nonevangelistic. They could do a great deal, but their ethnic traits and doctrinal/liturgical positions keep them from church-mutiplying evangelism. They have some renewal movements within their membership — retreats, conferences for deepening the spiritual life, and literature geared to life in Christ — but very little deliberate extension of the Gospel to ethnic

*On the local scene, conversion does sometimes bring harrassment and persecution. This must be granted.

groups outside their own community. The one exception to this of which I know is the remarkable Orthodox Syrian Church of western North America. This small denomination is made up entirely of *Caucasians* who have put on Christ in the Syrian Orthodox Church. They number perhaps 3,000 and have congregations in Los Angeles, Las Vegas, and a few other cities. The significance of the exception is great. Just as in the United States the Orthodox Syrians have won men and women *of another race* to faith in Christ and membership in the Syrian Orthodox Church, so they can and ought to multiply congregations among many or all the races, i.e. castes, of India.

Meanwhile *(c)* the Mar Thoma Church, by way of contrast, is full of one kind of evangelistic fervor. At Tiruvalla, K.V. Cherian, an able and devout Christian, runs a notable evangelistic center. Thousands gather there from all over the southern tip of India. Revival services in Malayalam and Tamil go on for days. Many make decisions for Christ. At the famous Maramon Convention, held in the sandy bed of a river, more than fifty thousand people each year gather and are addressed by famous evangelists from all over the world. E. Stanley Jones before his death had often spoken there, as have Edwin Orr, Abdul Huqq and others. The Mar Thoma Church has a missionary society which maintains more than twenty mission stations in Kerala, Kashmir, other states of India, and adjacent lands. In each station priests of the Church carry on mission work. At Tiruvalla the Church maintains the Golden Jubilee Evangelistic Center. Several sodalities (independent missionary societies of Syrians) doing mission work — some on American funds — are given a kindly blessing by the Church.

Nevertheless, it remains true that the Mar Thoma denomination neither does much nor intends to do much by way of evangelizing non-Christians. Its evangelistic work is directed overwhelmingly toward existing Christians. In the last fifty years it has founded very few Mar Thoma congregations of other ethnic units. Though there are thousands of Mar Thoma

Christians in the United States, it has planted no congregations of Caucasian Christians. A few Caucasians who have married Mar Thoma Syrians there may be, and these may attend Malayalam-speaking Mar Thoma congregations, but if so they are rare. In India, in the presence of powerful people movements to Christ among twenty-one castes and tribes, there is no cluster of recently formed Mar Thoma congregations. No substantial church planting has taken place. Mar Thoma mission stations — copying, alas, the institutional approach of Western missions— baptize very few non-Christians. This may be due to the fact that the Mar Thoma missions approached some of the most resistant segments of the population, or to a reluctance to start fully Mar Thoma congregations composed of people of other castes, or both.

A reaction to denominationalism also complicates the picture. The passion for church union plus nationalistic emotions have made it popular in India to castigate Western denominations for reproducing Indian carbon copies of themselves — Anglicans planting Anglican congregations and Methodists planting Methodist. As the Mar Thoma Church awoke to its evangelistic potential and privileges, leading Indian churchmen said to it, "Add the converts you win to the churches already there. Do not come in to plant a new denomination. We already have too many." The Mar Thoma Church heard this advice gladly. Because of its ethnocentricity (plus eighteen centuries of not baptizing non-Christians) it did not *want* to add non-Christian converts to Mar Thoma congregations or to start Mar Thoma congregations among other ethnic groups.

The net result is that this large, wealthy denomination of four hundred thousand souls is doing little toward the propagation of the Gospel in its native land. This is tragic.

Finally, *(d)* the St. Thomas Evangelical Church of India may prove the most evangelistic denomination of the four. Its theology and conviction demand vigorous evangelization. However, it is so newly on the scene that to date it has actually done little. It may yet recognize the great potential which all Syrian Churches have by nature and make significant strides toward propagation of the Gospel in India.

FUTURE POTENTIAL

Despite the somewhat disappointing picture which the past and present afford, all four of the major Syrian Churches possess *enormous evangelistic potential.* They are thoroughly Indian. They were in India long before many of the modern Hindu sects, such as the Kabir Panthis and the Sikhs. They are made up of men and women of ability. Both individual Christians and congregations have much wealth and learning, and Syrians, as we have seen, occupy positions of leadership in many sectors of life. They have, more than any other type of Church, close connection with the Churches of North America and Europe. And more than any other type of Church, they are open to the currents of revival and church growth flowing strongly through the Church Universal.

Further, in the providence of God, the now widespread Syrian denominations have come to their present degree of eminence, education, influence, and renewal at just the time when the evangelization of India is more possible than at any other time since the resurrection of our Lord. India has become a secular state. Enormous migration to the cities is going on. Indians are traveling abroad. Hindu missionaries are converting people to varieties of Hinduism in other parts of the world as well as India, and conversion has more or less ceased to be a dirty word. The rise of people movement denominations, in which marriage within the group is the prevailing pattern, gives repeated demonstration that "becoming a Christian" is not the same thing as "ruining one's caste."

To turn the corner, however, and transform these old nonevangelizing denominations — other countries have static Churches also — into Spirit-filled brotherhoods which spread the Good News spontaneously will require some or all of the following steps. These may be better stated than I have done here in tentative formulation; but something like them would seem to be necessary before Type 1 Churches can shake off their chains and rouse themselves to the call of Christ and the highest service of the motherland. I tender them, hoping they will be suggestive to readers.

1. *They must believe that faith in Christ is the pearl of great price,* to buy which a man will sell all he has; that God wants His lost children found; that the greatest gift the Church can give to India is multiplication of cells of Bible-believing, Bible-obeying, Christ-honoring Christians. These are the most potent element in any social reconstruction. Type 1 Churches must turn from any reduction of the Gospel, any low view of the Bible, any substitution of "other things" for faith in Christ. They must believe that salvation is by faith in Jesus Christ alone and acceptance of His Word as the only rule of faith and practice.

2. *They must learn effective modes of evangelism.* India is a vast laboratory in which it is easy to see both effective and ineffective operations. Much is being written these days on how peoples become Christian and the Gospel is communicated. Evangelism (which intends that unbelievers shall hear of Christ so winsomely and so persuasively that they pass through the waters of baptism and are incorporated in His Body) can be both taught and learned.

3. *Each Syrian Church must establish its own congregations in other ethnic units clusters.* India is a continent. Enormous populations are readily found in which there are no congregations, no Bibles, no Christians, and no evangelism. What Christians there are in government or other services have no relatives or loved ones in the surrounding populations. The web connections so necessary to the flow of faith simply do not exist. In these large populations of 50,000, 100,000, or more, the goal must be *clusters* of "our kind of congregations." A single congregation in this district and another single congregation two hundred miles away in another district will avail nothing. Single congregations face huge difficulties — for one, where will they find sons-in-law? Each

Syrian denomination should choose a mission field in which it intends to found many ethnically related congregations, all speaking the same language, of the same homogeneous unit, of about the same economic and educational level, and geographically close to each other.

4. *Syrian denominations must encourage the formation of apostolic bands,* like that composed of Silas, Timothy, Apollos, Paul, and Luke. The massive machinery required by Europeans carrying on missions in India across all kinds of linguistic and cultural chasms is not needed. Something much simpler and more apostolic would be better. These bands of missionaries (for that is what the apostles were) would learn the language of the people to whom they went, live among them, adopt their culture as far as possible, and spread the fragrance of Christ. It is as simple as that. Systems of support for these missionaries must be created, and systems of training them to be *effectively evangelistic in modern India* must be put into operation. The Friends Missionary Prayer Bands chiefly of the Nadar Christians of Tamil Nadu, which in 1975 had sixty-five missionaries in other parts of India, show that the task can readily be done by the well-to-do Syrian denominations.

5. *They must keep accurate records of the numbers of people of the world who have been baptized and added to the Body.* The newly baptized may be added to existing Syrian congregations, or congregations of daughter Syrian denominations. The evangelists may be lay or clerical, paid or unpaid. Evangelism may be of near neighbors in one's own tongue and culture or of unbelievers across deep chasms of language and culture.

Only by keeping true and accurate records will it be possible for each Syrian denomination to see what it has really been doing. Part of the cause for little evangelism is that priests and people alike have no idea how few they are bringing to the Lord, while in some parts of India sister denominations are bringing many.

More than one-sixth of all Christians in India belong to Type 1 congregations and denominations. Their average wealth, education, and status is far above the *average* of most other Christians. They constitute a rich but largely unused resource for the evangelization of India. Their adjustment to Indian culture is instructive for the other types. They pose an intriguing question to the Christian movement in India and other lands: Can a Church which insists on strict endogamy for itself spread the Spirit of Christ to other ethnic units, encouraging them to become Christian within their own ethnicity? Obviously the present procedure — by which an endogamous denomination refuses to convert members of other castes to itself — is necessarily fruitless. Is it time for a shift?

2

FULLY CONGLOMERATE CHURCHES

TYPE 2 is the most typical of all Indian congregations and denominations. It is found in every state and in almost every town and city. The leaders of the Church in India, by an overwhelming majority, worship in Type 2 congregations. Practically all missions at the beginning of their labors planted this type of church. Many missions have never founded any other kind. No wonder many church leaders believe that Type 2 is basically more Christian than other types — is in fact the *normal* sort of congregation and denomination, while all others are deviations from the true pattern.

Type 2 is also typical of churches founded by missionary labors in other nations. It is a common beginning form of the Church.

Conglomerate congregations and denominations, Type 2, are composed of Christians from many different castes and tribes. Each convert has come to Christ alone, *out* of the caste in which he was born.

Sometimes he comes by a truly spiritual conversion. He reads the Bible, meets the Lord in a dream or vision, and turns from his own vain search for *moksh* (release) to salvation by faith and God's sovereign grace. Sometimes he has come impelled by hunger, when famine swept the land. Dying people have been given food and shelter by missionaries, boys and girls by the hundreds placed in orphanages and cared for, given medical attention, education, and instruction in the Bible. Some, after the famine was over, went back to relatives. Some stayed in the orphanage. Those who stayed became Christians. Some converts have met Christ through the tender ministrations of Christian physicians and nurses. Some rescued women or child widows gradually learned of Christ and became Christians.

Conglomerate congregations were thus from the beginning made up of converts from many different caste backgrounds. The caste from which they came made no difference; they were all alike children of God and had by faith been born anew. They had become God's holy people. They lived above caste and tribe. The fact that converts in Hindu India are usually violently ousted from their castes, driven out of house and home and declared dead, fostered the process of conversion by abstraction. Pushed out by their own relatives and pulled into the Christian fellowship by those who welcomed and cared for them, they formed congregations of individuals.

The term conglomerate comes from geology and is described as a kind or rock made up of pebbles or other rock fragments washed into one place, where they are finally held together by a strong cement of hardened clay, silica or other binding material from the water that flows over them. The multiethnic congregation is precisely a conglomerate. Its members have come from many different castes — some high, some low — and each is part of the matrix of living rock. Multiethnic and conglomerate are synonymous terms for Type 2.

The process is entirely natural. Given the fact that no community wants its members to defect to any other caste, given the intense communal loyalty which is an essential part of the Indian system, there are only two ways in which men of caste can become Christian. (a) They can come out as individuals —

one-by-one-against-the-current, against the family, against the
jati or homogeneous ethnic unit in which they were born. In this
case they form conglomerate congregations, which in turn
produce multiethnic denominations. (b) They can come out
group by group, still against the caste (for the whole caste never
moves) but with enough of their fellows so that normal life along
the old pattern is carried on in the fast-forming churches. In this
case converts form people movement congregations which we
shall consider in Chapters 3 and 4. God has blessed and used both
ways.

THE MADHYA PRADESH PATTERN

Type 2 is the typical all-India pattern of Church, found in all
states; but it will be helpful to see how multiethnic Type 2
congregations and denominations arose in one particular state,
that of Madhya Pradesh. The process was complex and
developed in slightly different forms in most mission stations. As
we study the actual occurrences we shall understand more
thoroughly why conglomerates, so contrary to the Indian social
system, have become one of the two main kinds of Church and *by
all odds the most typical.* I have chosen Madhya Pradesh to illustrate
the process chiefly because I know that part of India well, but also
because it furnishes small illustrations of Type 3 and 4 Churches.
These will be seen as minor parts of the picture, Type 2
remaining clear.

Madhya Pradesh — formerly Central Provinces — is a large
state of 171,000 square miles in the very center of India, about
equidistant from Calcutta, Bombay, Delhi, and Madras. It is a
land of plains and valleys about a thousand feet above sea level.
Low hills and plateaus rise to two and in a few places three
thousand feet. The plains are densely cultivated. The hills are
covered with valuable forests. Coal is found in the eastern parts of
the state. The great steel city of Bhilai has been built during the
last twenty years in the southeast corner, where deposits of iron
ore, manganese, limestone, and coal are abundant. During the
last two thousand years Madhya Pradesh — the land of forests,

wild elephants, tigers, bears, and savage aboriginal tribes—has blocked North India off from South India. Travelers and armies went around it, either to the east or to the west.

In 1971 Madhya Pradesh had a population of nearly 42 million (up from 26 million in 1951) and a Christian community of about 100,000. Christians thus composed less than three in a thousand.

Map 2 shows the area, about six hundred miles from east to west, and (if we exclude the long southeastern projection) three hundred from north to south. The dotted black lines are the railways that tie the diverse sections together into a coherent whole. The capital city was for many years Nagpur but is now Bhopal. The towns and cities named on the map are the chief centers and were those in which missionaries first settled.

By 1860 most of the coastal regions of India and the great Gangetic plain had been occupied by missions. The center of the land lay untouched. Long inaccessible, it had only recently been opened up by the Bombay-to-Calcutta railway running through Jubbulpore, and later by another main line running through Nagpur. Incoming missions, therefore, landed at Bombay, proceeded "up country" by train, and then by oxcart to district headquarters sometimes fifty, sometimes two hundred miles from the railway. They arrived in small towns where Christianity was utterly unknown and was regarded — erroneously — as part of the invading power of Britain. Missionaries were frequently addressed as *"Sircar"* (government). Christianity was very strange. Missionaries learned the language without benefit of experienced teachers. They built residences, when they could buy a piece of land, or lived in rented quarters.

Typical missionary endeavors were extensive tours. A missionary would pile onto a bullock cart tent, beds, kitchen utensils, chairs, magic lantern, books for sale, and atop all a crate of chickens for eggs and meat, and set out in November after the rainy season to tour as many as possible of the hundreds of villages in the surrounding fifty-mile radius. Their camp set up in some center, the missionary and his Indian co-workers would preach from village to village to whoever would listen and invite

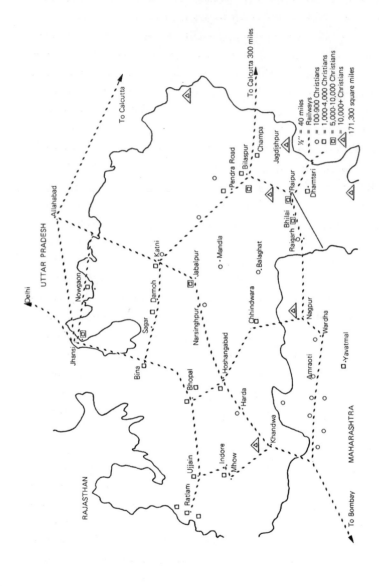

MAP 2—MADHYA PRADESH

RAJASTHAN

UTTAR PRADESH

Delhi

To Calcutta

Allahabad

Jhansi

Nowgaon

Bina

Sagar

Damoh

Katni

Pendra Road

Bilaspur

Champa

Jagdishpur

Narsinghpur

Jabalpur

Mandla

To Calcutta 300 miles

Bhopal

Hoshangabad

Chhindwara

Balaghat

Raigarh

Bhilai

Raipur

Dhamtari

Harda

Ratlam

Ujjain

Indore

Mhow

Khandwa

Amraoti

Nagpur

Wardha

Yavatmal

MAHARASHTRA

To Bombay

½" = 40 miles
= Railways
o = 100-900 Christians
⊡ = 1,000-4,000 Christians
▣ = 5,000-10,000 Christians
△ = 10,000+ Christians
171,300 square miles

them to come to the tent at night for magic lantern pictures and further conversation. Then on to another center.

This was seed-sowing evangelism. Tens of thousands heard, but few were convinced enough to become Christians. Sometimes laborers who worked on the mission buildings or as servants in the missionaries' homes heard often enough and had enough security to accept the new faith, but usually the friendly crowds heard, wondered about the strange new religion, bought a few books to read — and welcomed the touring evangelists the next year! The few converts who were made met with severe ostracism from their families and caste fellows. For a convert to be poisoned by his relatives was not unusual, since becoming a Christian meant traitorously renouncing his caste for the company of beef-eating Christians,* and being false to his gods who might be expected to take revenge on his relatives.

The earliest mission was that sent out by the Scotch Presbyterians in 1840 to Nagpur. About the same time, German Lutherans sent out four Christian artisans as missionaries. These walked to the highlands of Mandla district to evangelize the Gond tribe. Three of the four died within six months, and the fourth left that part of India. The Anglicans early occupied Jubbulpore. The Evangelical and Reformed of St. Louis, Missouri, settled in the region of Raipur in the 1860s. The Methodists came to Khandwa and Jubbulpore shortly after. The Christian Churches† opened Harda in 1882 and Bilaspur (walking there two hundred miles from Jubbulpore) in 1884. The English Friends, Swedish Mission, Canadian Presbyterians, American Friends, Free Methodists, American Mennonites, and General Conference Mennonites came in before 1900. All these were engaged in seed-sowing evangelism. Converts, one by one at considerable intervals, were gained and added to the small

---

*Eating beef to Hindus is as horrible as eating human flesh would be to Europeans. It is the ultimate sin — eating your mother.

†The Christian Churches, a movement whose adherents numbering a million in North America, carry out Christian mission all over the world.

congregations that arose at or near the missionaries' residences. There was no other way in which the converts could come. It was hard, if not impossible, for single converts to remain in their own homes.

In 1896 a great famine swept the area. For three years people died like flies. Whole villages were depopulated. The weaker families set out to look for food elsewhere. Some died on the road or in the forest. Unburied bodies were found under trees. Sometimes the children lived when the parents died. The government opened famine relief works, digging irrigation canals and artificial lakes and breaking stone for future roads. To check profiteering, missionaries were asked by government officials to visit these work camps, measure the work done, and pay the workers. Tens of thousands of children — boys and girls — were left on the doorsteps of missionaries. They took them in, fed them, built temporary shelters to protect them from the hot sun and torrential rains, called loudly for missionary physicians to come to India and help, started schools, and purchased land on which the hundreds of orphans in each area could work as they had been accustomed to do in their villages.

They also taught them the Christian religion. Those who after the famine remained in the orphanage generally became Christians and grew up in the atmosphere of an institution which was (and had to be) systematized after the fashion of Western schools. The children grew up very different from the villagers their parents had been. Converts of this sort added individuals from many castes to the small multiethnic congregations.

They were taught carpentry, blacksmithing, mason's work, and tailoring. Some became teachers in the schools or preachers who assisted in the evangelistic work. All without exception were pebbles, so to speak, in process of being formed into a living rock: the Christian Church. They had come from many villages. Many did not remember their castes. Some did, but coming from a low caste, did not wish to emphasize it. Some who came from a higher caste felt they had "ruined" their caste by interdining and living as one family with boys (or girls) of other castes. The missionaries did not feel it desirable to record the castes from which the orphans came; they believed they were forming a casteless Christian community which could be thoroughly Indian, speak Hindi as a mother tongue, eat Indian food, live in Indian houses, wear Indian clothes, and thus be the ideal Christians to communicate the Gospel to those who had yet to believe.

Orphanages of this sort were rapidly established in the late nineties by practically all missions: Canadian Presbyterians, Church of Scotland, Anglicans, Methodists, Free Methodists, Christian Churches, and the various others. As the work of the missions proceeded from year to year and decade to decade — in direct evangelism, orphanages, schools, medical relief, and public services of various sorts — the flow of converts varied from station to station and missionary to missionary.

Sometimes a great missionary (like Alexander Duff in Calcutta in the 1920s) through teaching the Bible and other subjects in the classroom, won a significant number of students to Christ. Sometimes an ardent Christian, Indian or missionary, who had employed a number of Indian workers on some project (building, famine relief work, or establishing a farm settlement, leprosy home, or the like) offered such financial security to those who left all to become Christians, and presented Christ so winsomely, that several of his employees became converts. Sometimes a physician or a teacher — Indian or missionary — so manifested the fruits of the Spirit and was so likeable and charming that Christians and non-Christians alike thought of him as truly God's man. He would win more converts than some very good missionary, full of good works, much prayer, and great knowledge of the Bible, whose life did not shine. Most of the new Christians brought none of their immediate relatives or friends. Now and then, however, some one of them — whether by some merit in himself or by the circumstances of having intimates who could be influenced — led a number of others to Christ.

Thus the one-by-one-against-the-current process of becoming Christian led to large multiethnic congregations in some places and small in others. Conglomerate congregations arose at all mission stations. *To join a community made up of individuals of many castes*, who in the various ways I have described chose to be known as Christians under the loving care of missionaries, is what it meant to become a Christian.

The resources of missions were distributed in the face of this actual situation. Most of the money went to the care of the communities of nontypical individuals which arose in the main towns and at the mission stations. Schools had to be built — the Christian community must not be illiterate. Hospitals or some kind of medical service had to be established — it would be irresponsible to have an orphanage with several hundred boys and girls and no physician to care for them when they fell ill. Substantial church buildings had to be erected in which the several hundred orphans and the mission staff could worship. Yet because the missionaries had come to India to propagate the Christian faith, they usually devoted a part of their resources to direct evangelism. The Canadian Presbyterians ruled that 50 percent of all funds from Canada must go to direct evangelism; but this was unusual. In many missions, direct evangelism received a quarter or less of the resources.

Moreover, a *theory* of missions which this process was building up, and a *theology* of mission which would support work resulting in small conglomerate congregations of educated, thoroughly Christian, and thoroughly decultured individuals, were both being developed. No one set about to prepare such a theory or theology to buttress the kind of work that was being done, yet both arose unconsciously as those who were doing the work and seeing conglomerate congregations rising on every hand (in very small numbers) sought biblical and theological justification for their labors.

That the growth of the Church was a slow process seemed inevitable in the light of Matthew 22:14: "For many are called, but few are chosen."

That the congregation was strictly noncaste seemed thoroughly biblical. Orphans, young men and women, married each other with no thought of caste, or rather, if they knew their original caste, rejoicing in cross-caste marriages. Did not the Bible say that all were sons of God and that in the Church there is neither Jew nor Greek, neither slave nor free?

That the vast majority of hearers rejected the Christian way was deemed something Christians should expect — was not the Lord Himself rejected and despised?

When rapid church growth in other parts of India was heard of, it was thought that it could not be really good growth. To be good, it had to be slow. And to be thoroughly Christian, converts had to come in one by one against the current of caste. A multiethnic community was *more Christian* than a monoethnic. A conglomerate congregation was a truly spiritual part of the Body of Christ. All this was theology formed to support the way in which Type 2 churches were being developed.

In short, Type 2 congregations (and gradually denominations) rose all across the Central Provinces as inevitably as the sun rises in the east. They seemed normal and natural. Type 2 was the Madhya Pradesh or Central Provinces pattern. It was also the typical pattern in almost every state in India.

The Thirty Missions and Churches

By 1959 thirty missions and Churches were at work in Madhya Pradesh. Each — with a few exceptions — was creating conglomerate congregations. Each denomination was a cluster of conglomerates, held together at first by the mission that gave it birth, and later by the emerging denomination and the web of marriage relationships that gradually grew up inside the multiethnic community.

A list of the missions follows, under the names of the denominations abroad which originally sent them to India. In the case of interdenominational missionary societies, their names are given rather than those of their Madhya Pradesh missions. In the case of the two Lutheran missions listed in column 2, the sending bodies were the Lutheran Church of Andhra and the Lutheran Church of Chhota Nagpur.

Old-Line Missions Established Before 1900	New-Line Missions Established After 1920 (mostly after 1945)	Service Organizations
Church of Scotland	Churches of Christ*	Mission to Lepers
Church of England	Conservative Baptists	TB Sanitarium
Evangelical Lutheran	Evangelical Alliance Mission	YMCA
American Methodist	World Wide Evangelistic Crusade	YWCA
Christian Churches	Pentecostal Church of God	ISSU†
Evangelical and Reformed	Oriental Missionary Society	
Mennonite, American	Full Gospel Christian Fellowship	
Mennonite, Gen. Conf.	Assemblies of God-North India	
Friends, English	Bible Crusade Missionary Society	
Friends, American	Andhra Evangelical Lutherans	
Canadian Presbyterian	Gossner Evangelical Lutherans	
Free Church of Scotland		
Roman Catholic Church		

As the missions moved into the 171,000 square miles, they generally occupied sections of the country where no other missions were at work. If the Friends were planting churches or doing mission work in one district, the next mission entering Madhya Pradesh went to another district, or at least to a subdistrict in which the Friends had no work. This arrangement, known as comity, presumably gave fair leeway to each sending body and prevented wasteful overlapping. Most of the missions hoped, prayed, and expected that numerous congregations would arise all across the territory they had occupied; they tended therefore to hold it for themselves and to resist others coming into "their" area. And had great Christward movements broken out, exactly that indeed might have happened. In the hundred years we are considering, however, from 1860 to 1960, no great movements took place. Thus Type 2 congregations in 1976 are usually tiny islands of Christianity in the midst of an ocean of Hinduism.

On Map 2, page 72, one can see the enormous areas in which

*The Churches of Christ, a movement whose adherents in North America number a million, began work in south east Madhya Pradesh in 1929.
†The India Sunday School Union.

there are no Christians. In only a few places does one discern concentrations of 5,000 to 10,000 and more (see double squares and double triangles on the map). Comity was a good system. It prevented duplication, but veiled the fact that it was wildly unrealistic to hope that the little congregations of a few hundred or at most a few thousand could, even with the help of missionary societies of the West, evangelize the huge populations in the midst of which they were located.

THE INDIAN DENOMINATIONS

By 1959, in addition to these missions whose controlling parent bodies lay outside Madhya Pradesh, mostly in America and Europe, a large number of local denominations had arisen. Every mission had planted its own denomination. In some cases this was a very small body composed of a few hundred members in half a dozen congregations. In other cases, the congregations as they were established became part of a much larger denomination. For example, Methodist congregations formed part of the Methodist Church in Southern Asia. Anglican congregations became part of the Church of India.

In 1959 the principal Indian denominations in Madhya Pradesh were: the United Church of Northern India, the Roman Catholic Church, the Anglican Church of India, the Methodist Church of Southern Asia, the Mennonite Church in India, the General Conference Mennonite Church, Friends Churches, the Christian Churches, and the Churches of Christ. Several smaller denominations also existed, together with some individual congregations which, though quite separate from one another, were often grouped under the heading of "Local Autonomous Churches."

In 1970 the Church of North India was formed, to which a number of denominations adhered. In 1973 the more conservative denominations joined to form the Federation of Evangelical Churches of India.

ARRESTED PEOPLE MOVEMENTS

While the small congregations of one-by-one-against-the-current converts were gradually being formed at or near the mission stations, the castes of India were responding to the Gospel in a more Indian way. Instead of single individuals deciding to become Christians and leaving their castes to do so — suffering severe ostracism in the process and cutting themselves off from their native stock — here and there groups of families all of the same caste or tribe decided to become Christian. Small movements to the Christian faith, running through a single caste, began. Since none of the Christian leaders in Madhya Pradesh, Indian or missionary, expected this kind of movement; since Hindus who felt vague urgings of the Spirit toward Christianity did not know how to go about it; since the dominant pattern was "one by one"; and since each caste vigorously resisted such a move on the part of several of its families — for these various reasons — many of these beginnings of people movements were halted. They died, so to speak, in infancy.

A people movement or group movement to Christ is a very tender plant, particularly in an area where the dominant pattern is one by one against the family. Unless such movements are recognized as precious gifts of God, prayed for, and tended with loving care, they very frequently stop after a few dozen or a few hundred have become Christian. Some revert to Hinduism.

During the last hundred years God gave to His obedient servants in Madhya Pradesh many beginnings of movements to Christ running through a particular caste or tribe. Each occurred within a total group numbering from perhaps fifty thousand to a million. Each held the potential of spreading throughout that caste or tribe. In other parts of India such movements have spread sometimes to fifty thousand, sometimes to a hundred thousand, and in a few cases to half a million persons. But in Madhya Pradesh no movement has grown large. All have been arrested.

The five listed below are well known, but many others arose which brought in smaller numbers and died earlier. Some died aborning. Some were bound to die, yet others perished needlessly. The Church in India must learn to recognize and value these precious beginnings and find out how to eliminate unnecessary infant mortality.

In the western end of Madhya Pradesh around the year 1900, the Balahi caste started to turn to Christ. Some Balahis opted for the Roman Catholic Church, some for the Methodist, and some for the Presbyterian, depending largely on where they lived. All told, out of several hundred thousand Balahis perhaps 20,000 became Christians.

In the southeast corner of Madhya Pradesh, for about a hundred years the million-strong Satnami caste has showed a mild interest in Christianity. More than a dozen small movements to Christ have occurred. Many individual Satnamis have become Christian. Probably today 20,000 Christians come from the Satnami background, but no sweeping movement has developed.

On the borders of Orissa, the Gara people movement has spilled over into the edge of Madhya Pradesh, and perhaps 4,000 have become Christians. Counting those who are Christians in Orissa, possibly 30,000 of the million Garas have become Christian.

In the southern projection of Madhya Pradesh about 7,000 Mehras are now Christian. This movement has taken in most of the Mehras in that part of the province. In terms of the *proportion* of the caste concerned, it is the most successful.

In the southwest, where Madhya Pradesh joins Maharashtra State, several small Mahar movements to Christ in several missions started back in the twenties and thirties. They were part of the great movement out of Hinduism led by Dr. Ambedkar which ultimately took three million into Buddhism. Had Ambedkar led his followers into Christianity, as many expected and hoped he might, the history of that part of India would have been radically altered. These small movements produced no concentration of Christians in any district; but 40 years later, the big city — Nagpur — had 14,000 Christians in it, according to the 1971 census.

These arrested people movements tell of a great hunger in the hearts of the oppressed and downtrodden. They long to leave Egypt for the Promised Land, but so far have been unable to do it except in these small numbers. The heart hunger continues in Madhya Pradesh and all across India. Christian mission and the Church of Christ ought to see in these people movements striving to be born *a truly Indian way of becoming Christian;* ought to encourage such movements to take place and nurture them once they have begun.

Small, arrested people movements in Madhya Pradesh feed Type 2 congregations and denominations. The process works as follows: The movement brings in a few dozen or a few hundred in scattered villages. These converts, immersed in a sea of caste fellows who consider them renegades, are uncomfortable. They commonly suffer harrassment of one kind and another. One by one they move to the center where a conglomerate congregation is — where other Christians live. Perhaps the rains fail and they go in to get work. Perhaps they put a boy into boarding school and move in to be close to him. Perhaps a daughter does well in school, goes on to nurse's training, gets a good job, and brings her old mother and father to live with her in the town. Perhaps a wife dies and the new wife does not like to live in the village. In many districts of Madhya Pradesh where there used to be small groups of village Christians there are now none. They have moved to the towns and joined the conglomerate multiethnic congregations there.

The Forty-two Districts

The size of Madhya Pradesh and the extent of its population is seen when one realizes that this single state, with 42 million inhabitants, has forty-two districts. The average for each, therefore, is about a million. Practically all districts were "occupied" by some mission. The mission stations were generally located along a railway (see map 2), which means that today in the towns along the railway lines one finds one or two churches per town. Cities generally have five to ten congregations. Each district will have a few hundred or at most a few thousand Christians. Tens of thousands of villages and towns off the railway, out in the plains and hills of this fair land, never see an evangelist, never in fact get a chance to hear the Gospel or read a Bible. The people who live there never walk past a church, or witness a baptism, or see Christians assembling for worship. No one there ever partakes of the Lord's Supper. As one views the map, so far as Christianity is concerned one may think of Madhya Pradesh as in absolute darkness, pierced here and there along the railway lines by the light of one small congregation. Great sections of the province are wholly unoccupied. No pastor, no layman, and no missionary ever sets foot there to preach the Gospel.

While one rejoices in the solidly Christian Type 2 congregations scattered thinly along the railways, our rejoicing must be severely tempered by the realization that each multiethnic congregations is necessarily surrounded by vast untouched populations which the multiethnic congregation is not reaching, *and does not particularly want to reach.* The castes are not "our kind of people." The conglomerate congregation is a different social organism. If it evangelizes at all (and most of them do little beyond passing out tracts), in essence it invites members of each caste to "leave your caste and join our community."

The caste system all over India inevitably produces in the total Hindu population a thin sliver of individuals who for various reasons are only loosely connected with or actually out of caste. Perhaps they have taken on a woman of another caste and been expelled. Perhaps they are being disciplined for some offense. Perhaps they have come from afar, cannot get a wife of their own caste, and realize that if they die they have no one to bury them. Perhaps they have had a horrendous row with their caste fellows. They may be highly educated and fed up with the caste system.

Or they have become Marxists and are rebelling against India's stratified society.

The multiethnic character of Type 2 appeals strongly to this mixed and tiny social minority. Through the years one of the main sources of converts has been persons either very slightly attached to or actually detached from their own hereditary castes. Districts with great cities in them have more of this type of person than those made up entirely of villages and small towns. So *multi*ethnic congregations have a better chance of spreading in cities than in villages. With *mono*ethnic groups, as we shall see in the next chapter, the situation is different.

WHERE ARE THE CHRISTIANS?

If Christians number about one in four hundred of the total population, this average must not mislead us. In the towns and cities they may amount to one or two in a hundred, but in many regions they are no more than one in a thousand or — in numerous subdistricts — one in ten thousand.

On map 2 the four symbols should be noted, with their locations. Tiny circles mean little groups of 100 or 200 Christians — one or two congregations. Each single-walled square means 1,000 or so. Each double-lined square shows that about 5,000 Christians (of all denominations put together) live there. Each double walled triangle indicates 10,000 or more. These triangles occur where arrested people movements to Christ have taken place, or Christians have moved into a nearby big city. Had the one-by-one-against-the-current mode of ingathering been strictly followed, the congregations and denominations of Madhya Pradesh would have been *much smaller* and even more scattered. The conglomerate church pattern in India produces small and very slow-growing churches.

Out away from the railways are a few congregations and former mission stations which I have not indicated on the map. They are so small that to show them at all whould give an erroneous impression of size and strength. They do not alter the conclusion I have stated that, with the exception of the congregations along the rail lines, Madhya Pradesh is in dense darkness so far as any knowledge of Christianity is concerned.

In most rural districts, the conglomerate church approach has resulted in small, sealed-off clumps of good Christians.

In the bigger towns and cities, however, where the larger mission stations have been, where mission institutions were built, and especially where the arrested people movements fed the local city churches, the situation is different. There you find substantial congregations of two hundred, five hundred, a thousand souls. These support their ordained ministers, attend church reasonably well, rear their children as Christians, and intend to stay Christian. Some are leading citizens of their towns. They push their young people on into education. They attend Christian Conventions and even do a little evangelism themselves. District superintendents and bishops live in the cities and are cultured, educated Christians.

Madhya Pradesh today and all its congregations and denominations are going through the pains of withdrawal of mission aid, which affects every type of Church.

MADHYA PRADESH PATTERN
COMMON THROUGHOUT INDIA

Since practically every mission in India started its work in a fashion somewhat like that described here for Madhya Pradesh, *it was inevitable that Type 2 conglomerates should arise all over the country*, despite the fact that they are very un-Indian. Conglomerates are the commonest type of congregation, not only in this province but in all parts of the land, except certain districts of the northeast and south where strong people movements have swept across a given caste or tribe. Even there Type 2 occurs in some *tahsils* or counties.

In each of the states listed below, the Madhya Pradesh pattern,

with many instances of Type 2 and a few small, arrested people
movements here and there, prevails.

> Uttar Pradesh
> Hariana
> Himachal
> Bihar (except for Chhota Nagpur)
> West Bengal
> Rajasthan
> Maharashtra
> Gujarat (except for the Dherd movement)
> Assam
> Bangladesh
> Karnataka
> Tripura

Even in Kerala, Tamil Nadu, Andhra, Meghalaya, and Manipur,
in districts and subdistricts unaffected by any people movement,
conglomerates are the typical form of congregation.

When one thinks of the Church in India, it is therefore fair to
think for the most part of multiethnic congregations. They are
typical in nine-tenths of the land area of the whole nation and
Bangladesh. The Indian Church pattern per excellence is the
conglomerate or multiethnic congregation and denomination.
Type 2 is the typical form of new congregations in many other
countries also, but distinctly not true in some.

MIGHTY LABORS OF
NATIONALS AND MISSIONARIES

During the last hundred and seventy years tens of thousands of
devoted Indian and European Christians have done an amazing
amount of work: preaching the Gospel, serving the people, and
propagating the Christian faith. Most of their labors have been
unrecorded and unsung. A few (such as Sadhu Sundar Singh or
Pundita Ramabai, William Carey, Bishop Thoburn, Dr. Scudder,
or Praying Hyde) have been written up; but for each of these

there are a thousand others whose good works are generally unknown. Yet they penetrated to every district and subdistrict. They learned the language, whatever it was, well. They lived among the people. They taught boys and girls — as a rule far more non-Christians than Christians. They healed millions of sick in dispensaries and hospitals. They translated the Bible and many other books. They learned Indian tunes and set hymns written in Indian rhythms to them. They toured the villages and the markets, the fairs and other gathering places preaching the Good News and being friends of all the earth. They maintained mission organizations in which Indians and missionaries functioned as parts of the team.

They baptized believers, organized them into churches, travailed with them till Christ was formed in them, loved them, prayed for them, wept and rejoiced with them. By incredible labors they created congregation after congregation — and most were conglomerates.

They influenced India in many ways. In earlier days, they opened the doors of the new scientific learning of the West to multitudes of eager young minds. They demonstrated a new kind of life in regions of India where it would not otherwise have penetrated for decades. They spread the knowledge of vaccination and other preventive medicine. They introduced new crops. They worked for more humane and just legislation for the oppressed; large numbers of the Depressed Classes and aboriginal tribes came to Christian faith through their efforts. These they elevated by fellowship and education till the cruel lie that the Depressed were inferior human beings was less widely believed, if not fully renounced. India's action in outlawing untouchability would never have been undertaken but for the labors of Christians.

Missionaries also touched and humanized the feelings of people in England, Germany, France, and other "sending" countries. In each of these, the missionary movement created huge numbers of supporters who prayed regularly for Indians, looked on them as "our friends and fellow Christians," gloried in

the lives of noted Christians such as Narayan Vaman Tilak and
Bishop Azariah, and gave unceasingly of their money and their
sons and daughters that the work of grace should proceed. All
this softened the feelings of the European ruler nations. It was no
accident that India won its freedom without a bloody war.
Clement Atlee, Prime Minister of England when freedom was ˈ
granted in 1947, came of a missionary family. His sister had all
her life been a missionary in Africa. Augustus Caesar, good man
though he was, would never at the very moment of his greatest
military power have granted freedom to Rome's most valuable
possession. But when the Christian people of England faced the
alternative of ruling India by force or yielding her freedom,
almost without debate they decided for freedom. Other factors
were certainly involved, but the considerable effect of missions on
the sending countries must be counted as one of the important
elements producing this amazing event.

The multiplicity of these labors and the commendable
achievements of many of them (for missions are a very wide and
wonderful enterprise) often blot out the central purpose of the
Christian mission: to propagate the Christian faith. While
cordially appreciating the multitudinous good results of mission,
in this chapter I have sought to depict the outcome of that central
purpose in its most typical form: Type 2, the conglomerate
multiethnic Churches.

EVANGELISTIC POTENTIAL OF CONGLOMERATES

Each type of Church has a different evangelistic potential.
Even if they were to put in equal amounts of time and devotion,
the end-result from each would be different. In proclaiming the
Gospel, each is really issuing a different invitation, since every
invitation to follow the Saviour also means "come and be a
Christian *along with us.*" Thus every type of congregation presents
a different option to those being evangelized.

My assumption here is that each of the nine types of Church is
presenting a biblical message. It is lifting up Christ Himself,

preaching the pure Gospel. The differences I shall speak of are not those that arise from heresy, ignorance, lukewarm witness, or unlovely witnesses. Such differences to be sure are found, as they are all over the world; and they are found in all nine types, the unique property of no single pattern. Consequently I shall not dwell on them here. They are the stock in trade of many who speak on evangelism and the Church and need not be repeated.

As Type 2 Christians and congregations witness for their Lord, *who hears them?* Who may be expected to respond — who is likely to accept the invitation? Evangelistic potential anywhere is conditioned by answers to these and similar questions.

1. Conglomerates have a powerful appeal to the thin sliver of humanity mentioned above which lies outside of or is loosely connected with the castes. Unaffiliated individuals are likely to become Christians in multiethnic congregations. This can be a truly religious decision. They live already in a noncaste society (i.e. outside the tight confines of any one caste) and will be in the same kind of society if they join a conglomerate congregation. Their way of life and that of the conglomerates have many things in common. But there are drawbacks. This small section of the population is made up, as we have seen earlier, of many who have broken caste laws and are either under discipline by their fellows or have actually been thrust out by them. Then, too, if they can easily join a Christian church, they can also easily leave it. As a rule this fraction of society is not made up of deeply religious men and women, and they may come to Christ largely for secular, materialistic, or social reasons. Nevertheless, the proclamation of the conglomerates to unaffiliated persons is quite likely to be heard.

2. A second group, more numerous than the first, also welcomes the Gospel from the conglomerates. Here we have members of ethnic units from which considerable numbers have become Christians. In fifty or more out of the three thousand castes and tribes in India, enough have become Christian so that the average member of the caste says, "Yes, some of our people have become Christians." Perhaps he says it in anger, deeply

resenting the fact. Perhaps he says it meditatively, believing it may be a good thing to be a Christian. Perhaps he knows that millions of Hindus have become Buddhists and that all Africa south of the Sahara is in process of becoming substantially Christian. Perhaps he holds that in the modern world freedom of conscience and of movement are good. Perhaps he knows of relatives who became Christians and prospered exceedingly. For these persons, numbering probably more than ten-million, becoming a Christian is such a reasonable procedure that they are not overly offended at the idea of joining another community. In fact, they do not regard the Church as really another community, since "many of our people are already in the Church."

3. A third group of persons, numbering many millions, is also at least slightly open to conglomerate Christian witness. These are those who have recently moved to some great city and are at loose ends there. They are learning many new ways and making many new friends. They are out from under the close supervision of parents and relatives, free to associate with Christians or go to a Christian church without fear of losing status. Furthermore, by virtue of moving to a new neighborhood and not being able to do all the things "our people always do back in the village where we came from," they have already moved out of the tight clutches of the caste system — at least temporarily. After a few years in the city (or a few months if they move into a neighborhood of their own caste and subcaste), if unacquainted with other horizons, they will establish anew in the city the caste friendships and bonds they had back in the villages. Then they will not be able to hear the Gospel proclaimed by multiethnic Churches. The "multiethnicness" will offend them. They will want association with "our kind of people." But for a short period great numbers of persons on the move can hear the Gospel witness presented by conglomerates. The Hindu refugees from Bangladesh in 1971-72 belong to this group and are currently somewhat responsive, even though back in Bangladesh.

When a conglomerate congregation shuts its eyes to the whole caste system and looks on all Indians simply as Indians, proclaiming the Gospel indiscriminately to all castes, it does not really see these three kinds of persons who can hear its message. A Christian from such a congregation therefore misses many opportunities. Unwittingly, yet deliberately, he sows seed on the path and in the brambles and the thin soil. Once he recognizes his own type of church and realizes that his message will generally be heard by special kinds of persons, he can sow most of his precious seed in soil he knows is good. Widespread blind sowing does — by accident — deposit some seed in good soil. But why sow blindly?

CAN MULTIETHNICS START MONOETHNICS?

This is a nice question. Are conglomerate congregations limited to the one-by-one-against-the-current type of church growth? Or can they light fires of faith which will spread throughout one caste and in it bring many to faith in a typical people movement to Christ? The answers are clear.

Historically most great people movements have risen as existing Christians of conglomerate congregations have led someone to Jesus Christ, and then he (for reasons largely unknown to the Christians) has led his own people — in India his own caste or tribe fellows — to Christ. In *Founders of the Indian Church,* many years ago, I related in popular fashion the lives of seven great Indians who started seven people movements which brought in millions of Christians. In a real sense those seven, though very humble men, were the founders of the Indian Church. Each was brought to Christ by a Christian belonging to a Type 2 congregation, who believed that coming to Christ one by one against the current was the best and maybe the only way in which men and women could come.

Consequently one must believe that multiethnic congregations *can* start monoethnic ones. However, all seven movements began unintentionally from the point of view of the conglomerate group. The existing Christians did not intend to start people movements. In fact, sometimes they resisted them. Each movement forced its way into the Kingdom almost against their wishes, certainly against their ideas as to how men and women ought to become Christians. We must therefore ask our question more definitively: *Can multiethnic congregations intentionally start movements to Christian faith running through a caste?*

The answer is a qualified affirmative. I have discussed this matter at some length in *Bridges of God* (chap. 9); let me here present a summary of the reply. Conglomerates can give birth to people movements provided that they:

Accept group ingathering as a desirable form of church growth and learn its pattern;

Concentrate attention on some homogeneous unit they deem winnable;

Encourage churches to develop *within* the communities of that unit; and

Win enough groups of that unit in a short enough time and a small enough area so that each convert comes into the Body *with some of his kindred.*

The conglomerate Churches of India and their great leaders, who are "convinced conglomerates", must learn that becoming Indian, becoming truly indigenous, means adopting not the outer trappings of Indian tunes and temple bells, but *the inner psychology of a pluralistic society.* Becoming Indian means planting the Church in every caste — without accepting the heresy that God made the tribes in different molds and that there are superior and inferior races. In is a heresy to believe that the inferior *must not* learn the sacred *shruti* (scripture) and must be content to be hewers of wood and drawers of water. The Church in India must both "plant the Church in every caste" and "press forward in establishing One Church in which all Christians are brothers" — *simultaneously.* The tasks are equally important.

3

MONOETHNIC CHURCHES
FROM CASTE

THE THIRD basic type of Church in India is the people movement
Church that arises from caste. This Type 3 is in sharp distinction
from the conglomerate or multiethnic type in which
congregations are formed as individuals from many castes,
converted one by one, join a single new community, and maintain
no link with any caste. Conglomerates or multiethnics not only
follow a new religion but also constitute a new social organism. In
monoethnic congregations and denominations, on the other
hand, the convert follows a new religion *but continues on in his
normal social organism.* To be sure, the old organism is changed —
sometimes very slightly, sometimes drastically — but it does not
disappear.

The same is true of monoethnic Churches from tribe, Type 4, with the essential difference that castes share a countryside with many other castes rather than occupying their own homogeneous territory. This, together with the presence of a unique tribal language or dialect and the fact that the tribes are not related to, or fully incorporated in, the elaborate and pervasive caste system of Hinduism — which extends throughout all India, and in which they are small enclaves, so to speak — makes it convenient to discuss them as a separate type.

A caste or subcaste is not a tribe, but since it practices endogamy and often has a highly developed and ancient tradition, each is in a very real sense a homogeneous people or "community."

The New Testament tells of the first people movement. On the day of Pentecost three thousand Jews came to believe in Jesus as Messiah and Lord. They were baptized. They received the Holy Spirit. They continued in the apostles' teaching and fellowship, in the breaking of bread and the prayers. Yet they did not cease to be Jews. They continued going to the Temple. They maintained the taboo against pork. They continued to circumcize their male babies on the eighth day. They observed the Sabbath, and refused to eat with Gentiles. They continued to take pride in the fact that they were of the tribe of Benjamin, or Judah, or Levi; continued to marry their sons to Jewish girls of the right subtribe and to enter into all the contractual relationships which that entailed. Their weddings were undoubtedly solemnized by Jewish rituals.

The illustration, to be sure, must not be pushed too far. Becoming Christian from a monotheistic faith is one thing, from a polytheistic faith something else. The Jews were the "People of God" before they became Christian. Marxists, Animists, Buddhists, and Hindus cannot be fully equated with them. Nevertheless, the example is valuable. It is biblical for people of a non-Christian culture to become Christian and bring over with them into the faith many components of their old culture. They can continue to speak their mother tongue. They can be tenderly affectionate toward their loved ones — probably more than before. They can discharge the duties of citizens in their own village, state, or city and in a thousand other ways retain cultural identity with their fellows.

WHAT TYPE 3 CHURCHES ARE

As monoethnic congregations arise in castes, several individuals — sometimes twenty, sometimes three, sometimes a hundred — decide together to become Christians. They come into the Church as one social unit. They remain in close contact with their caste, while in matters of worship, sacred books, doctrines of man, God, sin, salvation, the future life, and the like they become rigorously Christian.

People movements of this kind resulting in monoethnic congregations and denominations are characteristic of growing Churches in most countries, but are particularly natural in the Indian Church. If the multiethnic congregation is the most *typical* in India, the monoethnic is the most *natural*. A caste society inclines toward monoethnic congregations as water runs downhill. People who have been reared in a caste and think of themselves as members of a distinct group quite different from other men like to become Christians without "ruining their caste." As noted earlier, this phrase is used by Hindus to describe those who have left their caste, joined another caste, or become Christians. They have "ruined their caste" — that is, destroyed their caste status; they do not "ruin" the caste itself, although their defection may be regarded with anything from mild to furious regret, as well as — in some instances — mere thoughtful interest. But they have "made another father." Their natural father, the caste progenitor, was not good enough for them; they have betrayed him, have "made another father."

In a successful people movement to Christ these charges can not be leveled, with the same force because the Christians are still, to a considerable degree, one with their people. To be sure, since becoming a Christian means renouncing all other deities, religious allegiances, and scriptures and cleaving to Christ and the Bible alone, the strongly idolatrous section of the caste is commonly angry with them. So were the Jews with those who became Christians in Jerusalem. Christians may be boycotted, told they must use a different section of the river or pond to bathe in, and shut out of caste councils. In northern India, people movement converts hear "Hookah pani bund." (No more shall we drink water with you or smoke with you. You are no longer part of us.) Yet since the residences remain alongside each other as before, and since the Christians love their neighbors even more than before; since, also, groups of ten or twenty families help each other in time of need and cannot be badly hurt by boycott, the passage of time dissipates the anger. Non-Christians borrow tools or plowing animals from the Christians. A Christian housewife runs into a neighbor's house saying, "My fire has gone out. May I get a few coals?" and is not refused. Relationships are very apt to revert to normal, and the boycott ceases to be effective.

How Monoethnic Churches Arise

The heart of the people movement mode of becoming Christian — the unique process by which it occurs — is that instead of acting as individuals, men and women who want to follow the Lord Jesus talk the matter over with their intimates, sometimes for a week, sometimes for years, till a consensus is formed: that is, till some five or perhaps fifty are ready to participate in a decision to follow Christ. They become Christians and are baptized together. They worship and partake of the Lord's Supper as members of the same Body.

The process goes on in a caste which lives in many villages and is bound together by a web of blood and marriage relationships. Let us suppose that nine families in Sitapur have become Christians. The head of one family is Hira Singh. Hira's mother was born in

Rampur ten miles away, and her brothers, uncles to Hira, live there. His sisters are married to men who live in Nandghat and Baghmar, so Hira Singh has brothers-in-law in those two villages. In imagination we can easily construct the large network of relationships — aunts, second cousins, mother's relations, father's relations, and in-laws of many varieties — well known to Hira Singh in Sitapur. All these relations in a score of villages know that "one of us has become a Christian." Most are curious. Some come over to see what it means to be a Christian. When Hira stops in at their houses in the course of his work, he is plied with questions and his way of life observed. Soon some of the twenty groups of relatives will be saying, "Why should not we become Christian? It is a good thing to be Christian. Even the women who become Christians learn about God . . ." Then in one of the twenty villages a group will decide to repeat what has happened in Sitapur: they become Christian as a group.

This process, duplicated again and again, is the *people movement* and results in a cluster of congregations in which all the members are of one caste and many are interrelated. Men and women come to Christ with their relatives — husbands with wives, sons with fathers, four brothers and their wives together, leaders with followers, the weak with the strong. A segment of a social organism — a caste — moves to Christian faith and is followed across the months and years by other related segments.

This most natural type of Church in India is very widespread. Type 3 is found in most of the states, though *large* people movements from caste have taken place mostly in the south. It is important to note that Type 3 has developed almost entirely in the bottommost ranks of the caste system. In Figure 2 on the next page the column at the right represents caste society, about 500 million persons. These are distributed in five great divisions or compartments: the Brahman, Kshatriya, Vaishya, Shudra, and Low Castes. In each compartment are hundreds of castes. In the five taken together there are more than two thousand six

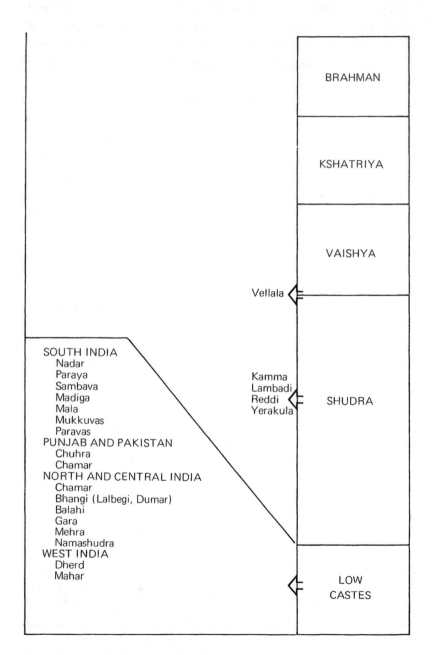

Fig. 2 Major People Movements from Caste

hundred.* A people movement to Christ could evolve through the process just described *in any one of these;* but as a matter of fact people movements have developed in only a few of the hundreds of Low Castes. Most of these are called Scheduled Castes or Depressed Classes.

Since each part of the nation has its own cluster of castes, in each region movements to Christian Faith have taken place in different castes. The left column in Figure 2 shows the major movements from the Low Castes in each region. For example, in South India seven large movements (Nadars,† Paravas, Sambavas, Malas, Madigas, and Mukkuvas and Paravas on the coast) have occurred out of the low caste. In West India only two of the Scheduled Castes have had large movements develop in them, Dherds and Mahars. Small arrested movements, not shown in Figure 2, have taken place in several others.

In South India, in addition to the above, we see movements of some size in four Shudra castes — Kammas, Lambadis, Reddis and Yerakulas. The Vellala Christward movement is the only one to develop in a truly middle caste. Vellalas do not like to be considered Shudras, yet do not claim Vaishya or Kshatriya status. Hence they are portrayed as between the Shudra and Vaishya sections.

*Estimates of how many castes and tribes there are and of which are castes and which are tribes vary greatly. J.H. Hutton's authoritative *Caste in India* (1961) lists 118 tribal names (p. 317-319); but some of these are counted as *castes* in many places. Thus Gonds in most districts of Madhya Pradesh are simply one cultivating caste among many. Tribes are continually becoming castes. Furthermore, some of the 118 tribes are really clusters of sub-tribes, some quite large. Thus Bhils, who might be supposed to be one tribe, are in reality many endogamous tribes each with a distinctive name. In one district, what are separate clans of one caste, in another are rated as separate castes. Consequently I have arbitrarily tripled Hutton's list and say "there are more than 400 tribes" and "more than 2,600 castes." The impression I wish to convey is that of very large numbers of endogamous ethnic units — castes and tribes.

†The communities in India are sensitive as to their ranking. Nadars have made great progress in the last hundred and fifty years and now rank as middle caste. Yet they were certainly a severely oppressed people when, between 1820 and 1860, they turned to Christ in great numbers. It is in historical perspective, not present status, that I classify them with others of low caste background.

While exact numerical proportions are impossible to construct — the scene is very complex — the following approximations convey substantial truth. In about 2,000 Shudra, Vaishya, Kshatriya, and Brahman castes, substantial and lasting people movements have developed in only 5 — that is in only 0.0025 percent of these castes. On the other hand in about 600 Scheduled Castes, substantial and lasting people movements have developed in 21 — that is in about 3 percent of these castes.

WHY TYPE 3 CHURCHES MULTIPLY

The two reasons for this are instructive. First, only to the Scheduled Classes have the benefits of Christianity appeared substantial enough to warrant a move to the Christian faith. In the Christian religion, members of the Depressed Classes were regarded as men, taught the same high religion that all Christians follow, taught the sacred book, and given the opportunity to become priests and pastors. Christianity taught that humanity was not divided up into high and low castes, with the Scheduled Castes occupying the very lowest niche, but that all were regarded as sons of Adam, hence all brothers. Furthermore, Christian missions established schools among converts from the Scheduled Castes just as readily as among the upper castes who were not becoming Christian. This opened the door to social and economic advancement. The benefits of Christianity appeared considerable.

Second, only in the Scheduled Castes did these benefits appear substantial *to large numbers of individuals at the same time.* Of the two reasons, the second is the more important. A people movement cannot develop unless many in a given segment of society come to hold a certain opinion at the same time. In the upper castes, many influential men were educated, wealthy, and well satisfied with the rank they had in the caste system. If there were some castes above them, there were also many below them. Here and there an individual felt the spiritual pull of the Christian faith, fell in love with Jesus Christ, saw that the Bible was the true book, came to know the power of Christ by personal experience, and became a Christian — but he came to this decision all by himself. In the Scheduled Castes, because of their oppressed condition, many were ready to hear the Gospel. As with the slaves in Egypt, the hand of Pharoah was so heavy upon them that they were ready to leave *in a body*.

A third reason is sometimes alleged: namely, that missionaries anxious to report large numbers of converts to their supporters in the West concentrated on the Depressed Classes and thus won many of them. Those who argue in this vein imply that if work had been done among the upper castes they, too, would have accepted the Saviour. No evidence supports this argument; the facts are all the other way. From the time of Robert de Nobili onward, the missionaries as they came to India worked primarily with the upper castes.

This was natural. They themselves were 'of European origin, and Europeans — traders, rulers, leaders of victorious armies — were men of substance and learning. Missionaries as a rule were educated. They liked and appealed to the upper castes; many missionaries concentrated on them. All missionaries who taught in schools (which enrolled chiefly the sons and daughters of the wealthy) of necessity worked with the upper echelons. Those who did direct evangelism spoke to the priests, the Brahmans, the literate, the upper castes. In Burma, Judson confined his efforts to the Buddhists, and when the Karen people movement started among the humble, was not at first interested in it. In the Punjab the Presbyterian missionaries wondered whether they ought to baptize Ditt and other Untouchable Chuhra converts, lest they prejudice the upper castes against them. Many a missionary has said "I would rather baptize one Brahman than a thousand Chamars." Whole missions never started work among the depressed, but stressed educational work among the upper castes largely on the grounds that the Depressed Classes were (as the Hindus always declared) inferior peoples who would never make good Christians.

Enough has been said to make clear that these group movements to Christ were not avidly promoted by missionaries. They occurred because Christianity offers substantial spiritual and material rewards, and because *large numbers* desiring these rewards were willing to follow the new religion to get them.

BATTLE AGAINST MONOETHNIC CONGREGATIONS AND DENOMINATIONS

A great battle over people movements has raged among Christians in India. From 1833 on Christianity was inevitably linked to the British Government. Government officials and the officers in the British Army were generally Anglicans and regarded missionaries — particularly Anglican missionaries — with respect. In turn, missionaries regarded officials as God's appointed rulers. Government officials dealt with the great: feudal lords, great merchants, landowners, temple potentates, kings and princes. It was natural for the missionaries, priests, and professors of the new and powerful rulers of India to begin their work with the upper castes, with Brahman pundits and the elite. That the Depressed Classes — known in those days as Untouchables, *Achhut* in Hindi — were becoming Christians was in fact distasteful to most missionaries before 1890. It would have been an unusual missionary who deliberately evangelized them. Sensible men do not start evangelizing a nation by preaching the Gospel to its slaves.

Though early missionaries thus worked very largely with the upper castes, nevertheless the oppressed of the land, listening from the fringes of the crowd, were deciding to become Christians and did here and there erupt into the Christian faith, in some places in great numbers.

When the Untouchables became Christians, they did so in a moving way. Their leaders had often been seekers after salvation in the Hindu system and were men of genuine religious discernment. They not only accepted Christianity, but believed and loved Christ, and He transformed their lives. They endured persecution for Christ's sake. They memorized long portions of the Bible. God was doing a genuine work of grace, and missionaries, when they came to a real sense of what was happening, rejoiced in it. The apostles in ancient Jerusalem accepted the spread of the Church to the Gentiles in Antioch with a similar, at first ambivalent, wonder and then rejoicing.

In India missionaries were assigned to shepherd the churches brought in by the "revival," as it was often called. Schools were opened. Pastors for village congregations were trained. The brightest boys were sent to high school and a few to college. *Strong people movement denominations came into being.* These hundreds of congregations were, however, made up of landless laborers, living in extreme poverty, at first 100 percent illiterate, and constantly treated by the upper castes as the scum of the earth. The little churches and denominations of "village Christians," to use a euphemistic term, living in hovels and worshiping in mud-walled "chapels," presented a marked contrast to the congregations of Anglican officials and educated Christians who attended well-built churches located in spacious grounds in the beautiful cantonment areas of Indian cities.

The missionaries engaged in educational and institutional activities in these cities, associating with government officials and regarded with favor by the upper castes whose young people they were educating, felt that theirs was the real missionary work and regretted the "mass movement Christians" who were so poor, so dirty, so uneducated, and brought so many problems into the Church.

While Type 3 congregations were arising among the Depressed Classes, Type 2 (conglomerate) congregations were beginning to form in the cities. These latter Christians, being fewer in number and living closer to the various kinds of institutions, were more rapidly educated. Occasional upper-caste converts from cultured families became highly educated and obtained good positions as teachers or government administrators. They felt humiliated to have Christianity known as the religion of the despised

Untouchables. (Even today in Andhra Pradesh, Christianity is spoken of as *Mala matham* or *Madiga matham* — the religion of the Malas and Madigas!) When the National Christian Council was organized in the 1920s, leading Indian Christians became its members and obtained an India-wide voice. Bishop Pickett recounts that in one of the very first meetings they proposed that the Council ban all future baptism of Untouchables and all mass movements. These were demeaning to the Christian faith. This popular proposal was supported by many missionaries in educational work.

Fortunately the great John R. Mott was at that meeting; his advice was, "Before you take that stand, make a careful study of the people movement churches [he called them mass movements], and when the facts are all in, then make your decision." His counsel was followed. J.W. Pickett (later to become a bishop) was appointed to do the research. The Institute of Social and Religious Research in New York City provided the funds.

Pickett did the survey between 1928 and 1931 and published his findings in 1933 under the title, *Christian Mass Movements in India*. In 1934 he became the Secretary for Evangelism for the National Christian Council and for three years lectured widely up and down India. With Singh and McGavran, he co-authored *Christian Missions in Mid-India** and also published his own *Christ's Way to India's Heart*. In all three his message, based on what he had found in his four-year research, was that the people movement churches, when well shepherded, were good churches and usually stronger than the conglomerate congregations (though he did not use either term).

He pointed out that the only place in all India where the higher castes were becoming Christian in significant numbers was Andhra Pradesh. There, observing the redemption experienced by the Malas and Madigas who had become Christian, the Shudra castes were espousing the Christian faith. Between 1925 and

*This influential book, now in its fifth edition and a revised form, has been retitled *Church Growth and Group Conversion*.

1935, 50,000 Kammas, Reddis, Lambadis, Yerakulas, and others had been baptized. Pickett called the people movement "Christ's way to India's heart." Figure 2 illustrates the position which these small Shudra movements hold in regard to the large people movements from the oppressed.

Simultaneously with Pickett's influential findings it became apparent that outside Kerala the only places in all India where Christians had any political power at all was where people movements had brought large numbers to confess Christ and be baptized. The implications of this newly discovered fact ended all talk of stopping the baptism of the oppressed; but it did not end the battle over people movements. To this day a substantial proportion of the leaders of the Christian Church in India are dubious about them. Some think that converts who come to Christ by groups cannot be genuinely Christian. Some think that the oppressed are a poor lot through whom to begin to disciple the peoples of the earth. Some fear the political repercussions. Some are horrified at the problems which poor and illiterate masses bring into the Church. There are those who realize that a Church largely from the Scheduled Castes and aboriginal tribes has great difficulty in being a truly *Indian* Church, in that it reflects the culture of the lowest ranks of society. Some maintain that the educated leadership of the people movement denominations and of their large congregations has absorbed so much training and Type 2 culture that it does not really represent its constituency.

On the other hand, many prestigious leaders of the Church see the miracles of redemption God has wrought in the lives of the Depressed Classes who have come to Christ in Type 3 congregations and denominations. Many leaders of these congregations openly thank God for the salvation He has worked in their lives. I heard one of the most highly placed ladies in India tell a city congregation how her own grandmother had come to Christ in a people movement from a low caste — and would never have come had it not been for that moment. Many Christian leaders see that some hundred million Indians* are going to move out of the religion that has held them in chains. Maybe they will go to Islam, maybe to Christianity, maybe to Buddhism, or perhaps to Marxism.

It is not too much to say that the most natural way for Indians to become Christians seems so strange to Western Christians and to the Indian leaders they have trained and reared in Type 2 multiethnic Churches that a considerable campaign has been waged against Type 3. The battle is by no means over. In the presence of great possibilities of people movements to Christ, *the major resources of the Church in India are spent for existing congregations and denominations, and for educational and medical institutions.* Very little is spent for evangelism among non-Christians. *Evangelism planned to elicit response to the Gospel running through a particular caste is almost nonexistent.*

To be fair, it must be said that monoethnic congregations are often difficult to shepherd and easy to neglect. Every people movement which is neglected, poorly shepherded, stagnant, or absorbed in party infighting makes some Christian leaders oppose all Type 3 evangelism. One can only pray that enough leaders will see that the royal road of the future, the truly Indian way of evangelism, is to pray for and encourage more and more such movements, recognizing them as *the most natural way in which men and women reared in castes can come to Christ.*

---

*Hutton, *Caste in India* (p. 198, 199) says that in 1933 there were 50 million Exterior Caste (Depressed Caste) people in India. He also says that the population of India at that time was 350 million. Since the population of India, Bangladesh and Pakistan (all of which were in India in 1933) is now 770 million (1976 World Population Data Sheet), the general population has increased by 220 percent. If the Depressed Classes population increased proportionately, it numbered 110 million in 1976. Perhaps 15 million of these are in Bangladesh and Pakistan, so we may say that there are "some hundred million" Depressed Classes people in India. In these matters exact figures are very hard to come by, for no one likes to be classified as Depressed Classes and what were counted as Depressed Classes in 1931 now aspire to be counted as something better. Definitions in each census vary. There can be substantial agreement, however, that there are indeed some hundred million victims of the Hindu social structure by whatever name they are called.

The sad fact is that when the Gospel was first proclaimed, God gave India hundreds of incipient people movements to Christ. Partly because Type 2 nationals and missionaries were so prejudiced against group movements; partly because they were working with the upper castes; partly because no one really knew what a people movement was, and the belief was nearly universal that the only right way to become a Christian was one by one, breaking out of caste, — for these various reasons *most beginning people movements died.* True, some were weak to start with. Even skillful nurture would not have saved them.

The most robust movements, however, grew vigorously. When this happened, *then,* finding themselves with large numbers of Christians and congregations on their hands, missionary societies and missionaries did devote considerable resources to shepherding the new Christians. Nevertheless, as we have seen, the problems brought into the Church by multitudes of low-caste Type 3 members made many Churches and missions seriously debate whether such movements should be encouraged.

Type 3 requires abundant nurture. It brings with it some cultural components which are sub-Christian; but also many strong and natural congregations. Indeed, the truly indigenous congregations and denominations in India come in only by the people movement route. They have a lovely Indian fragrance — of jasmine, mangoes, and curry.

As ways are found for the rest of the castes from which there have been no people movement, to come to Christ, many deficiencies of the movements that came exclusively from the victims of society will be overcome. The monoethnic Type 3 will indeed be regarded as Christ's way to India's heart. The Battle Against Monoethnics need not be continued. It must be ended.

Major People Movements From Caste

It would be possible to view each state in India and describe the people movement or movements which have taken place there.

But it will be sufficient to list them in four great divisions: South India, Punjab and Pakistan, North and Central India, and West India. Figure 2 tells the story.

In the south we begin in the sixteenth century with the great movement of two fishing castes (c.1534) along the southern coasts to the Roman Catholic faith. Tens of thousands became Christians. At the southernmost tip of India one can travel today for miles along the coast and always be in a solidly Catholic population. All the fishermen have become Christians, and their villages and towns are dominated by large church buildings. The process continued when the Nadars in what is now Tinnevelly Diocese and in Kanniyakumari, in the early nineteenth century, by a series of interrelated group movements formed Protestant Churches. In the Kanniyakumari District, 35 percent of the total population is now Christian — either Protestant or Catholic.

The Vellalas of Tamil Nadu, a great landowning caste of that state — who consider themselves above the Shudra castes — experienced a people movement to Christ in the nineteenth century. Nelson has a valuable section in his *A New Day in Madras* (1975:141ff.) on the Vellala churches. Theirs is the only sizable movement from a truly middle caste, though the Kamma movements of the last fifty years bid fair to exceed it. Vellalas and Kammas are forerunners of hundreds of movements which will occur in the "respectable" castes of India.

The low caste Sambava or Paraya caste became Christians in considerable numbers in the nineteenth century.

In Andhra Pradesh it was in 1870 and later that an urge to become Christian swept through the Mala and Madiga castes. These Scheduled Castes lived outside the village proper in what was called the *palem*. Since their very presence was thought to pollute, they had to live at a distance — perhaps a hundred yards — from the residential quarters of respectable castes. The movements resulted in congregations being formed in thousands of *palems*. Gradually these Christians built themselves church buildings, in the beginning mud-walled structures and later (in some cases) churches of permanent brick or stone in lime.

In the Punjab and what is now northern Pakistan, the Chuhras decided, in the vague ways that whole castes decide things, to abandon the Untouchable status conferred on them by Hinduism. Conviction in this regard increased in the 1870s and after. About a third of the caste became Christians, about a third Muslims, and about a third Sikhs. Had the people movement process been well understood and had missions been ready to receive whole peoples, no doubt a much larger proportion might have become Christian. The posture of the British Government is worth observing. It did not hamper movements to Islam or Sikhism, nor foster a turning to the Christian faith; it performed the function of a secular state and guaranteed the people the right to choose whatever religion they pleased. Together with the great movement from among the Chuhras, smaller movements from the Chamars took place here and there.

In the old Punjab (what is now Pakistan) the other Scheduled Castes, such as Kohlis, Ods, Bhils, and Meghwars, were not evangelized. It may be that they had not then become sufficiently responsive. Since 1960 they appear to be opening to the Gospel. It is a nice question whether movements develop when a whole caste ripens, so to speak, or when it is evangelized. And could evangelism which steadily held open to its hearers the people movement way of accepting Christ encourage such movements to break forth in a *slightly* responsive people? The answer to the second question is probably in the affirmative; as to the first, one must note that ripening is partly conditioned by the way in which evangelism is carried on. Missions need to discover much more about the limits God ordinarily places on these processes. History seems to record that many segments of society, many *ethne*, cannot hear the Gospel until certain conditions have been fulfilled.

Right methods and right men, both nationals and missionaries, sent by God, play a great part in the process. Acts of God, which in their breadth or subtlety we cannot really analyze, prepare whole peoples to hear the Gospel. When to such peoples disciples are sent, churches often multiply. It would be a mistake to restrict the

Gospel only to groups we think of as responsive. Often responsiveness is there and goes undiscerned. Ripe harvests go unreaped. The Kohlis in Sind, for example, have probably been responsive for the last hundred years, but have not been evangelized in the right way or sufficiently. Many other examples could be given.

In North and Central India no great people movements have taken place. In the United Provinces (now Uttar Pradesh) thousands of lowly Bhangis — sweepers — turned to Christ, and tens of thousands of Chamars in several districts became Christian, but the movements met with such hostility and countermeasures by the Hindus, led by the militant Arya Samaj, and the one-by-one pattern was so ingrained in Christian practice, that powerful denominations did not develop. The clusters of congregations remained small and separated. Bhangis lived four or five families to a village, and consequently a church of a hundred families (necessary to support its own pastor) was spread over twenty or thirty villages. Shepherding was difficult. Moreover, the entrenched institutionalism of the major missions diverted huge sums of money into work with the upper classes: schools, hospitals, and the like. Whatever the causes, people movement congregations and denominations in Uttar Pradesh did not prosper.

In Central Provinces (now Madhya Pradesh) and Orissa small movements of 10,000 to 20,000 took place in the Balahi and Gara castes. In Bengal (now Bangladesh) a small movement of a few thousand Namashudras arose around Jessore and Barisal; but in comparison with the educated Baptists of Calcutta the lowly Christians from the oppressed groups looked like third-rate believers, and their churches did not prosper or multiply. Was there lack of skill in shepherding, lack of resources allocated there, or were not enough Namashudras convinced that Christianity held substantial benefits for them? Were they shepherded by upper-caste Baptist pastors from the city instead of pastors developed from their own ranks — at home in their villages and powerful to tell their fellows of Christ? We do not know.

In the Himalayan mountains in the Almora District a series of very small movements took place *in the Shudra castes:* small numbers of barbers, blacksmiths, and carpenters became Christians. The villages in the hills were small. Artisans constituted only a few houses in each village, and the difficulties of shepherding were great. The churches did not prosper or spread.

In the southeast part of Central Provinces, in a population of a million Chamars (Satnamis, Chungias, and Kanaujias) small group movements kept occurring in the 1890s, the years 1910-20, and the 1930s. Some groups and individuals in these castes came to the Christian faith, but the big movement never occurred. In 1917, the leaders of 50,000 Chungia Chamars held a meeting at a place called Set Gunga to decide to become Christian; but they were not quite ready and put it off until the next year. A few years later they all became Satnamis.

The multitudes of famine orphans who were cared for in the early years of the twentieth century had very large numbers of Scheduled Caste relatives — for the oppressed are the first victims of any great famine. One wonders, if the missionaries of the time had held the people movement point of view — sought out the relatives and proposed to them that they become Christian without leaving their homes, accepting their own sons back as teachers and leaders — whether people movements might have been sparked. Or whether, on the contrary, the orphanages were so stamped with the one-by-one pattern, and the idea so thoroughly established of a Christian as an educated, *Westernized* person, that people movements in all that territory, ripe and ready to blossom, were actually headed off. We do not know.

Asking these questions does help one to see how peoples (both castes and tribes) in India have not become Christian. Whatever has happened in the past, in the future ministers and pastors, denominational executives, seminary professors, and intelligent laymen, too, should all understand *the most natural way* – the most Indian way — *in which caste people become Christians.* The Church in India should resolve that in the future that way will be pointed out again and again. Now would seem to be the time to present India's searching multitudes with the Gospel of liberation. Certainly nothing will confer on them so much strength and fulfillment as to become Bible-reading, Bible-believing, and Bible-obeying Christians walking in the power of Christ.

The most natural way is still not easy. The way of the Cross is never easy. Christians must not expect the privileged castes to batter down the gates of Zion in a rush to be baptized. Yet the Bible tells us that kings when they see Him will arise* and princes bow down to Him (Isa. 49:7), and commands us to disciple all *ethne.* All I plead for here is that, as in India the Church presses on to this goal, she offer all communities the option of becoming Christian in their normal ethnic groupings. Denominations and missions in other lands also should think in terms of such indigenous and natural people movements.

Evangelistic Potential of Monoethnic Caste Congregations

Monoethnics (one-caste congregations and denominations) have within their own groups great potential. Christians are related to hundreds of kinfolk who have yet to believe. Sometimes the connection is close and intimate, sometimes distant. As we have seen, Christians of such denominations generally maintain ethnic purity. They marry within the *ethnos.* Although there may be disapproval, they are definitely "our people." To become a Christian and join a *mono*ethnic congregation is to remain *one of our people.*

By contrast, among the multiethnics (again I am summarizing, for clarity and emphasis) to become a Christian means to "leave

*Ancient mark of great respect, since kings remained seated while all those of lesser rank stood.

our people and join another caste." One can hardly overemphasize the point. The decision to become a Christian in a Type 3 congregation is in fact mainly a religious one. The issue of caste is not involved. Whereas to become a Christian in a conglomerate (Type 2) congregation is largely a *social* decision: Do I want to become a member of another race, another family of man, another kind of people?

As a result, the evangelistic potential of people movement congregations and denominations is great; that is why they grow. The claims of Christ and the benefits of the Christian religion can be heard and seen without injecting the issue of leaving one's own caste and joining another. External opposition (Arya Samaj, Jan Sangh, et al.) may remain strong, but within the community the Gospel can be heard.

So long as the monoethnics grow, so long as a stream of new converts flows into the churches, evangelistic potential remains high. Hundreds of Christians say, "Just last year I was in your position. I was deciding whether to follow Jesus Christ or not. Remember, I am your close relative. I would not mislead you. When our people become Christians, God really blesses them. Come and join us." Those who hear the Good News are being invited to join the advance guard *of their own people* who have found a very good thing.

Once a Type 3 denomination has grown strong and has hundreds of congregations across the land, it constantly takes in a trickle of converts from its neighbors. Thus the Presbyterian congregations of the Punjab, Pickett reported in 1934, had won far more converts from the Muslims than all the specialized and scholarly missionaries to the Muslims put together. All across India non-Christians on the fringes of the Christian communities drop in at the church and come to love the Lord. They are employed by some well-to-do Christian, attend family worship in his home, and are led to Christ. Or they fall in love with some Christian girl, and that leads to conversion. Or some Christian prays for Christ to heal them, and He does, and they accept Him as Lord. More converts are added to *healthy* Type 3 denominations yearly in this way and by biological growth than were won in the rosiest days of the early people movements. When a Type 3 denomination gets sick and weak, however, the trickle of converts dries up.

When a people movement stops growing, is arrested and sealed off to families who marry largely within their own congregations, and develops quite separate from the idolaters, then evangelistic ‑potential rapidly declines. The myriad latent connections that bound Christians and non-Christians together are broken. Normal occasions for the flow of faith are greatly reduced. Each group really thinks of the other as a different caste. The people movement congregations lose interest in "those other people," while non-Christians feel a sense of revulsion in even thinking of "becoming Christian."

Examples of both high and low potential abound in India. The vigorously growing movement among the Adi Dravidas and Harijans in Tamil Nadu and Andhra Pradesh reported in 1976 by the Rev. Ezra Sargunam brought in more than a hundred congregations between 1964 and 1976. It expects to bring in another hundred by 1983. In it hundreds of new converts — like Andrew — find their brothers and sisters, aunts and uncles, close relatives and intimates, and bring them to Christ. Congregations spring up in many places. On the other hand, in the Tinnevelly Diocese about half the Nadars became Christians many years ago, and now the non-Christian half yields practially no converts. Christian and non-Christian have apparently decided to coexist. Christians seldom pray for the conversion of their fellow Nadars. I doubt that this is because they have ceased to believe that those who have no faith in Christ are lost. Rather it is simply easier to let one's neighbors alone. The two groups of Nadars have grown far apart.

Once a Type 3 denomination gets sealed off, it has less potential than Type 2. Because it is solidly of one people, it does not attract converts of other castes. It has ceased to burn with zeal to have its own non-Christian relatives become Christian and cares even less about its neighbors of other castes. Nadar Christians of Kannyakumari are a case in point.

Those who shepherd people movement churches are tempted to stop and consolidate. They slow down the number of baptisms until converts can be properly instructed. In some instances, they cease baptizing altogether. Fully granting the urgent need to instruct and nurture, one must nevertheless say that stopping to consolidate is always a mistake. Consolidation should be done *on the run*. The evangelistic potential of the new converts should be valued and used. They should be bringing their intimates to Christ. New congregations should be established. The caste should be discipled out to the fringes. If one denomination has insufficient resources to instruct and shepherd all who can be won, it should call loudly and insistently for other denominations to come and help. The brotherhood *of denominations* is very powerful and can be focused on every population prepared by God to start its march out of Egypt. If Moses cannot lead it out alone, he recruits Aaron. If the Church of South India cannot do it alone, it should invite Korean Christian missionaries, or Canadian, or Naga, or the Ceylon Pentecostals to take over five hundred villages of the prepared people and lead them into life eternal.

GREAT POTENTIAL ALSO
ALONG THE FRINGES

The glowing enthusiasm of a people movement in one caste often ignites men and women in another, neighboring caste. Faith begets faith. The Jewish Christian movements sparked a Christward march among Samaritans. When the Malas and Madigas became Christian, small Christward marches started in the Kammas and Lambadis. When 4,000 Mizos in the eastern edge of Tripura became Christian, several thousand nearby Darlongs and Riangs also turned to Christ in people movement fashion. Each people continued to marry within itself, but all belonged to the same Baptist Church. In the Koraput District of southwest Orissa where a Mehra people movement has prospered, about 800 Bhatras became Christian, kindled by the outpouring of God's mighty power on the Mehras. This soon stopped, however — allegedly because the rest of the Bhatras refused to identify themselves with what was predominantly a Mehra Church. Example after example can be given from all parts of India.

If these auxiliary people movements join the main movement they are quite likely to stop. The Bhatras want to be Christians but do not want to become Mehras. If, however, people of the newly awakened caste can become Christians while remaining themselves, there is reason to believe that their movements would prosper, in some cases more than the original one. Gentiles must not be required to become Jews when they become Christians.

One of the great needs of the Church in India is to understand the liberating decision of the Jerusalem Council in A.D. 52 that Gentiles could become Christians without taking on themselves the whole Jewish law — including, one would think, the law of endogamy *within the Jewish group,* whereby all who became Jews thenceforth married Jews rather than their own people. When the Church in India starts living according to this conciliar ruling and encourages congregations and denominations under the umbrella of the Church in India to arise in natural ethnic groupings, practicing their own endogamy so long as this seems natural, a new day will dawn.

This should not, of course, mean a separate denomination for every caste and subcaste in India, which would be both ridiculous and unnecessary. Many castes now use one Hindu temple, yet each cherishing and retaining its own particular ethnic character; so in the future natural clusters of castes will, while retaining their own ethnicity, worship in one church building — and why should they not call it a temple? (Acts 3:1, 5:42)

A problem certainly rises where, instead of a "natural cluster of castes," castes with a large social gap between them become Christian. In some parts of South India, these will *not* use the same building. Nevertheless since Christ does break down the wall of hostility among those who become His people, bringing them to Christ *in* their ethnic units *will*, with the blessing of the Holy Spirit, bring in *ever increasing measures of brotherhood.*

All church buildings would be open to all men, Christians and non-Christians alike. None is barred from the temple of God; but certain clusters of castes would tend to worship in one place and certain other clusters, according to convenience of residence and education, in another. Languages divide congregations very naturally and thoroughly. So do distances. Christians from the suburbs will not usually worship in church buildings in the center of the city. The weaver quarter of the town will likely build its own church, and the merchant quarter its own. Once the faith begins to spread naturally into every ethnic unit, while encouraging that unit to preserve its own cultural and ethnic treasures, we shall see places of Christian worship spring up spontaneously according to the convenience of the worshipers. Many house churches, with occasional joint services of worship, is the probable pattern of the future.

Just as today some associations of congregations prefer the Roman Catholic form of doctrine and polity, others the Episcopal, and still others the Congregational, and so forth, so in the future we shall see congregations and denominations arising and grouping themselves in various ways. What matter, if they all accept the Lord Jesus Christ as their Saviour and the Bible as their scripture, and cleave to none other? Some degree of structural unity is certainly desirable, but there is no need to deify it. The drive for structural unity must not be allowed to hamper and chain the spread of the Gospel. Believers in the many castes must not be forced to join the only allowable state Church; the day of Constantinianism is long past. Rather, as long as congregations and denominations rising in various linguistic and ethnic units are sound in regard to faith in Jesus Christ according to the scriptures, it would seem the part of wisdom to expect and to enjoy a very considerable diversity in the polities and structures of the various branches of the Church. The unity of the Church is unity in Christ and the Bible. Collusion between Church and state such that the Church could enforce unity — as it did in the Middle Ages — is not likely to occur in India. Even if it were possible, most Christians would regard it as a disaster.

In Africa, when the exploratory and mission-station-approach periods ended, indigenous *denominations* (not connected with any European mission or with any mission-connected Church) began to arise. Dr. Barrett, the Anglican authority, has counted more than six thousand of these — many very small. He deems about a thousand so syncretistic that they cannot be counted as Christian, and about five thousand basically orthodox. In terms of the typology we are following, *thousands of Type 3 monoethnic denominations arose.* One cannot help but wonder whether in the century ahead — if the Lord tarry — we shall not see in India a somewhat similar phenomenon. These indigenous Churches can, I believe, be helped toward biblical faith — if they are welcomed, and if existing Churches deliberately encourage them *and include them under their umbrellas, while giving them much liberty to be themselves.*

In South Africa, a Pentecostal Bible college enrolls leaders from many independent African denominations, promising that it will teach them the Bible but will *not* subvert them. It will expect to turn them back, as ministers deeply versed in the Bible each to his own denomination. This same policy is followed by interdenominational seminaries all over the world today. One hopes that similar intelligent assistance will be extended to the indigenous denominations likely to arise in many tribes and castes of India. Type 3 monoethnic Churches by the tens of thousands will need and welcome assistance, but not domination.

Thus, to sum up, Type 3 congregations and denominations raise serious questions as to the *right* relation of Christianity to that central though sometimes unadmitted component of India culture: caste. Is it biblically defensible to have congregations of Jews, Samaritans, and Gentiles meeting separately, or to become one in Christ must they all meet together? Is modern India successfully outgrowing caste, and ought the Church therefore to be leading the nation in establishing increasingly casteless societies (churches)? Ought those who desire to follow Jesus Christ to leave their castes and join Type 2 congregations — or stay in them and establish congregations of their normal companions and relatives? In short, are Type 3 congregations a legitimate form of church or a regrettable compromise? Should only Type 2 be established? Or, on the contrary, are Types 1, 3, and 4 (the last we shall examine in a moment) natural Indian forms of the Church, healthy and normal adjustments to Indian culture which Christians should therefore actively promote?

These questions are discussed throughout the present volume, and readers will be forming their opinions. Chapter 4 will add significant evidence.

Obviously the people movement to Christ will greatly aid the Gospel to spread through all six continents. The Indian example will therefore be significant for ministers, missionaries and missiologists in many lands.

4

Monoethnic Churches from Tribe

As NOTED earlier monoethnic Churches arise in tribes by the same process that operates in castes, and these I am calling Type 4. The people movement is born and develops in any homogeneous unit in any nation in substantially the same way. Having seen briefly how this works with the caste structure, we may find it helpful now to take a retrospective glance at the development of such movements in earlier times, before going on to their particular traits when tribal patterns are involved.

Monoethnics Through the Ages

One-people denominations have marked Christianity from the

beginning. The solidly Jewish Church described in the first chapters of the book of Acts was a cluster of congregations in which *all members were Jews*. All male Christians had been circumcized. All considered Abraham to be their father. A few years later, when the Christian movement spread to the Samaritans — half-breed Jews — between whom and the Jews themselves there was a great social distance, another cluster of congregations arose in which all members were Samaritans.

Somewhere around A.D. 300, the whole Armenian people accepted the Christian faith, and a very large cluster of congregations came into being in which *all members were Armenians* by race and language and all lived in one distinct country: Armenia. This cluster formed a national Church which exists to this day, even though greatly weakened by fanatical Muslim persecution.

When the Irish became Christian, they did so tribe by tribe — 127 tribes! Monasteries, in which a high type of Christian life and learning was maintained, arose where the chief lived. Not only did all the Irish become Christians; but all Christians in any one part of Ireland belonged to some one particular tribe.

The spread of Christianity across Europe is one long story of the awakening to Christ of distinct peoples, kinship groups, and tribes: Picts, Scots, Saxons, Angles, Danes, Frisians, Wends, Swedes, Vikings, Slavs, Magyars — one after another in different centuries, they decided to become Christian. In each case a one-people (monoethnic) denomination arose. *Every member of that cluster of congregations belonged to the one tribe.* Most of them practiced endogamy. Christian men of the tribe married women of the same tribe.

During the twentieth century, Africa south of the Sahara has been turning to Christ. In 1976 more than 100 million of its people were Christians. Dr. Barrett, the Anglican authority on Africa, says that by the year 2000 there will be more than 350 million. Again this great turning, the most notable ever to take place into any religion, has taken place tribe by tribe. Yorubas, Fantis, Ewes, Kikuyus, Zulus, Tiv, and hundreds of other tribes have become Christian *while remaining themselves*. All the Christians in each section of the land belonged to one tribe.

In African cities, of course, to which tribal people have flocked, Christians belong to many tribes. Nevertheless, even in cities one finds numerous one-tribe congregations and some one-tribe denominations.

In Asia one could easily find scores of illustrations. Two must suffice. In Burma, Rajah Manikam says, the Karen Baptist Church "is one of the strongest . . . of East Asia; its record of self-support has been the envy of many churches in this part of the world. Strong, self-reliant and vigorously evangelistic, it has produced some very fine Christian leaders" *(Christianity and the Asian Revolution,* 1955:259). The Karen is a one-tribe Church. To be exact one must say more. When I visited Burma some years ago I found Red Karens (Sagaw) and White Karens (Pwo). Each subtribe had a convention of its own. The congregations of each formed a distinct cluster. Each had its separate headquarters in Rangoon. In effect there were two Baptist denominations, entirely friendly to each other, but separate. In the Sagaw all Christians were Sagaws, and in the Pwo all were Pwos; with a few rare exceptions, each subtribe married among themselves.

In Indonesia, the great Lutheran Church of North Sumatria is overwhelmingly of one tribe: the Batak. In becoming Christian the tribe maintained its ethnic purity. With a few exceptions where Western-educated Bataks have occasionally married non-Bataks, Christian Bataks marry within the tribe. All the Christians in this branch of the Church Universal are Bataks. The tribal culture is enhanced, not destroyed. All congregations are Type 4; there are practically no conglomerates. In every congregation the membership is solidly Batak, and the leaders of the congregations and the denomination are Bataks.

GEOGRAPHIC AND LINGUISTIC
BASES OF TYPE 4

The geographic and linguistic explanation for one-tribe

denominations and congregations is the first that springs to mind. The essential difference between tribe and caste, as I noted in preliminary fashion on p. 94, is that the latter shares a region with many other castes, while the former is either the sole or the main ethnic group in a given district, valley, range of hills, or river area. In the old days, tribes held certain territories and drove off or killed all other tribes. Each developed a language or dialect of its own. When they started to become Christian, they did not consciously become one-tribe denominations; that was all they *could* become. It was impossible for Type 2 (multiethnics) to develop.

The monoethnic nature of tribal denominations often posed a problem to missionaries. When faced with a large number of small tribes, each speaking its own tribal tongue, missionaries tended to choose a single dialect (often that of whoever became Christian first), translate the Bible into it, teach it in the schools, and make it a standard language. In parts of East Africa Swahili has become the lingua franca. In northern Nigeria Hausa is widely spoken. In the West Cameroon, pidgin English is so common that the Bible is being translated into it.

Speaking generally, European rulers administrating large territories with many tribes in them considered tribalism a hindrance. It blocked progress and prevented the spread of learning. It created factionalism, made advance costly, and was a nuisance. Educated Christian nationals and missionaries thought it would be so much better if in Kenya, for example, everyone could speak Swahili — the Bible could be translated just once, into that language; a scientific Swahili vocabulary could be worked up; and glorious, inspiring worship in Swahili would enrich Kenyans of whatever tribe.

Despite all these assumed advantages to national administrators and missionary planners, however, the Kenyans became Christians tribe by tribe. Luo, Kikuyu, Kamba, Kisii, and many others moved to the Christian faith as ethnic and linguistic units. Congregations were solidly of one tribe or another (except, of course, those formed in great cities of educated Christians who worshiped in English or Swahili). Christians married girls of their own tribe and subtribe; they jealously preserved their own culture. They had become Christian, but — like the Jews in Jerusalem — had not renounced their tribe or caste.

In addition, consequently, to the geographic and linguistic reasons for monoethnic tribal congregations and denominations must be added this other factor: that tribes have a fierce loyalty to their own people. Type 4 congregations preserve ethnicity. They keep the blood pure. This enables them to become Christian without social dislocation. In one-tribe congregations, any member of *that* tribe can truly feel at home. In one-tribe denominations, all congregations go forward under their own leaders. They do not find foreigners over them as district superintendents, pastors, and bishops. The word *foreigner* refers here, of course, not to European missionaries, but to Christians of other tribes. To Nadar Christians in South India, for example, Syrian Christians are as "foreign" as are Koreans or Germans, in dress, language, customs, everything but the land upon which they stand.

As we press forward seeking to understand the Church in India, we would do well to value the insight that monoethnic congregations and denominations afford in regard to the spread and indigeneity of the Church. India is full of both tribes and castes. It is no use imagining they are not there. The joy with which some Christians hail every alleged breakdown of caste is not well based. Caste and tribe are in fact *not* rapidly breaking down, though in cities some of their exterior manifestations, such as the bans against interdining and studying or traveling together, are disregarded. Indian anthropologists tell us that caste and tribe continue strong and even develop new ways to express themselves, such as one-caste apartment houses in the great cities.

The Church, though it certainly promotes brotherhood, is not an antination or antitribe organization. The Great Commission does not read, "Go therefore and destroy *ta ethne.*" The task of the Church is to disciple *ta ethne.* Since for some decades high consciousness of ethnicity will still prevail, the Universal Church in the immediate future, as in the past, will include many one-tribe clusters, many national Churches over the world made up solidly of one kind of people, speaking one language. As great forces play upon the population of India — broadcasts in the standard languages, higher education, the pressures of trade and travel, commands of dictators or conquerors, and international ideals of one sort and another   some ethnic barriers will no doubt be eroded. Yet it is not the Church's business to destroy all languages but one, encourage interracial and intercaste marriage, and create a tribeless, casteless, raceless world.

Certainly as national cultures develop, trade languages become commonly spoken, and urban melting pots get hot enough really to melt their various homogeneous units, the Christian Church — with one Book, one Saviour, one Body of Christ, and one God and Father of us all — *will promote unity, brotherhood, amity, and recognition of a common humanity.* As India presses on toward building one strong nation out of the "United States of India," she will meet many of the same roadblocks we encounter in the United States of America. The presence of the Christian Church, which builds brotherhood *among* the languages, races, tribes, and castes of men and women, will help her to reach her goal.

The monoethnic Churches of India do not *promote* the caste system and segregation. Being Christian, they cannot and will not do this. But they do adjust to what is perhaps the greatest single component of Indian culture: namely, that it highly values the ethnic composition of all its peoples. As a nation composed of more than three thousand tribes and castes becomes Christian, it is natural for each *ethnos* to become Christian while yet in the stage of maintaining its high sense of peoplehood.

Is Animism the Cause of One-Tribe Churches?

A notable difference between people movements from caste and people movements from tribe is that the former have espoused Christianity from out of polytheistic Hinduism, the latter out of straight Animism. The tribes have no affection for Hinduism, whereas Hindus, of course, have marked affection: before conversion they have worshiped Hindu gods, used certain of the more popular Hindu scriptures, and given the names of Hindu deities to many of their children.

Yet coming from an animistic religion is not, I believe, a major factor in the development of monoethnic congregations; though once monoethnic (one-tribe) congregations are born, this element tends to make them stronger and more cohesive. Solidly animistic tribes move to Christian faith more readily than those which have partially adopted Buddhism, Hinduism, or Islam, but Animism does not of itself produce monoethnic congregations and denominations. There is nothing in Animism per se that inclines converts to prefer monoethnic congregations. The inclination arises from the fact that in tribes (and their distinctively Indian variation, castes) every member is intensely conscious of being different from all other tribes or castes. Where people-consciousness is high, monoethnic churches result.

WHERE ARE THE TRIBAL PEOPLE MOVEMENTS TO CHRIST?

When the tribal population of India is analyzed by racial origin, three major divisions are seen. In North East India one finds the Mongoloid tribes. These are yellow-skinned and their languages are related to those of Southeast Asia. In a broad belt running from northern Bangladesh to near Bombay are the Proto-Australoids such as the Santals, Uraons, Khonds, and Korkus. In the same territory, but stronger in the southern part of it, are the Dravidian tribes such as the Gonds and Bhils. The Proto-Australoids and Dravidians overlap. For example, Gond tribes are found in Korku territory and Uraon villages in Gond country.

In 1971, four small Baptist monoethnic denominations were

found, two in Assam among the Boros and Rabhas, and two in Orissa among the Khonds and Saoras. The 30,000 largely Lutheran Santals of West Bengal and Bihar are static, but across the border in Bangladesh, Santals for several years have been pouring into the Lutheran Church and now number more than 10,000.

In 1976, mostly in Nagaland and Manipur, there were over 300,000 Baptist Nagas; mostly in Mizoram and Manipur, over 300,000 Presbyterian and Baptist Mizos; in Meghalaya, about 200,000 Presbyterian Khasis and 100,000 Baptist Garos; in Chhota Nagpur, about two hundred miles northwest of Calcutta, more than 350,000 Uraons and about 200,000 Mundas have become Christians. Some in each tribe are Roman Catholics, some Lutherans, and some Anglicans (now Church of North India).

Incipient people movements to Christ have appeared elsewhere among a dozen or more tribes. Most of them are now arrested, though the tribes continue mildly responsive.

Some monoethnic clusters of congregations have formed and then very soon reverted to Animism. For example, south of Khandwa in West Central Provinces around the turn of the century about 500 Korkus were baptized. No missionary was delegated to push the movement forward, teach the converts, or give them intelligent care. An Indian worker sent there got into trouble with a woman, and the whole 500 reverted to Animism.

In the twenties and thirties perhaps 10,000 Bhils came to the Christian faith in Rajasthan, but when the missionary under whom the movement developed retired, the mission concerned allowed a vacuum of leadership, and the Bhils reverted in large numbers. Bhils number more than 2 million in Rajasthan, Gujarat, and southern Pakistan, and through the years have continued to show interest in the Christian faith. Currently Bhils in the southern tip of Pakistan are becoming Christian by the hundreds — another precious beginning of a people movement to Christ. However, to date, ten years after the first baptisms, no missionary or Pakistani evangelist has learned the Bhil language thoroughly and gone to live among them.

Thus the great people movements which have resulted in strong Churches are confined to Chhota Nagpur and North East India, but vital movements in Orissa, Bihar, Bangladesh, and a few other regions indicate that the approximately 40-million tribal population, scattered widely across the subcontinent, continues to be a receptive element in India. Tribes are found in every state. Even Kerala has forty-eight small tribes.

Many tribes in the Plains are in the process of becoming castes — another indication that caste remains strong in this country. Dyck has done a careful study of the way in which this takes place. His research, an M.A. thesis for the University of Manitoba, is an excellent statement of the anthropological mechanisms that operate to change tribe into something else. The tribe would normally use the same mechanisms to accomplish a move to the Christian faith. As Churches and missions seek to bring the divine life to the 40-million tribal population of India, the more they know about the ways in which tribals have become Christians and have become castes, the more effective their evangelism will be.

SHEPHERDING MONOETHNIC CONGREGATIONS FROM TRIBE

The fact that tribes live away from towns and in somewhat separate regions of the country has often led Churches and missions to try to shepherd them by remote control. People movements often start forty miles from a mission station. But beginning congregations of village tribals appear much less important to the missions than the educated communities in the towns. They are easy to neglect. Their care involves *learning their language, living among them, preserving their culture and sense of peoplehood, and developing a form of Christianity which makes them better tribesmen than they were before:* more courteous *in the tribal way,* more loyal *to the tribe,* more tender *toward their relatives and kinsmen,* and more concerned for the tribal welfare.

Furthermore, they must be taught many carefully chosen selections of the Bible. They must become people of the Book.

The biblical way of life must come to women, children, and day laborers as a richer, fuller way of living. Regular worship every evening must become a treasured custom. New clusters of congregations should deliberately use the tribal patterns of leadership, not those of conglomerate urban congregations. To take bright young men, send them off to Bible school or seminary for four years, thoroughly detribalize them, teach them the conglomerate urban pattern of Christianity, and then bring them back as pastors, is to court failure.

Their own leaders must be discovered, trained, and set to work as pastors, teachers, evangelists, elders, catechists, deacons, treasurers, and the like. To be sure, in the very beginning pastors of other ethnic units, who became Christians years ago, have to be used. As missionaries of the Syrian Church or the Mizo Church or the Churches of Nagaland or Meghalaya establish congregations among Bhils, Korkus, Gonds, or the Uraly of the Kottayam District, they will inevitably be the first leaders. Paul was the first leader of the churches in Galatia and boldly claimed that they were his children, that he was "in travail" with them over and over again until they should be formed in Christ (Gal. 4:19). But like Paul, as soon as possible the missionaries discover and train indigenous leaders from among the tribesmen and women themselves. These will be given increasing responsibilities, allowed to make mistakes, and picked up when they have fallen flat on their faces!

A system of support for leaders must be created which fits tribal villages. A system which works in a congregation of urban teachers, clerks, and factory workers all of whom are paid regularly in hard money, will not work in a village where the people seldom see much real money, and eat what they grow. Heavy reliance should ordinarily be placed on training unpaid workers. From time immemorial, tribal leaders have not been salaried men. The system of support for Christian leaders, if it is to succeed, must be economically possible to villagers who live on what they raise.

There is no escaping the period of travail of which Paul writes. The doctrine of the "indigenous church" must not be made to say that if the missionary will only keep out of the way, indigenous leaders will leap into being full-blown, thoroughly Christian and reliable. This distortion could gain credibility only in the tumultuous decades just past when the fever of transferring authority from Eurican missionaries to Latfricasian leaders had temporarily destroyed common sense.

Missionaries are an essential part of the spread of the Gospel and give birth to new churches. Like all good mothers they nurse their children and direct their ways. In the beginning, they have to be quite visible, transmitting the faith, translating the Bible, establishing new habits of worship and behavior, discouraging lying, hatred, and sexual sins, and encouraging mutual respect, love, and forgiveness of enemies. Having travailed, given birth, and cared for young churches, the missionaries (whether Tamilian or Naga or American or Australian) should turn over authority to indigenous leaders. These must be discovered, trained, and installed in their tribes. When the Mizos are becoming Christians, their permanent leaders must soon be Mizos — not Bengalis. When the Bhils are becoming Christian their elders and pastors and (as soon as possible) district superintendents and seminary professors ought to be men proud of their Bhil blood. Leaders who have grown up in boarding schools in Karachi or Ratlam will not do.

Travail must not go on too long. It must be followed by weaning and pushing out of the nest. Then the missionary goes on and repeats the process. Much of what I have written in *Understanding Church Growth* about the nurture of people movements (chap. 17) is applicable to monoethnic congregations and denominations from tribe and should be consulted at this point.

CHARACTERISTICS OF MONOETHNIC
CHURCHES FROM TRIBE

As we have already seen to some extent, churches from tribe differ from those arising from castes. They form in villages where everyone is either a Christian or a non-Christian of the same ethnic unit. Among the Uraons of Chhota Nagpur, everyone in the village is either a Christian Uraon or a *sansari* (worldly) Uraon — the designation used for those who have yet to believe. Thus the congregation, of necessity, is *part of the tribe,* just as congregations in Judea, as we saw earlier, were part of the Jewish tribe. Christian and non-Christian Santals are so much one tribe that they eat together, form work parties together, and celebrate common events together.

The intimate relationships which, in caste society, tend to be sharply broken on becoming Christian, in tribal villages tend to remain intact. For example, an animist family may have promised a daughter to another family, or actually married her to the boy by formal rites before puberty. Later the family becomes Christian. It nevertheless frequently honors its promise, and when the girl is of suitable age, gives her to the second family. The second family takes her, despite the fact that she now comes of a Christian family. Such maintenance of tribal relationships keeps open the pathway along which the Gospel spreads. The procedure should be carefully monitored. If giving daughters to non-Christian tribals always results in the girl being lost to the faith and the Christian family pulled back into animistic practice, it should be discouraged on the biblical grounds that Christians are not to be unequally yoked to unbelievers. But if, as a matter of fact, animist families to whom Christian girls are given in a few years come to the Christian faith themselves, then the congregations concerned usually consider that these families are really inquirers. No infraction of the apostolic injunction is involved in giving girls to them.

Another characteristic of *congregations* that arise from tribe is that they constitute *a cross section of the tribe as a whole.* Since the tribe is the sole population of the region, the denomination soon comes to be a good blend of its population. This is in sharp contrast to monoethnics from caste, which (so far) have brought into the Church almost exclusively the bottom ranks of Hindu society.

Being a true cross section of the whole population has marked advantages. It brings in leaders as well as followers, landed persons as well as landless laborers, upper ranks of society as well as lower. The Church in such areas becomes much stronger. For instance, in Meghalaya, Mizoram, and Nagaland, and in great reaches of Manipur (regions which have become full states) the Church has an independence, a stability, and an economic and social position it does not know in the rest of India outside Kerala. Only when people movements to Christ develop in the middle and upper castes — as they certainly will in the decades ahead — will other states in India know the liberation and lift that come from the Christianization of cross sections of the entire population.

One-tribe denominations (monoethnics) suffer from limited vision. They do not feel part of other tribes. They do not feel responsible for their Christianization or uplift. They are intensely interested in evangelizing their own tribe, but are somewhat indifferent to the spread of the Gospel to others. Jews have no dealings with Samaritans! We shall consider this again when we come to the evangelistic potential of tribal monoethnics.

I have spoken of the Church among the Nagas as if it were one Church, but in fact it is fourteen denominations, since there are fourteen Naga tribes and fourteen different Naga languages, some of which are mutually unintelligible. The Ao tribe became Christian first and most thoroughly. The Angamis have been most resistant — possibly because Angami congregations arose in and around Kohima and from the beginning contained many non-Angami Christians. Thus to the Angamis becoming a Christian probably looked like "leaving our people for a conglomerate congregation." The small Naga tribes in the northeast corner of Nagaland have been the last to become Christian. In 1970 victories of the Gospel were reported from that end of the state, in which noted headhunters were baptized. One had taken forty-seven heads!

If we are to understand the Church in India we need to keep clearly in mind the multiplicity of tribes and castes, not as an obstacle, but as the field in which the Lord calls His followers to labor. They must not labor as if tribe and caste did not exist, but should observe closely how the Lord has won whole tribes and castes to eternal life, and *duplicate those ways*. The hundred-year spread of the Gospel through the fourteen Naga tribes is replete with lessons for the rest of the Christian movement in India. It should not be regarded as a pattern applicable only in a very backward part of the nation.

One characteristic of monoethnics from tribe is that when members emigrate to other areas or to cities, they tend to re-form their congregations there. For example, about 1905 some Christian Uraons left Chhota Nagpur and walked southwest about a hundred miles to what was then the Native State of Udaipur, where Christianity was forbidden. No missionaries were allowed, and Christian immigrants would have been ejected. The seven Christian families concerned therefore entered simply as Uraons — which they were. They cleared the forest and made rice fields. They built no church building. They gathered in the headman's home every Sunday night for worship and sang the Bible through from beginning to end, using the Bible stories which missionaries had put into Uraon and set to Uraon melodies. Children learned the hymns — and therefore the biblical account — simply by being present when they were sung. In 1950, when I visited this congregation, the first European ever to set foot in the village, I participated in an all-night sing in the newly built church building. (In 1947 the Native States became part of Indian India, and freedom of religion was introduced.) I know of no conglomerate congregation which has lived "underground" for almost fifty years and during that time maintained Christian worship and consciousness of calling.

In Dhond, Maharastra, a company of Telegu-speaking Madigas who loaded the railway engines with coal — a dirty job — came there as Christians. Without any contact with the Australian Churches of Christ mission or the Marathi-speaking Church of Christ in Dhond, they continued as a Baptist congregation. Lutheran laborers from Chhota Nagpur who went to the tea gardens in Assam similarly carried their congregations with them.

Evangelistic Potential of Monoethnics from Tribe

Much of what has been written about the evangelistic potential of people movements from caste may be said about the movements from tribe. Within the group, both have a powerful appeal and a social motive for witness. In the tribe, they speak to fellow tribals not as outsiders but as living parts of the community. This is especially true if they remain strictly endogamous, marrying only girls of the tribe; use their tribal names — and, of course, language — and maintain the external appearance of tribals.

Tribals are not troubled by the dilemma of monoethnics from caste, in that the advantages of using the caste name must be balanced against those of declaring (in the case of the Scheduled Castes), "We are no longer Depressed Classes. We are Christians and no longer use our caste name. Untouchability and low-caste status have been done away with by our move to the Christian faith."

Though fully aware of the benefits of denying and forgetting the low-caste status, I am nevertheless of the opinion that the tribal is the better way. Claim the old name. Proudly confess: "Yes, we are part of the oppressed. They are blood of our blood and bone of our bone. We and they are going to fight for fair treatment. We have left the religion that gave us the low status, but we have not left our people. As Christians we are still Madigas, Parayas, Sambavas, Ods or Chuhras, and we are going to lead all our people out of Egypt into the Promised Land."

Are the Pagans the True Tribals?

As one-tribe congregations and denominations multiply in India they are hearing and will continue to hear the counterclaim of their pagan fellows: "We are the true tribals. You have left the old ways."

For example, more than half of all Khasis in Meghalaya are now Christians, but during the last few years the animist Khasis — especially the highly educated — are declaring: "We are the true Khasis. We follow the old customs. We have not betrayed our tribal heritage. You Christians are no longer Khasis, you are traitors. We shall not become Christians."

As we have seen again and again, in various ways, this nationalistic fever commonly plagues the process of turning to Christ. It cannot be entirely avoided, since Christians have indeed left the old animistic worship. They no longer fear evil spirits. They no longer placate godlings and ghosts. They do ban premarital sexual intercourse and, — in the few tribes where it has been practiced — the age-old custom of head-hunting. Furthermore, Christians more than pagans have welcomed education, have become literate, have sought government posts, have become teachers and doctors, lawyers and geologists, and so on. More of them have moved to cities and been urbanized. The old prescientific way of life seems unreasonable to Christians.

All this is certainly true, and in the light of it the angry claims of the pagans have a slightly hollow sound. They themselves copy the Christians in scores of ways. They also drive cars and read books and electrify their houses as soon as they can. This being said, however, it is necessary to add that Christians can readily outdo the pagans in maintaining those components of tribal culture which mark Khasis as Khasis, Nagas as Nagas, Mundas as Mundas. Tribal dances can be taught in Christian schools and become a part of Christian festivals. Tribal dress can be ruled the only acceptable dress on formal Christian occasions. Glorifications of the tribal ancestors and early tribal heroes can become part of the body of learning the Church transmits. Each denomination has a wonderful system of teaching the truths it considers worth conveying to the next generation. It would be no trick at all to add to biblical materials some historical lessons which glory in tribal history and achievements.

Monoethnic congregations and denominations ought to renounce some multiethnic or conglomerate traits, probably adopted down the years almost unconsciously as Christians from conglomerate denominations were hired to teach in their high schools or seminaries; or as tribal leaders went to Serampore or Yavatmal for prolonged periods of study in those renowned interdenominational institutions of higher learning. Tribal leaders who have gone abroad for education need to be particularly careful lest on their return they introduce ways of worship or behavior which are unnecessarily foreign.

The goal that should dominate all worship and Christian training is, of course, first that it be *thoroughly biblical and Christian*. But great care should be taken that it be also *tribal and indigenous*. The wedding ceremony, for instance, does not need to follow the international model that arose in the West. It could be deliberately patterned on the tribal mode — beautified and enhanced by suitable Christian scripture and freed of any crude or coarse elements. Similarly, seeking God's blessing on the sowing of seed, reaping the harvest, dedicating a new house, and beginning a journey could easily be cast in the traditional tribal mold. In Chhattisgarh in early August baskets of newly sprouted grain are taken first to the temple and then to the river, where they are consigned to the water. Nothing need prevent this rite — as part of asking God to bless the fields — from becoming a colorful part of Christian worship. The baskets can be taken to the churches, impressive passages of scripture read, and specially suitable prayers offered. In short, many tribal customs can be baptized into Christ and used.

Tribal Christians' potential for evangelism will be greatly augmented if their loyalty to the tribe and affection for all tribals is constantly demonstrated. As noted earlier, Christians should be *better tribals* than non-Christians: more concerned for the tribal good, more intelligent in seeking it, more honest in handling tribal money, more generous in aiding the needy of the tribe, prouder of being tribals. Christians, if they will, can easily outdo pagans in the claim, "We are the true tribals. We honor the ancestors more. We work more for tribal uplift. Come join us. Christ will give you power, and you will be better tribals."

Discipling Tribes Out
to the Fringes

In many tribes only a part have become Christian   about half the Garos remain to be won. About 40 percent of the Khasis, 30 percent of the Nagas, 95 percent of the Khonds, and 80 percent of the Rabhas remain outside the Church. Non-Christian tribals in growing up have no scripture, no house of worship, no knowledge of God, and are swept automatically into the worship of idols and (equally detrimental to their welfare) into materialistic secularism.

It has been easy in the past for Christward movements to stop with only a part of the tribe converted. Once stopped, the Christian section remains Christian and the others become content to remain non-Christian. The two groups learn to coexist. In effect, two tribes have been formed, and marriage relationship between them grows less and less. In deliberate contrast, the tribal Church should bend every effort to *evangelize its own people out to the fringes. Each tribal Church should claim the whole people for Christ* and pray earnestly for God to pour out His Spirit on all, to the end that all may come to a knowledge of Him.

Tribal Missionaries to
Forty Million Tribals*

Here and there strong tribal denominations have sent missionaries of their own to distant segments of their tribe, and even other tribes. For example, the Baptist Church of Mizoram since 1971 has been sending more than a dozen missionaries to

---

*Depending on which census is followed and how one counts them, the tribal population in all India will vary from 30 to 60 million.

help disciple the Riangs and other tribes of Tripura. Recently the Presbyterian Church of Mizoram raised a hundred thousand rupees to begin and maintain a mission to the Meiteis of Manipur. Garo Baptist missionaries have been sent to disciple the Garos in Bangladesh. In 1936 I personally played a part in getting the Rev. Urbanus Kajur of Chhota Nagpur, an Uraon, to become a missionary to the Uraon villages along the eastern edge of the Bilaspur District of Madhya Pradesh.

Such beginnings as these are good, but inadequate to the contemporary opportunity. The tribes of India are on the march. They will become Marxists, Hindus, Christians, or simple materialists; they will not remain Animists. *Thousands of missionaries* are called for. A Christian tribal population of more than two million could easily send such a number. They need not be graduates with theological degrees — and indeed, should not be. *They should be intelligent and devout tribals.* They should learn the new language thoroughly, receive careful training in cross-cultural evangelism, and be assigned to certain receptive populations of tribals, maintained there by the prayers and offerings of the sending congregations. Both the senders and the tribe being evangelized would be abundantly blessed. The sending congregations should normally expect their missionaries to come home for several months every three years and to mail regular prayer letters back to their supporters. Tribal missionaries would be given a year or more to learn the language of the tribe to which they will minister. They should establish a way of life very close to the tribal pattern rather than copying the European life-style, which unfortunately sets so many European missionaries apart from the common people. Motor transport, refrigerators, extensive libraries, typewriters, and the like are not necessary. The tribal missionary must look and be thoroughly *of* the people. The scale of living should be about that of Christians in the sending churches, and somewhat similar to that of the tribals being evangelized.

To be avoided at all costs is sending tribal missionaries to the most resistant spots in India where all previous missions have failed. Receptive populations on the edges of existing movements should be sought out. Santal missionaries from the rapidly growing Santal churches in Bangladesh should go to concentrations of non-Christian Santals in other parts of the country. Konyak missionaries ought to go to the Kond Hills in Orissa, where Baptist congregations have already risen among the Khonds, and a population of at least 100,000 awaits evangelization. Were ten Ao missionaries to be located in the little-reached part of the Khond tribe and evangelize and plant congregations there for twenty years, they could have a profound effect. Presbyterian Khasis might well explore and claim a Bhil area in the extreme west of Rajasthan, where the congregations they would establish would become part of the Presbyterian wing of the Church of North India in Gujarat and Rajasthan.

Groups of missionaries should be sent. Present practice in "India-based missions," which assigns a single missionary family to one district and another to a district two hundred miles away, is erroneous. It guarantees that the converts won will find themselves lonely individuals or lonely small congregations with no option but to marry into and add to the scattered conglomerate congregations already found in those parts. Thus any tribal movement to Christ becomes impossible. Instead of this mistaken policy, groups of tribal missionaries should occupy a whole district or subdivision *(tahsil, taluq)*. Each missionary would be responsible for evangelizing perhaps ten villages, in one of which he would live. All missionaries would be within walking distance of other missionary families.

Their converts would also be within walking distance. Tribal congregations, as they arose, would have marriage relationships with each other and enough weight soon to become a force for good in the population. In time of need, each Christian could help the other. Annual gatherings would take place without cost for train or bus travel, in the open air, at favorable times of year. Tribal missionaries should avoid like poison the old pattern of European missionaries who claimed huge territories, located themselves in central towns, and traveled by horse carriage and later by motor car. Tribal missionaries must be much more like the *peregrini* (Irish tribal missionaries), who between A.D. 400 and 1000 fanned out across Ireland and then across all north Europe and greatly aided the conversion of the tribes there. They went on foot. They lived off the land. They slept in rude houses and carried with them precious manuscripts of only a few portions of the Bible. In these days of the printed page, this last need not, of course, be copied.

Since tribal denominations arise where the tribes are strong and where Christians are the dominant population in all the towns and countryside, non-Christian pressures against the missionary movement cannot be brought to bear on the sending churches. The churches need fear no one. Their leaders can laugh at the temptation to adopt such an overly irenic stance toward Hinduism that conversion is renounced and the establishment of congregations and denominations on new ground regarded as an unfriendly act. It is not that, of course. The friendliest action possible toward non-Christian neighbors is to make available to them, warmly yet modestly, without trying to force anything, the power and wisdom of God in Jesus Christ the Saviour.* We are concerned here with the profoundest possibilities in life, which should be open — in an understanding way — to everyone to choose for himself if he discovers their life giving quality.

But where Christians are a tiny minority in the population it is sometimes difficult to see this. The long history of the Syrian Church bears eloquent testimony to the possibility that a minority denomination may have difficulty in maintaining the fire of evangelism.

Tribal congregations and denominations have tremendous evangelistic potential. It is so far largely undeveloped, but holds bright promise for the future. If the tribal denominations can

---

*Readers who desire to think through more carefully the right relationship of Christians and the Christian Church to the social structure of India, so heavily dominated by tribes and castes, may wish to follow this chapter by turning to Appendix B where the matter is discussed at some length.

catch a vision of their power and believe that God has raised them up for just such a time as this, they will play a most important role in the expansion of Christianity in India.

5

Modified
Multiethnic Churches

Fully conglomerate congregations and denominations are not
made up of equal numbers of Christians from a dozen or more
ethnic backgrounds. The essential characteristic is not equal
numbers from many communities, but rather Christians from
several diverse groups, or castes, living together as one
community — intermarrying, interdining, and behaving in
general as one people. There is no loyalty to any one caste. The
only community for which Type 2 has love and allegiance is the
Church. Type 2 congregations are usually established on new
ground as the faith spreads across India.

With the passing of years, however, here and there a movement
to the Christian faith running through a caste starts in the
neighborhood of these conglomerate congregations. This people
movement may indeed occur in either a caste or a tribe. Instead of

142

converts coming one by one against the will of their families, they come group by group *with* their families. Instead of being thereafter shut out by their native community, leaving their ancestral homes and coming to live at or near the Type 2 congregation, they stay on in their villages in the houses they have built, cultivating their fields and enduring whatever harrassment or persecution befalls them. They have become Christians, but they have not left their people.

When the people movement is large and scores of thousands become disciples of Christ, establishing hundreds of churches across the plains or the hills, then within a generation the fully multiethnic congregation at the center has been transformed into a fully monoethnic congregation. A few of its members may still be Christians of other backgrounds, but for the most part teachers, pastors, district superintendents, bishops, and even physicians are of the main body of Christians. In Nagaland they will be dominantly Naga. In Mizoram they will be dominantly Mizo by tribe. In Tinnevelly Diocese they will be Nadars. In Andhra Pradesh they will be of Mala or Madiga background. To be sure, the Church all over India makes sufficient effort to play down castes so that in Andhra Pradesh, if an able pastor of Kamma or Brahman background serves faithfully and really loves the majority community, he can be and often has been elected to high office. But in general leaders are of the same community as the rank and file of members.

When the people movement is weak and small, and comes to a halt after it has brought in a few hundred or a thousand or two, the situation is otherwise. Then the fully multiethnic character of the congregation at the center is modified. Multiethnic leaders continue for some time to be the best educated. They set the tone. Marriage into their families is desirable. The rural Christians of the people movement only gradually come to town. They form at first a tenth and then a quarter or a third, and finally two-thirds or three-fourths of the community.

When an arrested people movement from Community X occurs, the conglomerate congregation in that district soon comes to have many members of Community X. When the Chamars of Ballia District in Uttar Pradesh had a small people movement to Christ, the conglomerate congregation in Ballia town began to get many members of Chamar background. Conglomerate congregations in the Presbyterian and Methodist denominations in Gujarat, after the Dherd movement, gradually became Dherd in complexion. In Jagdishpur in Madhya Pradesh the small, fully multiethnic congregation of 1925 by 1975 included many leaders of Gara extraction.

If the nearby people movement is small and arrested, the multiethnic character of the town congregation is modified. While most Christians gradually come to be of that one community, some are of others. Some have moved there from other districts and are necessarily of other stock. The congregation appears to be thoroughly conglomerate, even though most of its members are of one background; but the appearance is misleading. It is really quite a different organism, to which the term *modified conglomerate* may properly be given.

Modified conglomerates — Type 5 — in which from half to nine-tenths of the members are of one ethnic strain, are widespread in India. At one end of the distribution they shade off into pure conglomerates. At the other they look very much like the monoethnic congregations in towns and cities.

The "pure" multiethnic, having been gradually and heavily infiltrated by members all from the same ethnic background — Bhil, Mahar, Santal, Namashudra, Rohidas, or some other community — yet retains something of its conglomerate nature. It stoutly maintains that caste is nothing. It still considers it ill-mannered to speak of it. For a while church offices continue to be held by the ablest persons, regardless of caste or tribe background. But the whole congregation has become a different kind of thing. *It is a conglomerate which has within it many members who know themselves to be of one caste or tribe and who live and vote that way.*

These modified conglomerates, as I have said, are common in many parts of India and add an interesting complexity to the

Church. They occupy a halfway position between Type 2 and Types 3 and 4, falling along a line of distribution, as noted, from those which are almost fully multiethnic at one end to the almost fully monoethnic at the other. In between are most of the modified conglomerates, which may look and sound like the "pure" article but are in fact quite different. If we are to understand the Church in India, then pastors, administrators, missionaries, and laymen alike need to distinguish betwen fully multiethnic and *modified* multiethnic congregations: Types 2 and 5. Administrators who fail to discern the difference, are likely to expect conduct from Type Fives, of which they are incapable. Appointments, which are bound to fail and arrangements, which ought to work but don't, damage the Cause. Type Five is a unique kind of congregation.

Type 5 Has Many Disadvantages

Modified conglomerates introduce tension into the congregations and denominations. Suppose the denomination has thirty congregations, and the arrested people movement has brought large numbers into seven of these. The twenty-three fully multiethnic congregations will have a higher standard of education than the seven into which many illiterate adults have come by way of the people movement. The twenty-three will speak the standard language fluently; the seven will tend in many homes to use village dialect. Leaders of the twenty-three congregations will be elected to key positions. Soon the seven will form a visible block of somewhat backward Christians.

If the situation is reversed, and among thirty congregations twenty-three have been increased by the converts of the people movement, then the seven fully multiethnic ones are likely to feel oppressed and neglected. Power will be exercised by the more numerous congregations.

All this leads to factionalism. As the Church in India derives from a society numbering more than three thousand castes and tribes, each of which has intense self-awareness as a separate race or group, it is inevitable that the Church itself, made up of many homogeneous units, will have *a tremendous emotional diversity within its overarching theological unity.* At its worst it will break out in factionalism and party strife. There is no way to avoid this save that of all Christians so feeding on the Word of God and being so filled with the Holy Spirit that while we each remain separate and utterly ourselves, we all esteem others more highly than ourselves. This is a long discipline.

Another disadvantage of modified conglomerates is that they want to be pastored by their own sons, which makes the location of pastors difficult. Most denominations train pastors or ministers in a seminary or Bible school with other prospective ministers from all over a language area. Thus we have theological training schools which serve all the Hindi-speaking area, all the Marathi-speaking area, and all the Tamil-speaking area. Seminaries which use English as a medium of instruction bring in men and women from any state. These all-India training institutions in English remind one of those of the Middle Ages in Europe, which taught in Latin; prospective priests came from native stocks which spoke German, Gaelic, Saxon, Norwegian, French, or Spanish, but they learned in Latin.

The all-India seminaries today use English. The assumption is that on graduation such pastors can go to any congregation anywhere and minister satisfactorily. But this is not true.

Each homogeneous unit congregation is usually best cared for by one of its own sons. In the small denomination used as an illustration above, the pastors of the twenty-three fully multiethnic congregations ought ideally to come from those congregations, and pastors for the seven modified conglomerate congregations ought to come from the caste that now makes up most of their members.

This is difficult to implement. Moreover, superintendents and bishops tend to feel that it is not right. Christians ought to accept pastors of whatever racial background. Really good pastors of whatever race or group ought to love and care for their people no matter what small differences in ethnic makeup there may be. All would agree that this is the ideal. All would grant that it is much easier to allocate pastors when one can disregard the color and composition of each congregation, considering it "just Christian." Nevertheless, one continually sees pastors who do not fit their congregations simply because they are not of the homogeneous unit concerned. I am thinking of a finely educated pastor, of good mind and friendly nature, who a few years ago watched helplessly while his congregation divided. He was of a fully conglomerate background and had truly risen above caste. His congregation had perhaps a hundred members of like mind, and three hundred who were conscious of coming from one caste. Against his wishes, the pastor found himself becoming the leader of the hundred and the "enemy" of the three hundred. They did not like him, and perhaps he did not really like them. Attendance waned. Giving went down. Yet he himself was an able man destined for high office.

This disadvantage in Type 5 is substantial. The formation of smaller and smaller parties in each congregation, on all kinds of real and fictitious issues, must certainly be resisted. Yet the pastoring of Christians and the extension of the faith *is* closely tied to leaders being recognized as "our kind of people."

Another disadvantage is that, up to the present at least, modification in the makeup of Type 2 congregations has tended to lower the standards achieved by the pure conglomerates. People movements have occurred — so far — chiefly in the Depressed Classes and the aboriginal tribes. These have brought with them the mentality of the oppressed and the underprivileged. The redemption which the Christian faith affords and the lift which the Church and the mission give, help to dissipate some of the evil aspects of that mentality, but some still continue. Consequently the modified multiethnics are burdened with problems of various sorts: quarrels, party strife, poverty, irresponsibility, infidelity, and the like. These failings are found in all lands and among all races; but Christians from upper-caste backgrounds commonly believe that Christians from Depressed Classes have more than their fair share of them.

Type 5 — Modified Multiethnics — Also Have Many Advantages

There are actually *more* Christians at present in modified conglomerates than in pure conglomerates. Much larger numbers have in this way become Christian, for the very reason that people movements — even when soon arrested — remove the greatest barrier to conversion: namely, the necessity to renounce one's race. As we have seen, in a people movement converts come *with* their families and *with* at least some of their caste or tribe fellows. Consequently, many more become Christian. The modified conglomerate congregations are therefore bigger, have more members.

It is common in some quarters (particularly those where the Church has not grown well) to scorn "mere size" and to look on bigness with contempt. Denominations which have not grown often pride themselves on their smallness. It becomes an unwritten article in their creed that they are seeking *good* Christians, not more Christians. Phrased in this way, what is a virtue — the search for spirituality — becomes a vice, an idolizing of littleness. The three thousand on Pentecost and the multitudes who, flooding into the early Church, experienced the exceeding great power of God, warn us not to belittle numbers. Numbers of the redeemed are important. When good shepherding is provided, growth improves quality. Indeed, as long as two men can lift more than one (and pray, give, and praise God more than one) there is no basis in either scripture or common sense for regarding numbers of Christians as contemptible.

Thus modified conglomerate congregations, as a rule, are bigger. They can give more to the Church. Their members get good positions in many industries; they become part of the urban social fabric more rapidly and in many more ways. Bigger congregations sing better, begin more new congregations, present more candidates for the ministry, and become independent of the foreign mission sooner. Their members cast more votes. In the late twenties leading Christians were advocating putting an end to people movements; they brought in too many problems. Then in the thirties, the Government of India established legislative assemblies to which such citizens as received enough votes could be elected. Leading Christians, elected to the legislative assemblies by the votes of their rural members suddenly ceased to despise people movements!

In fact, some of the real problems of beginning denominations and congregations are precisely those of littleness. Until they grow much bigger, these will not go away. That modified conglomerates are bigger brings marked advantages.

A distinctive advantage of Type 5 is that they are substantially more indigenous than the pure conglomerates. Members of the latter have come in one by one to already existing congregations and simply take on the color of the congregation. The single convert as he joins an existing church has very little power to bring over any substantial part of his cultural heritage. Existing Christians set his pattern. This means that he eats what they eat, earns his living as they do, and worships in well-established modes. For years he remains a humble member of his new society.

But with even small, arrested people movements the situation is different. Converts come in groups, and staying on in their ancestral homes, perhaps for many years or permanently, bring with them their own way of living. If they are weavers, they continue to weave. If they are peasant farmers, they continue to farm. Their lives are not lived near the central church, but out in the villages where they seldom see "emancipated" Christians whose external mores they are accordingly under less pressure to copy. So they retain a great deal of their basic culture — often, indeed, too much. Some of their superstitions come in with them.

Modified multiethnic congregations thus have a more Indian look about them. This Indian look is constantly eroded where it has to give way to the old multiethnic pattern; but some of it survives.

Modified conglomerates have a much larger evangelistic potential than pure conglomerates. Some, and sometimes most of their members come from one or two castes or tribes and have relatives in them. Thus they have multitudinous points of contact and can speak to their own brothers and sisters and cousins. They can talk about common ancestors. They can say with simplicity and truth, "I was like you. In fact, I am one of you. I belong to such and such a clan. My sisters have married into such and such *gotra*s (septs), and what the Lord did for me he can do for you. When you trust the Lord Jesus you are not denying your people, you are simply joining us who are fulfilled members of the caste. Do, dear cousin (or brother or sister), come into the rich, full Christian life with me."

And the ways in which people of that caste live — all the delicate points of their culture: the kind of food they eat, the kind of houses they build, the little jokes that pass among them, the way they look at other castes, all are known to hundreds of Christians in modified conglomerate, Type 5 congregations. When they evangelize, they do not go out to preach to "those people," but rather go to "tell our own dear ones of the Great Treasure." Like the disciples of Jesus in the first instance, they can go without "purse, bag, or shoes." They will find hospitality in the homes of relatives.

It is not surprising, therefore, that all across India Type 5 is winning more converts to the Christian faith than Type 2. The more modified they are, the greater their potential. Large numbers are not won at once, but a steady trickle of converts comes in.

Often these come when humbler members of the Christian

community through friendship or marriage lead members of their former caste to Christ. The process frequently begins with caste members who have felt an urge to become Christian and have sought out their kind of people in the Christian fold, and formed friendships with them.

The chief evangelistic potential, perhaps, and certainly the one with the greatest possibilities is that modified conglomerates can learn the people movement method of coming to Christ more rapidly than fully conglomerate Christians can. Each type of Church loves and uses *its way* or presenting Christ and bringing men and women into the divine life.

Conglomerates know the one-by-one-against-the-current mode; it is the way they have all come. It is the way they have seen, and what they think the Bible teaches. This, they think, is the right way to evangelize. We can all agree that "one by one" is one of the two ways God has used and is using in India to spread the Gospel. Yet it is a slow way, necessarily confined to those who are ready to leave their family setting. It is a foreign way. Caste India does not like it, for it threatens family solidarity.

Modified conglomerates, by contrast, know (sometimes rather hazily) the people movement way of becoming Christian, which God has also used and blessed in India. Many of their parents and grandparents have come that way. Presumably modified conglomerate Christians could learn it gladly.

All about the congregations and denominations in India lie unbelievable numbers of men and women securely positioned in the strong surviving caste structures of the modern day. They are not accessible to the one-by-one-against-the-caste approach to the Saviour — they know really nothing of Him — but they might hear the Gospel if it were possible to follow Him by group action within the castes, so that while retaining nine-tenths or more of the culture of the family, those who become Christian could still follow Christ Jesus. This is not theory, it is accomplished fact. This is the people movement which has created denominations in most of the states of India, and large denominations in several of them.

Scripture may be cited against this, as well as the biblical examples I have noted in its favor. But the bleak truth is that those who are willing to give up *everything* for Christ — including their relation to the only human setting they have ever known — are few in any land. True and deep commitment to Christ is more likely to come in what seem like reasonable circumstances, fostered by kin contacts, than in special situations fostered by pleasant people who are not of our background and ethnos.

Were Christians of all sorts — all across India — to learn the people movement way of becoming Christian (the second way God has blessed in India to the growth of the Church), the possibility of the spread of the Gospel would be enormously increased. Modified conglomerates, because they are more indigenous and are interlocked with natural ethnic units at more points, can learn this pattern rapidly and willingly.

We should keep in mind that this mode of becoming Christian has been abundantly blessed by God. The strength of the Church in India is largely due to people movements to Christ which have erupted now and then from the earliest days till the present. All Christians in India ought to learn it. Pickett called it Christ's way to India's heart. It is thoroughly indigenous. The modified multiethnic, I believe, can learn it more rapidly and willingly than some other types of Indian Church.

THE TIME IS SHORT

I have shown, I think convincingly, that modified multiethnics have many contacts with their own kind of people who have yet to believe, and most of whom have yet even to hear about the Lord. But these contacts disappear with the passing of years, and modified multiethnics gradually become fully multiethnic congregations. In the first generation, Christians have many relatives among the non-Christians and know them well. In the second generation they have many more relatives, but know them not nearly so well. In the third and subsequent generations,

Christians have very little knowledge of relatives in their former castes. If they know of them vaguely, they are often ashamed of them or at any rate mutually hesitant and embarrassed. They do not attend each other's weddings and funerals. Gradually each becomes a totally different segment of society.

Thus the evangelistic potential of Type 5, if it goes unused, tends to diminish with the passage of time. The more biblical and educated the Christians become, and the more they marry Christians of other caste stocks, the greater the social distance between them and their own kith and kin. Thus the larger evangelistic potential they once possessed steadily diminishes and may even entirely vanish. Leaders of the Church need to maintain contact by every possible means. Literature claiming whole castes for Christ and declaring to them that "you and we are one people" ought to be written and distributed in large quantities.

Marxists, Buddhists, and orthodox Hindus are all vying for the hearts of the multitudes. Christians who have hundreds of thousands of close relations in the castes ought to value these contacts and by every means seek to preserve them and win these relatives to Christ.

PART II
THE FOUR
SECONDARY TYPES

6

URBAN CONGLOMERATES

UP TO THIS point in our discussion of conglomerates and modified conglomerates, I have been speaking of congregations and denominations born in villages and town where the Gospel is first proclaimed and congregations first begin to form. Historically this has happened in and around mission stations in the large villages or towns which were headquarters of subdistricts and districts. In the very beginning, when whole cities were assigned to Anglicans or Presbyterians, the multiethnics arose in great cities also. Thus the congregations in Bombay planted by the Scotch Presbyterians in the 1850s were thoroughly multiethnic.

In this chapter we turn from the hundreds of districts to the big cities. In modern India the rush to the cities is on. Great cities growing rapidly greater mark the nation. New cities are being built. Old cities are being enlarged. Bangalore has ceased to be a pleasant retirement town and become a huge manufacturing metropolis. Vizagapatam is now a major port. The sleepy village of Bhilai with 4,000 inhabitants has become the steel city of Bhilai with a population of a quarter of a million.

Christians move to the cities as readily as non-Christians, if not more so. As a result, city congregations are increasing rapidly by transfer growth. Let us see how this creates Type 6 congregations: the urban conglomerates. Figure 3 below illustrates the process.

In India before freedom, the main old churches in most central cities were found in the cantonment area. This was essentially an army town outside the "Indian city." In the nineteenth century, English officials and regiments of the British army were quartered, not in the Indian city proper but outside it, in buildings on a hundred- or five-hundred-acre plot of land. Individual houses were set up on acre or half-acre lots. The bungalow, garden, servants' line, stable, and carriage house were invariable parts of the residence. Wide streets lined with shade trees, suitable drainage ditches, and clearly marked commercial zones (bazaars) were parts of the cantonment.

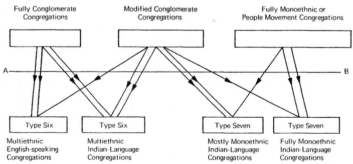

Fig. 3 Urban transfer growth influenced by ethnicity. Christians coming from district congregations to the city distribute themselves into type 6 and type 7 congregations.

In towns and cities which had cantonments, missionaries usually bought property and built their churches, schools, hospitals, and residences either in the cantonment or in open country on the edge of the Indian city. This was not, as ill-informed critics suppose, because they wished to put a distance between themselves and the people, but because — a hundred years ago — it was difficult and often impossible for Christians to purchase property within the cities. When churches were built, they were necessarily in the cantonment. Teachers in the schools and workers in the hospital lived on mission properties near the church. Some members of Anglican and Scotch Presbyterian congregations were English (government officials) and lived in the cantonment. These found it convenient to attend if the house of worship was nearby.

With the tremendous growth of Indian cities after World War II and the passing of the British Government, not only do Indian officials now live in the pleasant residence of what used to be the cantonments, but the cities themselves have flowed out around the old army towns. The latter no longer form separate settlements loosely joined to the Indian cities; they are now surrounded on all sides by rapidly growing sections of the metropolis. A factory employing 5,000 workers is built on a main road four miles west of the city center which used to be the cantonment. A suburb of 20,000 people rises there. Among these are perhaps 500 Christians. They are assured of welcome by the big churches four miles away, and may join one or another, depending on their denominational preferences. But four miles is a long way to go. Bus fare costs. Someone must be left in the house. Night meetings are difficult to attend. It is almost impossible to take non-Christian friends four miles to church, so the city-center congregation develops a membership part of which lives at a distance and seldom attends. And many of the 500 Christians in the factory suburb never join any city-center congregation.

In 1973 Professor Middleton of Union Biblical Seminary in Yavatmal found that in the city of Nagpur, in the 1971 census, 14,000 had reported themselves as Christians, but all the city center churches put together had only 3,000 members. Eleven thousand Christians — who intended to remain Christians — were not members of any Nagpur congregation. They thought of themselves as members of the church in Amravati, or Janjgir, or Mungeli two hundred miles away, and sent a little money there now and then. But they were scandalously neglected and in danger of becoming Christians only in name.

Professor Middleton, as a project for some of his students at the seminary, had them search for Christians from Chhatisgarh (the southeast part of Madhya Pradesh, two hundred miles east) and found more than a thousand. He instituted a search for Marathi-speaking Christians who had moved to Nagpur from east Berar (fifty to three hundred miles west of Nagpur) and found more than a thousand. He had his Telegu-speaking students search for Telegus from Andhra Pradesh living in Nagpur, and found several hundred Christian Telegus, most of whom had no church home in Nagpur. He also had a few ardent Christian Tamil students, but they could find no Tamil settlements in Nagpur. Then one day Dr. Middleton was speaking in Madurai in Tamil Nadu. Returning by train he met a Tamilian gentleman who lived in Nagpur, was employed by an Indian firm there, and was moreover a Christian! He had never attended any of the city-center (cantonment) churches and felt that Nagpur was a foreign land. He knew of other Tamilians who worked in Nagpur and thought a Tamil church might be established there.

Similar conditions are found in Delhi, Bombay, Bangalore, Calcutta, Allahabad, Bhilai, and other rapidly growing cities. Christians are flooding into them and finding places to live, but these are seldom near old congregations. Such Christians can and should be formed into new urban congregations. These will be Type 6.

CHRISTIANS FROM FULLY
MULTIETHNICS FORM TYPE 6

In cities, Christians from fully multiethnic congregations in the districts regroup into multiethnic congregations, but with some differences. George Samuel — who lived in Bombay for ten years before he came to the School of Missions in Pasadena and wrote his master's thesis on "Growth Potential of Urban Churches: A Study in Bombay" (1973) — distinguished two types of urban congregation which have arisen from Type 2 and Type 5 back in the districts. His findings are illuminating as to the socioeconomic structure of urban congregations and denominations in India.

If Christians who move to the city are highly educated, function in English, and belong to the professional and managerial classes, they join English-speaking multiethnic congregations. These are very thoroughly multiethnic, drawing their members indiscriminately from Christians of all ethnic backgrounds. It makes no difference whether a man is by background a Naga, a Paraya, a Chamar, an American, a Brahman, a Kayasth, an Anglo-Indian, or a Rajput prince. If he operates in English, has a high income, and associates with other English-speakers, he commonly worships in an English-language congregation. Here caste is never mentioned and racial background is ignored; Christians are simply Christians, educated citizens of the world and ardent Indian nationalists. They put a distance between themselves and denominations and congregations still immersed in the mire of caste feeling and strictures. These English-speaking congregations Samuel called "multiethnic English."

As Christians with less education move to the city, they function in their own mother tongues. Let us suppose that the city is Bombay and those coming in have grown up speaking Marathi. When they move to Bombay they will feel at home in a Marathi-speaking congregation. Whether they are Lutherans, Methodists, Anglicans, or Nazarenes will make some — but not much — difference. Should there happen to be a church of their own denomination close at hand they will worship there. But since denominations do not have churches in every part of that great city, Christians from conglomerate congregations in Pune, Buldana, or Amravati will in Bombay join the nearest Marathi-speaking conglomerate.

This will be *very thoroughly multiethnic*. Because its members have come from multiethnic congregations back in the districts, and because (coming from many districts and denominations) they are necessarily from many ethnic units, these Type 6 congregations are wholly divorced from caste. Together with multiethnic English congregations they display an antipathy to caste which is truly remarkable. They do not want to hear it mentioned. They live above caste. In their polite society the word is never used. They consider themselves simply Indians, totally above the old caste system. This is one of the benefits, they believe, of being a Christian: it has lifted them out of the morass of caste.

Similarly Hindi-speaking Christians coming to Bombay from fully multiethnic congregations in upper India to work in the factories and on the docks may learn enough Marathi to get around, but will want to worship in Hindi. This is their mother tongue and what they speak in their homes. They will join Hindi-speaking multiethnic congregations. Whether they were Presbyterians, Wesleyans, Lutherans, or Baptists in upper India is a matter of secondary importance.

All these thoroughly conglomerate congregations which worship in Marathi, Hindi, Gujarati, or other languages, Samuel calls "multiethnic Indian-language churches." He discusses this point extensively in his chapter in Hedlund's fine book, *Church Growth in the Third World* (1977).

In this fashion, in all large cities multiethnic congregations arise whose members have come from the multiethnics back in the districts and *have become more multiethnic by the move.*

CONGREGATIONS FORMED BY CHRISTIANS
FROM MODIFIED CONGLOMERATES

Modified multiethnics or conglomerates, it will be recalled, arose in towns where people movements had occurred in the district. While the congregation at the center remained multiethnic, it gradually became heavily dyed, so to speak, with the color of one caste, from which most of its members came. What happens when Christians from *modified* conglomerate congregations move to the big city?

Mr. Samuel found, quite surprisingly, that many such Christians liked to join "mostly *mono*ethnic congregations." That is, their caste affiliation back in the district bulked larger than anything else. If they came from congregations in Maharashtra where most of the members were of the Mahar caste, for example, they liked to join Marathi-speaking congregations which were heavily Mahar in ethnic composition (this being what "mostly monoethnic" means). If they came from congregations in Kerala where most — but not all — members were Syrians by community, they joined "mostly monoethnic Syrian" congregations in Bombay. Similarly, in Bombay one can find mostly monoethnic Madiga, mostly monoethnic Mahar, and mostly monoethnic Nadar congregations. These mostly *mono*ethnic congregations are properly listed as Type 7 and will be fully discussed in the next chapter. However, since they come into being when Christians from modified multiethnics back in the districts move to the big city, I mention them briefly here.

Mr. Samuel divided mostly monoethnics into two types: mostly monoethnic Syrians and mostly monoethnic others. The distinction is valid, but for convenience I am noting only a single type: "mostly monoethnic urban." It is important to hear what Samuel is saying. He asserts that *when conglomerate congregations back in the districts have arisen mainly from one caste, then ethnic considerations dominate when those Christians come to Bombay.* They join, *not* multiethnic congregations which happen to speak their language, but *mono*ethnic congregations where they find Christians both of their own language and their own community. Christian migrants to the city seek out their own kind of people. This is natural. Who will get them jobs in the city? Their own relatives: brothers, sisters, cousins, uncles, sons. Who will put them up in their homes for a few months? Who will help them out when they are in trouble? The big city is a dangerous place for one with no relatives and merely friends who speak the same language. Ties of blood and marriage are much stronger. So Christians regroup *both according to language and whenever possible according to ethnic ties.*

As we study the congregations that arise in cities as the Christians migrate there, we see that they form several distinct types. In this chapter I am focusing on three of these. Christians from multiethnics and modified multiethnics back in the districts, on coming to the big city are likely to regroup themselves into (1) multiethnic English-speaking, (2) multiethnic Indian-language — both of which are very thoroughly multiethnic — and (3) mostly or fully monoethnic,. Indian-language urban congregations. The first two of these are Type 6 and the third is Type 7.

The diagram in Fig. 3 on p. 158 will help us to see what is happening (here also I am somewhat anticipating our next chapter). Congregations in the big city lie below the axis *AB*. To the left are the multiethnic English-speaking and Indian-language congregations; these are the most completely multiethnic. At the extreme right lie the fully monoethnic congregations, which are still substantially if not entirely endogamous. Toward the right, not far from the fully monoethnics lie the "mostly monoethnic" congregations, which are so slightly conglomerate, so heavily of single-caste origin, that they are *almost* monoethnic. Even more than the modified conglomerates back in the districts, these are of one caste.

As we study the diagram we note that the *district* congregations from which all these migrants come — above the axis *AB* — can be grouped in three main blocks: fully conglomerate, modified conglomerate, and people movement. When Christians from any of these move into the city, they regroup into Types 6 and 7. The lines and arrows connecting the district blocks with the city blocks of church members show where the migrating Christians have gone. The transfer growth of the big-city congregations comes in different proportions from the district blocks.

The multiethnic English-speaking churches, as we have seen earlier, have grown chiefly when highly educated members of fully conglomerate congregations back in the districts moved to the city. But a smaller number have come from modified conglomerates, and a few (not shown in the diagram) come from the people movement congregations.

The flow into multiethnic Indian-language congregations comes about equally from the fully conglomerate and modified conglomerate congregations. A few also probably derive from the people movement congregations. Since however these have usually come through some town congregation in which people movement Christians lived while getting their education back in the district, this element did not seem appropriate to include on the diagram.

The modified multiethnics in the districts also feed the "mostly monoethnics" in the city and occasionally the fully monoethnic congregations there, too.

Thus the big city has acted as a shunting yard. It has directed Christians whose consciousness of ethnic origin is slight or nonexistent into the highly multiethnic Indian-language and English-speaking congregations, while those whose caste or tribal feeling is strong have been shunted into congregations where the person who does not belong to the dominant community is in a minority. His children are likely to marry into the dominant community and thus become more monoethnic than ever.

Evangelistic Potential of Big City Conglomerates

So far big-city conglomerates — Type 6 — have not shown much evangelistic potential. The big city is where Christians get lost, not where they are apt to convert others to Christ. George Samuel's research indicated that in Bombay the only congregations actually adding Christians to the Lord were of the monoethnic Indian-language type. Multiethnics seem unable to bring non-Christians out of their tight caste societies into the strongly anticaste, multiethnic churches. The English-speaking multiethnics were the least potent, with the Indian-language congregations a close second.

The reasons for low evangelistic potential are clear and have a great deal to do with the relation of individual Christians and the congregations they form to the society in which they live. How does that society perceive them? How does the Christian perceive his society? What does it mean to "become a Christian" vis-à-vis the caste from which men and women are being invited to follow Jesus Christ? As I have noted earlier and repeatedly, the *structure* out of which conversion to Christ and His Church is taking place is of enormous importance. Does the convert leave that structure or remain a part of it? Any understanding of the Church in India, where the caste system is in fact still so highly influential, requires the utmost attention to the relations of Christians to caste society. The city congregations — both those now in existence and those which will form in the years ahead — enable us to see these relations quite clearly.

Highly educated Christians, for example, who worship in English-speaking congregations, associate with English-speaking non-Christians in the business and government world. These are very largely of the upper castes and look on all Christians as essentially low-caste people. So while such Hindus may on occasion visit English-speaking congregations, they cannot imagine themselves joining them. As earlier noted, consciousness of caste, the close ties of blood and marriage, and pride of peoplehood are very high in the upper castes of India. All these would be sacrificed were they actually to join a Christian congregation — even an English-speaking one. It would mean leaving their own caste to join another.

Bearing this unfortunate but very commonly held feeling in mind, one is tempted to conclude that the urban multiethnics, particularly the English-speaking congregations, have small evangelistic potential. They are winning practically no one to their fellowships. Since most of their business associates are upper-caste people in good standing, most of those to whom these Christians naturally witness by life and word find it extraordinarily difficult to imagine themselves becoming Christian. .

Remembering however the great power of the Gospel, and the way in which through the centuries the Risen and Reigning Lord has called great as well as small to serve Him, a sounder judgment would be that Type 6 — the multiethnics in the great cities — have potential if they evangelize the winnable. Four segments of urban society appear open to them.

1. Beyond doubt, all great cities contain large numbers of displaced persons out of touch with their families and castes, learning new patterns of living, able to attend Bible study groups without let or hindrance, able to eat with Christians and worship with them. Cities are anonymous places, where for the most part one can do as he pleases. It was in the cities of the ancient world among just such urban multitudes that the Church experienced its first huge growth, and this in the face of violent persecutions which broke out again and again for nearly three hundred years.

Urban English-speaking conglomerates *can* grow; but they will have to find the "good soil" in which to plant the seed. They will have to look attentively for displaced persons who will yield themselves wholly to Jesus Christ as Lord and Saviour — who will become Bible-reading and Bible-obeying Christians. The fine Christians who make up the English conglomerates must then make these thoroughly a part of their fellowship.

2. A fringe of high Indian society is thoroughly disenchanted with the caste system. Its members have traveled abroad and come back to India to suffer severe culture shock. Or, on political grounds, they believe that the division of India into several thousand castes weakens the nation and they want to minimize caste. In either case they can hear the Gospel from a section of the Church which is aggressively anticaste and enthusiastically for a style of life which never mentions it.

3. A small part of the upper echelons of urban society tolerates cross-caste marriages. Three in ten thousand marriages in Bombay in the sixties were cross-caste. Those few who have married out of caste ought to feel close to Christians who worship

in very thoroughly conglomerate congregations. To these openly cross-caste marriages may be added a large number of common-law unions such as are found in every great city, where a man of one caste has taken in a woman of another. Both (were the facts known) would be out of favor with their respective castes. Both have an uneasy conscience in the matter. Theoretically both ought to be able to hear the Gospel from the multiethnics and to become part of their fellowship, regularizing what may often be a deep and innocent relationship apart from the bars of caste.

4. A fourth good opening for the Gospel, maybe better than the first three, is for members of Type 6 congregations to evangelize certain receptive units of urban society. Every city has them. These are persons who, back in their districts, have experienced people movements to Christ. They know that "our people have become Christians in some numbers. We can become Christian without leaving our people." The multiethnics can evangelize these receptive segments, encouraging converts to join existing churches or to form new monoethnic congregations.

Big-city multiethnics should note carefully which modes of presenting Christ *are actually leading others to eternal life.* They should practice those modes. They should observe which segments of urban society are in fact accepting Jesus Christ as Lord and Saviour and forming congregations of worshiping Christians and should evangelize those and similar segments.

I believe that Type 6 *multi*ethnics could — if sufficiently motivated, if filled with the Holy Spirit — establish *mono*ethnic congregations. In the Central African Republic, in the capital city of Bangui, a large central congregation with members of many tribes living in many of the precincts *(mohullas)* of the city resolved to start congregations in each precinct. The local members of a precinct simply evangelized their own relatives and fellow tribesmen and incorporated them, *not* in the multiethnic congregation at the distant center, but in a monoethnic precinct congregation which met just around the corner.

Urban multiethnic congregations have Christians from many different caste and language backgrounds. The account in the book of Acts can be duplicated. Men of Cyprus and Cyrene on coming to Antioch can speak to the Greeks also. Christians now in a multiethnic congregation can, on coming to their own kind of non-Christians living near them, speak to them also, *and form them into a congregation of that particular ethnic unit and that particular language.*

Type 6 city congregations have great gifts. Their members hold good jobs. They are highly educated. They come from the best Christian families back in the districts. They are financially secure. They are more open than any other type of Christian to the influences of the world Church. We must believe that God has brought them into existence in order to play a great part in the discipling of the *ethne* (the *jatiyan*, Matt. 28:19 in Hindi). That they are not doing so now is something that can be remedied. The great abilities of pastors, ministers, bishops, and seminary professors might well be devoted to finding ways in which this powerful section of the Church in India can become more evangelistically potent.

7

URBAN MONOETHNICS

As MONOETHNIC congregations were born back in the districts, a natural and correct name for them was people movement congregations. The movement would start in some one people (caste or tribe) and bring thousands to the Christian faith by conversion from pre-Christian belief.

In the rapidly increasing urbanization, however, monoethnic congregations have been formed *not* primarily by streams of converts out of other religions,* but by people movement Christians migrating to the city and there re-forming into

*The great original people movements to Christ did touch some urban settlements of their particular castes, leaving congregations of Chuhras, Madigas, and others in the old cities, where colonies of these castes already existed in 1900. Such congregations may reasonably be called people movement congregations, since they came in by such a movement in the first place. Yet for ease in discussion, I refer to them also as urban monoethnics — for they certainly are one-caste congregations.

congregations away from their original ones. Hence in the big city such churches can scarcely be classified as direct "people movement congregations" yet are properly called monoethnics, for they maintain much of that one-caste or one-tribe structure.

Three kinds of urban monoethnic congregation are found — taking them in the chronological order of their appearance: those formed in the first instance out of caste, out of the Syrians of Kerala, or from tribes. We shall examine these instances of Type 7 one by one.

URBAN MONOETHNIC CONGREGATIONS FROM CASTE

First to appear in the big cities were the urban monoethnic congregations of Nadars, Madigas, Malas, Chuhras, and some others who migrated to the great growing urban centers to work in factories or railway yards, as servants in well-to-do homes, or sweepers in employ of municipalities. In far-off Dacca in Bangladesh in 1974 I ran across 6,000 Telegus (Madigas) who were employed by the sanitation department of the municipality.

Christians of these castes came to cities with non-Christian caste fellows. Economic opportunity offered jobs, and people looking for work moved in response to it. Migration is seldom easy. It involves uprooting and leaving loved ones; exile, expense, and the danger of being stranded in a far country. Migration becomes possible chiefly when "many of our caste have gone, have prospered, will help us get settled and get jobs, and will bury us if we die there."

In this manner non-Christians and Christians alike of the oppressed castes went to the tea gardens of Assam, the rubber plantations of Malaysia, the sugar estates of Fiji, and the factories of Calcutta, Bombay, Bangalore, Delhi, Madras, Nagpur, and other manufacturing centers.

Historical Perspective

During the years 1880 to 1940, as the first few Christians

moved to the city they naturally joined the small *multi*ethnic congregations their own missions had established. They came in small numbers and became parts of the mission station communities. They worshiped in the big brick churches built by the missions. Small multiethnic communities already lived in the school compound, the mission compound, or some convenient plot of land purchased by the mission. As Christians from rural congregations came in, they settled in or near these centers.

Occasionally a factory, railway colony, or industrial development of some sort made it possible for Christians to settle in or near them. There would be enough so that new congregations could begin. Missions would often purchase land there and put up a chapel or church building.

The first congregations in cities tended to be conglomerates, for the simple reason that Christians from many castes came to live there. But when a people movement took place in the mission territory back in the districts, then migrant Christians of that one caste background began to be the principal part of the big-city congregations of that denomination. The Telegu Baptists furnish a good illustration. The congregations in Madras City have an interesting history. Beginning in 1878 the Baptists (whose field was in what is now Andhra Pradesh) established a mission station in Madras City, where 100,000 Telegu-speaking people lived whom no other mission was evangelizing. No other mission could do so, for none had Telegu-speaking evangelists or missionaries. By 1930 two Baptist congregations had been established, one at Perambur and the other at Vepery. One pastor, the Rev. T. Rangiah, looked after both. These Christians were mostly Madiga by background, but some were Mala (both, of course, Telegu speaking). Vigorous evangelistic work was carried out by the missionaries, mostly among upper-caste Telegus; but almost all the converts came from non-Christian Malas and Madigas. Consequently the two congregations became modified multiethnics; most of their members were of either Mala or Madiga background.

A process which has accelerated since 1947 created small

Baptist congregations in many nearby settlements: *pakuthigals* or *palems*. The reason for the change is clear. As the big city grew, Telegu-speaking people from the north poured into it. They tended to settle in one-caste communities. Telegu-speaking Kammas, Brahmans, Malas, and Madigas all came in; but each group liked to live with its caste fellows. Christians of Madiga background lived in Madiga communities and formed Madiga congregations — monoethnics. Similarly, Malas formed Mala congregations. When converts were won by near-neighbor or family evangelism, they too of course added to the existing monoethnic congregations. When local chapels were built, they naturally served the people who lived near them. If the *palem* was Mala, then the congregation was monoethnic Mala. If the *palem* was of Madigas, the congregation was monoethnic Madiga. If the settlement was a mixture of the two, then the congregation tended to be a two-caste (duo-ethnic) community. These did not thrive as did Christians of one community.

In terms of our typology, by 1970 in Madras City, among the Telegu-speaking immigrants the two big modified multiethnic Baptist congregations — Type 5 — had given birth to twelve Baptist churches and twenty-two centers (churchlets). Most of these were monoethnics, either Madiga and Mala, i.e. Type 7.

After 1940 the process illustrated by the Telegu Baptists in Madras City, with minor variations, took place in many large cities. Working-class Christians coming in from the districts tended to regroup themselves in monoethnic or duo-ethnic congregations. These found it possible to grow by conversion from their own caste fellows among whom they lived. Occasionally, when numbers were small, migrating Christians (especially if they were highly educated) formed multiethnic congregations, but among the urban working classes monoethnics appear to be the preferred pattern. *The process is unplanned.* No one determines that "our new congregations shall be monoethnic." Rather, as congregations form, *they are naturally conditioned by the language and social structure of the people who constitute them.*

Housing

Christians in people movement denominations back in the districts are rural poor, often illiterate and generally landless. When they migrated to the big city they were very different from those who had been parts of the privileged conglomerate congregations at the old mission stations, benefiting by the high degree of education there available to become teachers, nurses, skilled labor, technicians, foremen, inspectors, or managers of some sort.

Rural Christians arriving in the city went to squatter towns, shack towns, congested quarters — to the *pakuthigal*s or *palem*s described by Dr. Amirtharaj Nelson. In Brazil these sections of cities are called *favellas;* in Ghana, *zongos.* They are a regular part of the rush to the city. Waste land costs little or nothing. Mud walls and roofs made of odds and ends or thatch offer protection from sun and rain and a modicum of privacy.

Recently government and industry have been building concrete high-rise workers' quarters with water and sewer systems; but with the population explosion and the tremendous urban development, rural slums seem likely to appear again and again.

While city Christians of rural Harijan background arrive poor, they must not be thought of as poverty-stricken refugees. Many get good jobs and regular wages. Some grow to be skilled labor. Bit by bit they improve their houses, which however still remain rather primitive — but then, so were the houses back in their villages. The school system in cities is good. Children grow up literate. Many graduate from high school. These Christians advance to the place where they build their own chapels and churches. The fantastic price of city land keeps churches from multiplying as they should. Modern missions should allocate funds to help new city congregations buy suitable plots of land and put church buildings on them.

But buying land and building a church is not the only approach. Churches can multiply where no land is bought at all.

This was the pattern of the early Church for perhaps a hundred and fifty years. The Methodists in Bombay have multiplied ethnic congregations over the past two decades. According to the Rev. Justin Harris, they have done so in every case without a building. Christians have been gathered and churches formed which meet in any sort of space available. In short, today's approach to the city must be flexible and may entail fantastic multiplication of worshiping groups which witness and serve in house churches. One large congregation in Seoul, Korea, in 1979 had 1,345 house 'churches which met in homes all over that large city. The same could happen in Delhi, Madras, or Calcutta.

In India, city Christians of this rank in society stay "Christian by caste" even when living far from a church they can attend. This is one of the more hopeful signs. It means that when the Church or mission modernizes itself to the point where it is multiplying congregations in the rapidly developing suburbs of the city, it will find groups of "born Christians" already there. These must be formed into congregations, fed on the Word, and led into deeper experience of the Saviour and more obedience to the Lord.

Evangelistic Potential

From the point of view of the spread of the liberating Gospel of Christ, urban monoethnics, Type 7, are most important. Frequently they are the only city churches which are growing by communicating their faith to those who have yet to believe. As George Samuel's study in Bombay so well proved, the more prestigious congregations — English multiethnics, Indian-language multiethnics, and Syrian congregations of various sorts — very seldom introduced any non-Christian to Christ; but many urban monoethnics from caste won a steady stream of converts. This is the more remarkable since the great denominations and the missions concerned did not recognize this fact and made no special effort to encourage Type 7 congregations to propagate the Gospel. Urban monoethnics have great evangelistic potential.

A principal effort therefore of all denominations, church

leaders, seminaries, missionaries and ministers should be to make urban monoethnics aware of their unique abilities, and help them in every way to exercise them. In every large city the denomination which has congregations there and the mission which assists it ought to locate a team of ministers whose sole task would be to help the urban monoethnics from caste plant many daughter churches. Every such congregation ought to have a new church committee, exactly as it now has a Christian education committee and a property committee. The new church committee would continually survey the developing city to discover groups of unshepherded Christians and other groups of receptive city people who have not yet accepted the Saviour. The committee would also arouse the whole congregation to the spiritual need of both these groups and urge every member to consider himself or herself a bearer of good tidings.

Home Bible studies in sections of the city where receptive segments of the populations live — where Nadars, Malas, Adi Dravidas, Vellalas, Madigas, Kammas, Garos, Khasis and other similar ethnic groups have settled — should be vigorously promoted. In each study group the aim would be to have more non-Christians than Christians. If only Christians gather to study the Bible, the outcome is spiritual illumination for the Christians, but little overflow to non-Christians. Where the Bible study group contains several seekers, there it has evangelistic potential of a high order.

Missionary societies should make available grants for new buildings. Home Bible studies often grow into home churches; but since city quarters are cramped and small, congregations need soon to get larger places in which to meet. Since property in the big city is enormously expensive, the new small congregations need help either from the denomination or from the assisting missionary society.

Any strategy for urban evangelization in India today must take seriously the high evangelistic potential of the urban monoethnics.

URBAN SYRIAN CONGREGATIONS

The oldest Christian Church in India is the Syrian. As we have already seen, it is strictly monoethnic. Every member of the Syrian Church (all four major denominations and the minor too) belongs to the Syrian community (caste) and marries within it. Hence all the Syrian denominations must here be classified as *mono*ethnic, Type 7 Syrian Churches when constituted in the cities.

However, as we saw in Chapter 1, they differ greatly from the monoethnics from caste coming from people movements in the bottom ranks of society. The monoethnic Syrians may have arisen eighteen centuries ago from Jewish synagogues, upper-caste converts, people movements from the upper castes; or by immigrants from Syria and what is now Iraq. But for the last thousand years the Syrian Church has been a one-race denomination with high standing in the community, and ranking with the upper castes. Its economic position was good. It was a responsible business community. As in the Hindu upper castes generally, any member who did not obey the social rules was expelled, fell into the lowest ranks of the social order, and disappeared. In short, Syrian denominations are monoethnics which did *not* arise in people movements from the lowest castes.

For the past several decades these Syrian monoethnics have also been migrating to cities all over India. They are highly educated people and find their way into many professions and businesses: education, chemistry, engineering, publishing, government service, nuclear science, aeronautics, the army, and many other careers. They are hard-working, reliable, intelligent, and regarded as valuable employees by most firms in India.

When a few Syrian families find themselves in a large city, they worship in an existing congregation—Church of North India, Baptist, Church of South India, Methodist, Lutheran—it makes little difference (though, because of the intense struggle in the seventeenth century to free themselves from Roman Catholic engulfment, Orthodox and Mar Thoma Syrians never worship in Catholic congregations). They fit in and are quite cooperative. They strengthen the congregation, but very seldom become an integral part of it or marry into its community. Their own clergy visit them from time to time; for Syrians, the only valid communion services are those performed by their own clergy. The Orthodox are more strictly separated from other denominations than the Mar Thoma.

When enough Syrians are found in any city, a bishop from Kerala visits them, installs an ordained priest, and organizes a congregation which later builds a church. It is now a fully constituted Syrian Church (Orthodox, Mar Thoma, or St. Thomas Evangelical) in Bombay, Delhi, Madras, or perhaps Calcutta. It is, of course, a Type 7 congregation: fully monoethnic.

Urban monoethnic congregations from the Syrians are different from the Syrian communities back in the homelands. In certain districts in Travancore they form 50 percent of the population. In big cities they are 0.1 percent or less. In Kerala they are the dominant Christian communities; in great cities only a small congregation among many large ones of other kinds of Christians. In Kerala, when one thinks of Christians he thinks of Syrians, but in Delhi one thinks of Anglicans, Presbyterians, Methodists, or Roman Catholics.

The members of the Syrian Type 7, moreover, live scattered across a whole city (except in some parts of Bombay). Their normal companions are Christians of other denominations. Perhaps they teach in a theological seminary or college, and all their intellectual intercourse is with Christians who think of the Syrian denominations — if at all — as rather quaint forms of the Church. Furthermore, urban monoethnic Syrian congregations live intermeshed with non-Christians of ability. Syrians work at adjoining desks, form parts of the same faculty, have superiors and subordinates who are Hindus of many sects, or Marxists, or Muslims. Much more than back in the districts and farms of

Kerala, urban monoethnic Syrians rub shoulders with some of the 600 million Indians who in 1976 were of other faiths.

Evangelistic Potential

In consequence of all this, the evangelistic potential of Syrian Type 7 ought to be very high — instead of which it is practically nil. Let us see why.

These urban monoethnic Syrian denominations arising all over India are extremely important for understanding the Indian Church. Their strict endogamy is an adjustment to Indian culture. They maintain it as entirely legitimate and not in the least militating against their earnest and sincere practice of the Christian faith. The Reformed Syrian denominations (Mar Thoma and St. Thomas) are just as endogamous as the Orthodox and Roman Catholic. They like the Syrian community, they believe in the stock from which they spring, they know that a close relationship whereby all one's relatives are of one particular ethnic unit has marked advantages.

While they do not like to be referred to as a "caste," they are determined to preserve their purity of blood. If pushed to defend the practice, they will point out that Europeans in India commonly marry other Europeans, and indeed Anglicans for the most part marry Anglicans. I have never heard a Syrian scholar present a thoroughly biblical defense of endogamy, but am confident that this will soon be forthcoming.

The theological and biblical issue is precise. Can a truly Christian Church, faithful to the Bible and obedient to the risen and reigning King, practice endogamy or allow any of its sections to practice it? For instance, could a Methodist denomination in Andhra Pradesh, of dominantly Mala background, expel a believing member for marrying a Christian of Madiga background?

Since the New Testament does not mention marrying across race lines as a sin, can any denomination disfellowship for it? The question is related to — but not the same as — that of whether a

Christian Church can expel members for making and selling liquor, trading in opium or narcotics, enlisting in the army, owning slaves, joining the Marxist party, or taking communion in a Christian Church which does not believe in the apostolic succession.

In addition, however, two weighty considerations must be borne in mind. First, since about the year 1800, Indian Churches and missions have taken the position that the Christian Church will make no adjustment to caste. Caste is wrong. It teaches that men are made in different molds, and this teaching is contrary to the biblical doctrines that all men are descendants of Adam and hence brothers, all are alike sinners in need of God's forgiveness, and in Christ there is neither Jew nor Greek, neither slave nor free, neither male nor female. All are one. The middle wall of hostility has been broken down, and we have all been reconciled by the blood of the Cross. (Before 1800, Christians from the upper castes in churches of South India were seated separately from Christians from the lower castes and given the communion first. Robert de Nobili adopted many Brahman practices and behaved like a Brahman teacher.)

Second, in the world today a tremendous battle against racism — any kind of discrimination based on race — is being waged. The Christian Church has taken a strong stand that all races are equal, no race privileged above the others. In the Church we are all brothers and sisters. The whole thought of superior and inferior races must be fought and destroyed. The Hindu social system is based on the doctrine that God Himself (the great God Brahm) created men in different molds. The Brahman he created from His head, the Kshatriya from His arms, the Vaishya from His thighs, and the Shudra from His feet. Any acceptance of this heresy, from the Christian point of view, is an unacceptable adjustment to culture — so great an adjustment that when it is made the Christian faith is destroyed. As the theological and biblical issue is debated in India and around the world, these considerations must be borne in mind.

The present book does not enter the lists for or against the position held by the Syrian denominations. It merely points out that all Type 7 congregations (the highly favored ones from the Syrian community, the highly handicapped ones from the Depressed Classes, and the powerful ones from tribes in North East India) do practice endogamy and intend to continue it. They hold that it is quite possible for a community to maintain ethnic purity and be thoroughly Christian. They would agree that endogamy is an adjustment to Indian culture, but would stoutly argue that the adjustment has been made on every continent, and in India by the missionaries themselves for the last hundred years, and is a normal part of the expansion of the Church in a caste-bound social order.

Probably all the Type 7 denominations I have mentioned would say: "Some of our members do marry people not of our ethnic unit, and we have not excommunicated them. If our members refuse to give husbands and wives to children of such unions, that is not a church decision but a *personal* one. It may not be ideal, but under Indian conditions it is not wrong, either. What is possible and right in the atomistic society of England and America cannot be imposed on Churches of India. We must be free to make decisions which fit our conditions and enable the Christian faith to prosper here.

"The battle for brotherhood is peculiar to the white race, which has been shoving dark-skinned races around. Let white Christians repent of their sins. We quite agree. But that does not mean that Indian denominations cannot make rules for their own sons and daughters which are essential for their welfare."

A further consideration necessarily comes into the picture. To date, no monoethnic denomination has built into its program of evangelization a *deliberate* appeal to other castes to "form yourselves into congregations in your caste or tribe, as we formed ourselves into congregations within ours." The Syrian denominations could easily make such an appeal to the upper castes.

Unconscious appeals of this sort have probably been made. As the Nagas of Nagaland evangelized the Thankul Nagas of

Manipur, it is reasonable to suppose that they encouraged the Thankul Nagas of Manipur to form Thankul Naga congregations and even denominations. The Ao Nagas form a quite different endogamous unit from the Konyak Nagas, and the Angamis do not intermarry with the Thankuls. Whereas in much of plains India the Gospel means "Believe in Jesus Christ and become a Christian in the existing Christian community," it is clear that in the hills of North East India the Gospel means "Believe in Jesus Christ and become a Christian in your own racial community."

One wonders whether both Syrian Type 1 and Type 7 may not in the near future pioneer a form of evangelization which meets the opposition of caste by saying something like this:

"We are thoroughly Christian. We value highly the salvation we have in Jesus Christ. We invite you to become Christians like us. This does not mean 'Join our congregations.' On the contrary, it means 'Form your own congregations within your own castes.' Preserve any degree of endogamy you desire. Of course, as biblical Christians who take the Lordship of Jesus Christ seriously, you will believe that mankind is one great brotherhood, and in Christ there is no real difference between races and castes. Being in Christ is truly so tremendous an experience that all cultural distinctions whatsoever pale into insignificance.

"However, the degree of endogamy which you desire and which you believe is consonant with Christ's will for you is your business, not ours. We intend to keep our Syrian ethnicity. You may do likewise. Keep your distinctly Brahman, Nair, Chetty, or European ethnicity.

"In great meetings of the Church, all will partake of the communion together, and since interdining is already going on in all universities and many cities and liberated sections of the Indian people, we believe that you will welcome such a symbolic affirmation of the unity we have in Christ.

"So form your own congregations. In Andhra these may be strictly Kamma or Reddi, or made up of believers from several of the Shudra castes who live in the villages. As Christians you will marry, in the future as in the past, within the confines of the Kamma and Reddi communities. You are free in Christ to do as you wish in regard to these matters. Come join us in joyful worship and full obedience to the Lord Jesus as He has pleased to reveal Himself in the Bible."

As we consider evangelistic potential, we must make clear that urban monoethnic Syrian congregations today do *not* carry on any such evangelization. Indeed these, in a desperate attempt to preserve ethnic purity, carry on very little if any evangelization of non-Christians. A few devout evangelists may speak the words, but the paltry outcome in terms of converts from the ranks of atheists, agnostics, idolaters, and materialists indicates eloquently that effective evangelism is being done in the smallest possible way, if at all.

Urban monoethnic Syrians should compare themselves with urban monoethnics from caste. These humble congregations of factory workers and unskilled labor are continually winning fellow ethnics into their own congregations. Syrians cannot do this — *they have no non-Christian fellow ethnics.* In Indian cities today there are hundreds of thousands who regard Christians as "our own people, who have gone on further than we have. When we become Christians we remain our own kind of people. We do not leave our caste, we simply join the advanced, liberated section of it." In Indian cities today *very few* non-Christians if any regard Syrian monoethnic congregations as "our own kind of people." Consequently, if Syrians are to be effectively evangelistic *they must find segments of the population with which they can talk, whose members will listen with pleasure. People of those castes who believe may then be formed into congregations.*

URBAN MONOETHNICS FROM TRIBE

The great cities of India are curiously devoid of large numbers of tribals. The smaller cities in North East India, such as Shillong,

Agartala, and Imphal are of course filled with them, but I am speaking now of the manufacturing complexes of over a million.

The tribals have had plenty of land, have liked their way of life, and have not flocked to the city. The Uraons and Mundas have moved to the tea gardens of Assam, but not in any large numbers to the factories of Calcutta.

Consequently we are dealing with urban tribal congregations as these arise in towns and *small* cities. If a tribal congregation is formed near an educational institution — as for example Jorhat Seminary, or a Presbyterian high school or college in Shillong, or a Baptist city church in Imphal — it will likely be *multi*ethnic at a high educational level. It will include Christians from all tribes. It will have one church building and one service in English for educated people or in the language of the area. In that church, Christians from several tribes will worship, rather pleased at the intertribal nature of the congregation. Pantribalism is popular today — it sets tribals off from Hindu India.

But if large numbers from each of several tribes live in any city, then, particularly at the lower educational level, *mono*ethnic congregations flourish. The same psychological social and linguistic considerations that cause Swedish immigrants to the United States to prefer congregations of Swedes, worshiping in Swedish, eating food that Swedes like, enjoying Swedish humor, and marrying the best girls in the world (Swedish, of course), operate to help tribals to form monoethnic urban congregations.

Evangelistic Potential

This is very high. Cultural compulsion of all sorts operates in favor of tribal men and women becoming Christian on migrating to the city. The animistic gods have been left behind in the hills. The advanced section of the community is beyond doubt the Christian. To become Christian is to step up in the world. Among the many new ways learned in the city, the Christian ways seem highly desirable.

But if a city congregation of tribals (tribal Type 7) carelessly ceases to evangelize and multiply congregations, the processes of secularization go on apace and in a few years the pagan tribals have hardened into sophisticated materialists who believe that the good life is theirs already — why become Christian? Urban monoethnic tribal congregations, therefore, are in a position of great importance. Modern Churches and missions,* give high priority to helping urban monoethnics from tribe to *disciple all of their own tribe living in the city, and to do it soon.* Vigorous multiplication of congregations among city tribals is urgent.

And missions! I vigorously dissociate myself from a strange contemporary aberration which affirms that missions are outmoded and no longer needed. The best research indicates that only about 500 million non-Christians in the world *can* be reached by the near-neighbor evangelism of existing congregations and denominations. That leaves more than 2,400 *million* who can be reached *only by missionary efforts.* Naturally "modern missions" include missions from all six continents. The task is immense.

8

THE GREAT CONGLOMERATES

IT HELPS in understanding the Church in India to realize that about 83 percent of its members are found in eight great conglomerate denominations. These superdenominations, as it were — federations of many types — may be conveniently designated as Type 8 Churches. Most are stronger in one region than in others, but with two exceptions all can lay claim to be all-India Churches. Naming them in order of their emergence we have:

	Millions of Members in 1977
1. Roman Catholic Church	8.5
2. Methodist Church of Southern Asia	.9
3. Federation of Evangelical Lutheran Churches in India	.8
4. Church of South India	1.6
5. Council of Baptist Churches of North East India	1.1
6. Presbyterian Church of North East India	.3
7. Church of North India	.6
8. Federation of Evangelical Churches of India	.2

186

The following diagram, figure 4, gives an idea of their comparative strength in 1977. The blocks indicate total community including infants and casual Christians. Communicants or full members in each case will, of course, be fewer.

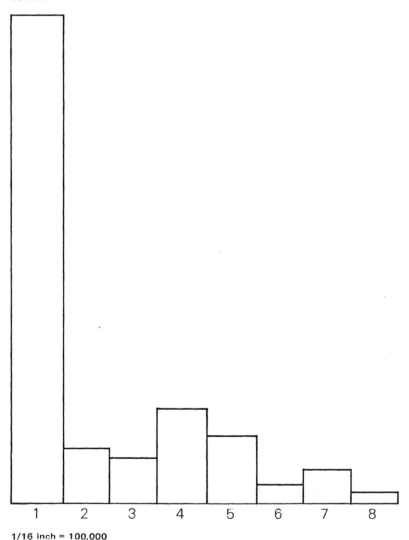

1/16 inch = 100,000

Fig. 4 Comparative strength of India's Great Conglomerate Churches In 1977. Numbers refer to list opposite.

The numbers given in the table p. 186, also for total community, are 1977 estimates* based on censuses and memberships in 1968, 1971, 1975 and other recent dates. The 1981 government census will, no doubt give slightly different figures. Yet the overall impression will remain substantially unchanged.

In making such a classification, we must face the question as to how large a membership a denomination has to have to be counted a *great* Church, and for the purposes of this volume I have set the number arbitrarily at 100,000. This is why some Churches found in several states are not included; they do not have enough members. A couple of Pentecostal denominations which have grown vigorously are still well under 100,000 each. Local autonomous churches are found all over India, yet I doubt if all their members together would add up to 100,000.

Each Type 8 Church is composed of Churches of Types 2, 3, 4, 5, 6, and 7 and is thus a thorough conglomerate. Each is made up of congregations and clusters of congregations which are linguistically and ethnically distinct. For example, in the Roman Catholic Church, which has a total community of about 8.5 million, are congregations speaking Hindi, Tamil, Telegu, English, and *all* the other major languages of India. The Catholic superdenomination is a mixture of big monoethnic and small multiethnic Churches.

Similarly the Federation of Evangelical Lutheran Churches in India is a combination of very dissimilar monoethnic denominations (Types 3 and 4) in Andhra Pradesh, Chhota Nagpur, Assam, Tamil Nadu, South Orissa, and West Bengal. In the cities it also includes a few multiethnic Types 2, 5, and 6, and monoethnic Type 7. The Federation worships in six major

*To obtain the most accurate figures possible — in a much debated field — I wrote to Dr. David Barrett, the world authority, Editor of the World Christian Handbook to be published in 1978 or 1979. In February 1977 he kindly gave me the above figures and the following for other groups which cannot be called Great Conglomerates: Orthodox Syrians 1,400,000; Mar Thoma Syrians 400,000; and other Christians in many denominations "at least a million." Thus total Christians in India numbered in 1977 16,800,000.

languages — Hindi, Tamil, Telegu, Bengali, Oriya, and
Assamese, and in at least three tribal tongues: Santali, Uraon, and
Munda. It includes the ethnic Churches of Uraons, Mundas,
Santals, Meharahs, Parayas, Sambavas, Malas, Madigas, and some
others. In each, 95 to 98 percent of the members are of that tribe
or caste.

The Council of Baptist Churches and the Presbyterian Church
in North East India, like the Roman Catholic Church, are each of
one ecclesiastical and doctrinal family. They are the most regional
of the great conglomerates, with few congregations outside the
states of North East India. Nevertheless, since they are made up
of denominations of many different endogamous tribes,
speaking mutually unintelligible languages, and some
multiethnic congregations of converts from many castes in the
plains of Assam, they must be classified as Type 8.

The Church of North India and Church of South India,
though very largely confined to North and South India,
nevertheless rank as Type 8 denominations.

CHARACTERISTICS OF TYPE 8

Type 8 Churches — consisting of groups of what I have called
denominations or Churches — are powerful associations of
people movements from caste, people movements from tribe,
pure conglomerates, modified conglomerates, urban
multiethnics, and urban monoethnics. Associations may be
organized as Federations, United Churches, or Churches, it
makes little difference. They function in much the same way.

Type 8 has many advantages. It protects small units of the Body
against local selfish parties which favor their own relatives, sell
and "eat" church properties, and administer a cluster of
congregations from a very limited or parochial point of view.

It approaches government much better than small units do.
These greater Churches plead their cause from strength,
speaking for large bodies of Christians with a single voice, and

thus avoid confusing government with many rival and conflicting claims and points of view.

They look good to mission boards from overseas. When these believe that "mission work" consists entirely in helping young Churches, they want to deal with responsible bodies which can make and carry out long-range plans. The world Christian enterprise is looking for something to take the place of the strong, dedicated missionary societies of the past. The great conglomerates appear to have sufficient size, weight, ability, and organization. They have not to date shown evangelistic concern, but they may develop it. So missionary societies based in Eurican lands like to deal with them.

The great conglomerates also appear to bypass the meaninglessness of Western denominational divisions. The argument runs as follows: Each Protestant denomination in Eurica arose to reform a corrupt condition there. In India these corrupt conditions do not exist, so why confuse listeners with conflicting emphases which are not germane?

There is some truth in the argument, but it is nevertheless an oversimplification. Many basic issues are just as relevant to India as to the West. Does *biblical* baptism require conscious repentance, conscious belief, and conscious obedience, or is it a rite analagous to circumcision? Does the true Church arise where two or three are gathered in Christ's name and He is there in the midst of them, or only where a bishop in the apostolic succession from Peter is present to give sanction to it? Is the Bible the written Word of God, or is it a human record of past events whose truth and authority each Christian and each denomination is left free to judge?

These issues and others like them lie at the root of the denominational divisions in the West, and all are relevant to the Indian scene. Furthermore, as we shall see in the next chapter, when the Church grows strong in any land it develops valid denominations of its own. As it begins to ask its own questions of its own environment, clusters of congregations decide that they must interpret the Scriptures in their own way. It is impossible to have one monolithic Church, unless (as in the Middle Ages) the Church controls the state. This it is not likely to do in India in the foreseeable future, nor would most Christians want it.

Great conglomerates have disadvantages also. They are heavy with machinery. The properties inherited from the powerful Church of England and the missionary societies may easily in modern India be taxed out of existence. Managing these properties, paying taxes on them, and keeping them repaired is a tremendous task. The railway fares and days consumed in all-India meetings of far-flung small clusters of congregations eat up a disproportionate share of their small resources. Something simpler and more local and indigenous to each of the multitudinous regions of India will work better.

To be sure, each of the great conglomerates has its sections, its dioceses, its language areas. Each has substantial local autonomy. The conglomerate therefore, whether called a Federation or a Church, has considerable flexibility. Nevertheless these super denominations are heavy with machinery.

These Type 8 Churches do not represent the heart concerns of their very different clusters of congregations, which are intensely local and ethnically and linguistically unique. For example, the Rev. Imotemjen Aier, in his research into the growth of the Garo churches in what is now West Meghalaya, points out that whereas the Bengali and Assamese languages, written in the Devanagari script, were the prestige languages of North East India, the Garos hated alike these languages and the script in which they were written. They had for centuries regarded the people of the plains as their enemies and did not like learning to read in that enemy script and language. When the missionaries put Garo into *Roman* script, it helped materially in the discipling of the Garos. Whether a great conglomerate would have had grace and imagination enough to recognize this regionalism and enthusiastically bend toward it is an open question. A strong characteristic of all Type 8 Churches is to play down regional differences. "A silly tribal prejudice," such as I have just described, could easily be scorned. Printing the Bible in Roman might well be held an unnecessary and damaging concession to local factionalism, which would not sit well with the government.

A third disadvantage is that the great leaders of large federations and associations have been exposed to and some have been greatly influenced by Western liberalism. With few exceptions they are men who have had years of training in Europe and America. Such training feeds back into influential church positions some men who have become substantially Westernized. Two areas in which Westernization is particularly damaging are views of Scripture and supraracial views of society.

In regard to the former, the West is currently making tremendous efforts to adjust its beliefs to the scientific world view which has swept across the common people of the Western world with such force. But the common people of Hindu India do not yet hold the scientific world view. They quite comfortably continue their worship of spirits and gods. They and most Christians believe in their scriptures with an ardor and certainty like that of Western Christians two hundred years ago.

In the West, latitudinarian views of scripture are held in the hope that they will commend the Gospel to scientific man. But the receptive segments of Indian society are largely untouched by scientific agnosticism. They need ardent, not lukewarm views of scripture. They need biblical truth categorically stated, not carefully hedged about with conditions. They want certainty. If told that honest doubt is a good thing, a sign that the person is seeking God, they will turn to "real" religious leaders who have no doubt at all that their message is ultimate truth.

Indianization may or may not involve using the classical Indian dance forms, singing Indian lyrics set to Indian music, or stating Christian truth in the philosophical terms native to India; but it *must* mean stating the truths necessary to salvation with certainty in thought forms which Indians immersed in caste society can recognize. *Becoming a part of the Body of Christ must appear possible to listeners.* Till this happens they have not really heard the Gospel.

The supraracial outlook on society which is tremendously

popular in Western culture has been accepted by most Indians educated in the West. They never question it; they have been thoroughly converted to the supraracial outlook. When these men are elected to positions of nationwide influence they are in danger of confining the Churches to a static pattern congenial to the antiracial convictions of Eurican Christians. If the present 16 million Indian Christians (about 2.6 percent of the total population) are held to a strictly supracaste position, and all movements to Christ running through castes are forced either to discontinue or to join the existing conglomerate Church, it is entirely possible that the twelve hundred year static condition of Christianity in the Middle East will be reproduced in India. The contented posture of the Syrian Churches of Kerala indicates that such an outcome is more than possible. Christians frozen into nongrowing, supracaste ethnic blocks for a century would have great difficulty in beginning to grow again.

That Type 8 Churches are urban-dominated tragically magnifies this disadvantage. Their chief leaders have by education and extensive experience become cosmopolitan citizens of the world. They do not see things primarily from the perspective of their numerous rural members.

As we saw earlier in other connections, the seminary professors, district superintendents, executives of various sorts, and bishops have of necessity to live in towns and cities. They associate very largely with educated urbanites, read modern books and magazines, address meetings of other leaders, see problems in the large, attend international gatherings, and *think in multiethnic terms*. This has some advantages, but it also means that they often look with proud annoyance on that most Indian of all cultural traits: communal mentality.

Akin to this is the fact that many important leaders have grown up in conglomerate congregations and are thus personally members of no great Indian caste. If by chance they are personally of a people movement from caste, they are likely to be sent to lead sections of the Church where they can administer impartially because they are related to no one.* The arrangement is good in some ways, but in highly ethnic India it adds to the feeling that "when we join the Church we must leave our own people." We have noted that in 1926, the leaders in the National Christian Council almost passed a resolution banning all further conversions from the Depressed Classes. When one sees the myopic upper-class interest which alone could have given rise to such a deliberate policy, he realizes how easy it is for leaders of conglomerate Churches to forget or deny their ethnic connections. The great conglomerates in India are in constant danger of forgetting that Christian leaders of ethnic Churches must identify with the racial aspirations of those Churches and do battle for those ethnic blocks.

One of the reasons the great Ambedkar did not become a Christian was well expressed in what he told Bishop Pickett, recounted in the latter's *Christ's Way to India's Heart,*

When I read the Gospels, the Acts of the Apostles, and certain passages of St. Paul's epistles, I feel that I and my people must all become Christians, for in them I find a perfect antidote to the poison Hinduism has injected into our souls, and a dynamic strong enough to lift us out of our present degraded position. But when I look at the Church produced by Christian Missions in the districts around Bombay [mostly conglomerates and modified conglomerates] I have quite a different feeling. Many of my own caste have become Christians and most of them do not commend Christianity to the rest of us. Some have gone to boarding schools and have enjoyed high privilege. . . . What sort of people are they? Selfish and self-centered. They do not care a snap of their fingers what becomes of their former caste associates so long as they and their families get ahead. . . . Indeed, their chief concern with reference to their old caste associates is to hide the fact that they were ever in the same community. (pp. 29, 30)

---

*In the great people movement Churches, of course, one finds exceptions to this generalization. The CSI bishops in Kanniyakumari and Tinnevelly dioceses would usually be Nadars. The Presbyterian moderator in Mizoram would be a Mizo. The executive secretary of the Konyak Baptist Council would be a Konyak.

Highly educated cosmopolitan Christians in India meet their greatest challenge at the point of ethnic identification. That leaders should be highly educated, have a broad outlook, executive experience, impartiality, and world vision is all to the good; but for them to hide the fact that they were ever in the same community drastically diminishes effective presentation of the Gospel. Rather than have leaders who stand above all communities, much is to be said for those who deliberately identify with and champion the units to which they belong.

John Knox prayed, "Lord, give me Scotland or I die." He was a great Christian, but also a great Scot. In any controversy about the rights of the English and the Scots, he was solidly on the side of the Scots. No leader of the Scottish Church who maintained a strict impartiality — neither English, nor Italian, nor French, nor even Scotch — could possibly have won Scotland to the reformed faith. Ambedkar could not have said of John Knox what he did of the elite leaders of some conglomerate congregations around Bombay.

India is simply not going to be converted into conglomerate congregations and denominations. No conceivable extension of a small dribble of converts leaving many castes and tribes and coming one by one into multiethnic Churches will win 2,900 and more ethnic units in India to Christ. God is using and will use the small trickle. Across the years it will bring in many; but it is not enough. When India is won to Christ, it will be in a series of movements to the Christian faith running through the castes, which will allow men and women to become Christian without renouncing their race —*jati, ethnos*. This is abundantly seen in the Syrian Church, the Mizo Church, the Naga Church, the Nadar Church, and every other great Church in India.

The Rev. Gordon Soddy, a British Baptist missionary of experience, was in 1975 engaged in writing the history of the Baptist Union of Bangladesh. He believes that for any Church to be strong it needs to "get into a natural social community." He writes, "A natural social community helps the formation of a stable church." Speaking of a successful church-planting minister, he says, "He established a viable church that still exists because he got into one particular community and held onto it." Speaking of the weak Baptist churches in two districts, he says, "Dacca and Commilla never managed to capture a community." (Quoted in the preface of Peter McNee's *Crucial Issues in Bangladesh*, 1975.)

Many Indian leaders do everything *but* what will enable them to "get into a community" and multiply churches *there*. Consequently conglomerate congregations and denominations of a few hundreds or thousands arise in the midst of receptive *millions*. The eminent leaders of Type 8 Churches are in grave danger of so glorifying "supracastism" that they will discourage movements to Christian faith running through caste even more than urban missionaries did. That they will do this for the most part quite unconsciously merely adds to the danger.*

UNITED CHURCHES AS CONGLOMERATES

The great conglomerates have arisen in two ways: (1) Five powerful missionary societies from the West have carried on enough mission and fathered enough people movements to Christ so that each has hundreds of thousands of Christians of its persuasion. These constitute five of the large Type 8 denominations: namely, the Roman Catholic, the Methodist, the Lutheran, the Baptist, and the Presbyterian. Then (2) three instances of Type 8 arose as several denominations united to form a larger one. This pattern created the Church of South India, the Church of North India, and the Federation of Evangelical Churches.

Time will not permit recounting the history of each of the United Churches. Nor is it necessary to do so. United Churches have been forming in most lands of Asia, and the process in all

---

*The most vigorous criticism of this book will likely come from leaders whose thinking is thoroughly conglomerate. They easily assume that their multiethnic policies and convictions are the direct product of faithfulness to the Bible.

cases is substantially the same. Let us therefore look at the best known United Church — the Church of South India — and briefly recapitulate the steps by which several denominations merged into one.

Some missionaries and some nationals in India began quite early to consider it desirable for several small denominations (especially those of similar doctrine and polity) to form one Church. Thus in 1901, after years of negotiation and conference, three small Presbyterian Churches, planted in India by two Presbyterian missions from Scotland and one from America, were merged into one. They were all in the extreme south of the country. The advantages in training and placing of ministers were substantial.

Between 1901 and 1908 the process went a step further. The Congregational Mission from the United States and the London Missionary Society decided that their Churches believed substantially what the Presbyterians did. The advantages to their congregations of being parts of one strong South Indian Church were attractive. Numerous conferences and conversations on church union were carried forward. In 1908 a new constitution was adopted which had previously been ratified by the Congregational and Presbyterian Churches and missions. Thus the South India United Church (SIUC) came into being.

In 1910 the Anglicans entered into annual conversations, consultations, and negotiations about forming a Church which would unite the Congregational, Presbyterian, and Episcopal doctrine and polity. The plans were criticized by some as a surrender to the doctrine of apostolic succession. Other men, such as Chakkarai and Devasahayam, criticized the proposed Church as too Western; they feared the Church in South India would be solidified in Western molds. Nevertheless, year after year the conversations went forward, and difficulties one by one were ironed out. Ways were found of bridging the gaps, formulas devised which would enable each side to agree to union.

For example, ordination by bishops who had themselves been ordained in the apostolic line was deemed essential by the

Anglicans. This meant reordaining all ministers and missionaries in the SIUC. The South India United Church, on the other hand, with its strong inheritance from the Congregational and Presbyterian Churches of England and America, could not countenance reordination, which implied that theirs were not real ministers. A compromise was finally worked out: already ordained ministers of the SIUC were to be accepted in the Church of South India exactly as were already ordained ministers of the Anglican Church; but all *new* candidates for the priesthood (ministry) were to be ordained in the Episcopal tradition by bishops who had themselves been so ordained.

The Anglican wing of the new Church had to pay a price for this departure from the rules of the Church of England: the Church of South India would be technically out of communion with the Church of England (though actually in very close fellowship) till such time as all its ministers were "properly" ordained. The full story is fascinating and well worth reading, but cannot be told here. Thus, item by item, over twenty-two years a plan of union was hammered out which allowed these very dissimilar denominations to merge. The Church of South India was inaugurated in 1947, just after World War II.

One of its attractive features was that bishops of the new Church were to be chosen from among the leaders of SIUC British Methodist and Anglican Churches. Thus the most powerful leaders of all the Churches concerned, conscious that they themselves might be made bishops for life in the new Church, had the strongest motives for urging union. They were already powerful executives. The Episcopal office guaranteed lifetime tenure.

In a similar fashion the Church of North India was formed. It too had a Presbyterian nucleus to begin with. It pulled in the British Methodists, British Baptists, a part of the Christian Church Disciples of Christ, and of course the Anglicans. The problem of reordination it solved as follows: leaders of all the uniting denominations, using a most carefully developed formula from which each offending word had been deleted, *laid hands on each other's heads.* In the Anglican and Roman Catholic understanding of the rite of ordination, it takes three bishops, each of whom has been correctly ordained in the apostolic succession, to ordain any other bishop by laying on of hands and saying the right words with the right intentions. Thus the ceremony which was to unite the ministries had to make it possible for three Anglican bishops to lay hands on all non-Anglicans becoming bishops of the new Church.

To avoid implying that the ministries of the Presbyterian and other Churches were invalid, the Presbyterian and other denominational leaders also laid their hands on the heads of the Anglican bishops. Thus what gifts and powers each Church possessed were held to be transmitted to all, and the appearance of reordination was avoided.

The coming of the Anglicans into these two Churches brought them vast properties: the great church buildings at state capitals and important cities, the National Church in New Delhi right next to the Lok Sabha and presidential palace, and other inheritances from the established Church of the British era.

All this gave the United Churches a new sense of power and progress. They had demonstrated to the world that the union of denominations was possible even across the tremendous gaps between the Congregational and Episcopal forms of polity and doctrine. The movement toward church union in the United States which has animated the breasts of several of the larger denominations has drawn substantial encouragement from its success in India.

With the formation of the United Churches, three of the eight great conglomerates now possess apostolic ordination. Five do not, and hold that it is not a biblical mark of the ministry.

The United Churches and indeed all Type 8 Churches are in fact more federations than single denominations. Each original denomination and each regional and ethnic Church retains a considerable character of its own and a freedom to do what it wishes. This is not so much a carry over from "western denominationalism," that favorite whipping boy of chauvinistic champions of unity, as it is a manifestation of the multi-sided ethnicity which is an essential feature of the Indian scene. All over the world, as well as in India, society is composed of thousands of homogeneous units. The Church, as it arises in each, of necessity adapts to the culture of each. *Particularity* is of the essence of flesh and blood Churches. Each while conformed to Christ on one side, is conformed to the beautiful language, culture and ethnicity of its own homogeneous unit on the other.

How far such cultural adaptation should go is a nice question. Carried too far, it destroys the Church. Not carried far enough, it guarantees that the Church will appear as a foreign intrusion and lose evangelistic potency. Christians, whatever their ethnic or regional bias, must, of course, cleave to One Lord, One Saviour and One Book. The Lord and Saviour are closely defined in the One Book. No other book may be regarded as authoritative infallible scripture. The ultimate measure is the Bible. The Christ worshipped and obeyed by Christians is not the cosmic Christ of theosophy, but is Jesus Christ who became flesh and lived amongst men and is revealed in the Old and New Testaments. But having said this, I hurry on to say that considerable adaptation to culture should go on. As I wrote to Dr. M.M. Thomas in 1973,

> This is the time for the Church to flow into as many of the myriad cultures of India as possible — changing them as little as possible in the direction of any Western form of Christianity, preserving as much as possible of the precious culture of each segment of society — in India, of each caste — bringing it in fact to its own perfection which was intentioned by God, and was made possible in Christ. And building into it the righteousness which is from God, through the Holy Spirit and the unique revelation of God's will which He has given to the world in the Bible (p. 146-147).

Where the line must be drawn between legitimate cultural adaptation and unacceptable religious syncretism is a most important and difficult question. We shall be answering it for the foreseeable future. I have discussed this matter at length in *The*

Clash of Christianity and Cultures. Here it is sufficient to say that as the Christian Faith spreads through the 3000 and more castes and tribes of India, it is desirable that it take on much of the color of each. That is what in part adaptation to Indian culture means. An illuminating instance took place in the state of Manipur. There the Church had started among the Thankul Nagas and then spread to the Kukis. In the beginning, the Baptist Council was perforce a Thankul organization in which every member was a Thankul. When a few Kuki congregations were founded, a Kuki pastor was elected to the Council and found himself very much in a minority there. It was entirely natural that, as soon as there were enough Kuki congregations, they formed a separate Kuki Council. The older leaders, who had hoped for a single Baptist Council for all of Manipur State, regarded this development as a backward step, a triumph of tribalism, a splintering of the Church. They might better have considered it a legitimate and desirable adjustment to the social milieu, which would aid in bringing the whole Kuki nation into the freedom of Christ.

No Church in India can spread throughout the multitudinous pieces of the Indian mosaic *and* at the same time be a monolithic totalitarian organization. Even the Roman Catholic Church, which has the name of being one, is in reality a federation of denominations. The Latin Rite Roman Catholic Church of the Mukkuvas, along the southern tip of India has an internal life very unlike that of the Syrian Rite Roman Catholic Church and that of the Hindi Rite Roman Catholic Church of Chhota Nagpur. Each of these three denominations has arisen in a separate caste. Each is of necessity different. The principle is that as the Church spreads into caste after caste, it is *desireable* that it take on the color of each.

To be sure, it will also baptize that caste into the unity of Christ; but unity will manifest itself in a multiplicity of practices, policies, political postures, and social stances. Diversity in unity must be the watchword of the Church in India — as well as in the rest of the world. The rights of each ethnic Church, as well as each region, exist in tension with the rights of the whole denomination. Just as states rights and national rights in the United States have clashed over a period of two hundred years, so we may expect regional and ethnic rights to clash with "whole Church rights" in India. That is, in part, what adjustment to Indian culture means.

GROWTH PATTERNS

Five Type 8 Churches, including the two United Churches and the two Federations, have grown little since World War II. They have increased by biological growth but have had little conversion growth.

This was a surprise, because the argument most commonly used for church union was that it would make the Church more credible and hence more evangelistically potent. John 17:20,21 was always quoted: "That they may all be one . . . that the world may believe." It was argued that many Hindus would long ago have become Christians, but confused by many Churches did not know which to choose. Between 1925 and 1947 the following story was frequently told: The Iravas in Kerala, who number about a million souls, seriously considered becoming Christians. But then someone asked, "Which Church will you join — Mar Thoma, Roman Catholic, Anglican, Lutheran, or Basel Mission?" The questioner went on to say, "The Iravas are now one caste, one big family. When you become Christian in different Churches, you will be forever separated." Whereupon the movement toward Christ subsided.

The story is, of course, special pleading. The Iravas did not become Christians, but for reasons much more powerful than this oversimplified version. Nevertheless, the uniting denominations did generally believe that one Church would be evangelistically more potent than the many.

However, during the thirty years since the Church of South India was formed, far from growing more rapidly, it has not kept pace with the growth of the general population. Dr. C.N. Raju's

study, *Are the CSI Churches Growing . . .?* (1965) proves that the
rate of growth of the Church of South India between 1952 and
1962 was 1.39 percent *less* than that of the population.
Unfortunately the Lutheran Federation and the Methodist
Church seem to be following the same static pattern. The Church
of North India and the Federation of Evangelical Churches of
India are too recently formed (1968 and 1974) to have established
a trend, but their constituent bodies have not been growing. One
conference of the Methodist Church — in west Andhra Pradesh
— grew very satisfactorily (doubling in the twenty years after
1948) through an ongoing people movement to Christ from the
Madiga caste. The rest of that Church showed chiefly biological
growth.

To be fair to the five nongrowing Type 8 Churches, one has to
point out that the last thirty years have entailed tremendous
adjustments. The missionary system of the previous hundred and
fifty years has been — by the mainline boards at any rate —
largely dismantled. The Christian community is in a state of shock
and is going through withdrawal symptoms.

In assessing the situation, positive and negative factors must be
balanced. On the positive side, Christian radio is heard all over
India as it has never been before. The Every Home Crusade with
an Indian staff of over eight hundred full-time workers has done
a tremendous job in placing a suitable tract in every home in all
India. Evangelistic crusades by noted Christians have presented
the Gospel to scores of thousands. Despite this, however, the
great conglomerates have been growing slowly. Radio and
literature seldom result in men and women accepting Christ as
Saviour and becoming responsible members of His Church. They
may sow a field or ripen a harvest; they do not carry ripened
sheaves into the Master's barn.

On the negative side we must place the following facts:

Most Type 8 Churches have turned away from sustained effort
to win non-Christians to faith in Christ. Most congregations are
baptizing very few of their non-Christian friends and neighbors.

Working out relationships with mission boards overseas has

kept the great conglomerates too busy to evangelize non-Christians.

Keeping various parts of each great Church happy and properly represented in the national administration has proved a bigger task than anyone anticipated.

Fear of Hindu oppression has led some Christian leaders to play down evangelism.

A spate of lawsuits which have arisen as missions withdrew* has dampened the ardor of Christians and made them wonder if they have anything to say.

The erosion of biblical certainty among educated leaders of so many Western denominations and seminaries has infected enough upper-echelon Indian leaders to reduce the desire to evangelize.

The new philosophy of mission, which places major stress on development and very little on evangelism, has almost squeezed evangelism out of the program of most main-line denominations.

All these factors, in different measure in each section of the Church, have diminished evangelistic potency and go far toward explaining the thirty years of chiefly biological growth.

Three of the great conglomerates, however, have shown considerable increase. The first is the Roman Catholic Church, which has been making steady progress, partly by taking over neglected Protestants left stranded by the Protestant dismantling of mission, but more by an inner dynamism which keeps people movements active. And the two Protestant super denominations in North East India have grown fairly well. The reason is not far to seek: they are made up of monoethnic denominations from tribe, and some of these have been growing healthily by the people movement.

It appears that in modern India, if a great conglomerate fathers people movements to Christ, it grows. If it does not father them, it becomes sealed off and static.

---

*These lawsuits concerned mostly who owned church buildings and other properties and had the right to use and sell them.

Evangelistic Potential of
the Great Conglomerates

The eight great conglomerates are great umbrellas under which many types of congregations and denominations are brought into one organization. *Each part of a Type 8 has to be administered as a separate block or denomination.* Its particular and peculiar problems must always be considered and its leaders chosen from within the linguistic and ethnic block concerned. Even the Catholic Church (which has the name of being one Church) is in reality a federation of denominations. For example, the Fishing Caste Catholics along the coast of the southern tip of India follow the Latin Rite, while their close neighbors are Syrian Rite Catholics. Yet the two are light years apart. They have very little to do with each other. They also have very little to do with the 400,000 Catholics in Chhota Nagpur.

The larger forms of government possess marked administrational advantages, as we have already seen, but so far — loose as they are — have not shown power to adjust sufficiently to the enormous diversity of the Indian scene. It may be that decentralized denominations, which allow and encourage more freedom of action, entailing the risk of heresy or deviationism, will be the form that fits Indian culture. Certainly Hinduism has steadily resisted any organization of its religious life into one monolithic structure. The question is: Does indigenous Christianity *in India* mean one Church with one creedal statement, one order of priests, and one authoritative head of the Church, or does it mean many administratively separate Churches held together by an inner binding loyalty to Jesus Christ (not the "cosmic" Christ) and His living word in the Bible?

However we answer that question, the fact of the matter is that federations, united Churches, and large denominations are here today and will be here tomorrow. One may ask, therefore, how effective they are for the propagation of the Gospel. Since I have already discussed their present growth patterns, we may now go on to ask: How can they be made evangelistically more effective?

"Triumphalism" toward other Christian Churches must be avoided. We are happily leaving behind an era in which many denominations (some very big and some very small) imagined that they were the only true Church. They wasted much energy fighting other branches of the Body of Christ. This mind-set has not entirely disappeared, but the coining of the term *triumphalism* to denote an arrogant conviction that "our branch of the Church alone will triumph" has helped render such a position less and less reasonable.

While each denomination properly considers its grasp of truth truer than that of others, today most of them also grant that as long as another denomination is firmly based on the Bible and is living in conscious discipleship to Jesus Christ it is also validly a Church. Hence it is an ally, not an enemy. Only God knows which existing forms of the Church will survive and do best, or whether He will create new and better forms. In the years ahead, therefore, effective evangelism will be furthered by each Church working ahead, doing God's will as it sees God's will and counting all other Christian Churches as part of the Church Universal.

To be evangelistically potent, Type 8 must actively evangelize those who do not yet believe in Christ and for the most part have not yet heard of Him. The housekeeping tasks of administration and the nurture and education of existing Christians must not shut out the greatest service Christians can render to their non-Christian friends, i.e. telling them about the Saviour and persuading them to become His disciples. The courteous approach to non-Christians, of listening before we speak and of understanding the religions of those to whom we communicate the Good News, must mean *more* evangelism, not less. If we really love our neighbors as ourselves, we will make every effort to share with them the treasure God has given us to carry in these earthen vessels.

To evangelize effectively, Type 8 must make their constituent parts intensely aware of how the Churches in India have arisen — all nine types — and how each may, in its own sphere, be a good steward of the grace of God. The steady emphasis of this book has been to point out the real evangelistic potential of each type and to identify such segments of the population as each may reasonably expect to bless by the proclamation and living of the Gospel.

The great conglomerates need to be sensitive to the values and aspirations of ethnic units within their territories which want to move to the Christian faith. Some of these movements may appear regrettably local or caste-limited ("castey"), but this is added reason to encourage them to adopt that faith, while steadily pointing out that it is possible only on grounds of biblical authority. Within the wide limits of that authority, each *ethnos* has complete freedom to chart its own course, choose its own leaders, and bring in its own cultural components. The great denominations have power; but they will misuse it if they try to force caste-wise movements to Christ into multiethnic Churches. Particular societies must be respected, their cultures appreciated, their webs of relationship preserved, their family loyalties enhanced. Type 8 can do this, but it will take conscious effort. For example, in some sections of India today, as several ethnic units have come to Christ they have demanded separate synods, associations, unions, conferences, or prebyteries. The National Church (a great conglomerate) has deplored this, insisting that the demand was no more than local factionalism and was fracturing the unity of the Church.

It must at once be granted that large units are easier to administer than small (I have said this before), and that the "curse of caste" has been that it divides society up into a multitude of small units intensely conscious of their separate identity. Nevertheless, curse or no, *this is the kind of society that exists in India.* The Church has two options before it: *(a)* it can fight all diversity, look on all manifestations of ethnic pride and regionalism as dangerous, and yield to them only when it must; or *(b)* it can simply accept the diversity of India's society as a given, exactly as it now accepts the extreme heat of May and June as one of the facts of life. If several thousand from some new ethnic unit pour into the Church and then demand that they be given a conference or presbytery of their own — a Konyak Naga Union for example, quite separate from the Ao Union — it would be cheerfully granted. The great Church might debate the matter with them, discuss its practicability, cost, relationship to the overarching unity of that Church, but under option *(b)* the Church would not consider the decision a matter of conscience or of loyalty to Christ and His whole, universal Church. In this writer's opinion, option *(b)* seems more likely to enable the Gospel of Christ to spread to the waiting multitudes.

The great Churches, however, also have a duty to teach the unity of mankind (all are sons of Adam) and the unity of the Church (it has one Lord, one faith, one Book). The Church is also a part of modern India which on the political level is pressing forward to a form of society in which Indianness bulks larger than communal affiliation. On both counts, the Churches should encourage many forms of action above and beyond all ethnic differences. United conventions and conferences will bring together Christians of all parts of the Church, across all denominations. The upper levels of ministerial training will take no cognizance of ethnic origin — all candidates will train together. Literature will constantly speak of mankind as one and stoutly maintain that one of the greatest blessings of the Christian Church for India is a consciousness that all men are equally valuable and there are no superior and inferior castes. Symbolic acts on an all-India — or even regional — scale will emphasize the unity all Christians already have. They eat together, attend each other's funerals, and as far as *the Church* is concerned may intermarry.

The conviction that underlies the writing of this book is that all the Churches of India, and perhaps the great conglomerates more than some others, can be evangelistically potent. They face the most responsive India ever to exist. The sowing of nearly two hundred years of modern missions has prepared a huge harvest. The multitudes moving to the cities are more receptive than they could have been in their ancestral villages. The acids of modernity are eroding traditional faiths. Active Marxism and anti-Brahman movements in the south are creating great vacuums of belief, in which men and women eagerly listen to all kinds of new gospels. The Indianizing of the Churches and the diminishing foreign missionary presence are saying very clearly that Christianity is an Indian religion. No disloyalty to Mother India is involved in becoming a disciple of the *Nishkalank Avatar* — the Sinless Incarnation.

The Type 8 denominations are already doing something to deepen the spiritual life of their congregations — they are already training ministers in fine seminaries in various parts of the land and carrying on a massive program of good works. They are ardent Indian patriots and commend great India on their travels abroad. They have good standing in the eyes of their fellow Indians.

If, together with fervent faith and intense patriotism, they now observe the sociological conditions and compelling cultural elements that incline men toward accepting the Saviour; if they study carefully the ways which God has blessed to the increase of His Churches and duplicate those ways among those whom He has prepared to start the march to the Promised Land, then *great growth of the Church can be theirs.* They can be the greatest blessing to the nation, and effect the most radical liberation of the peoples who believe and resolve to walk in the Light.

9

THE INDIGENOUS CHURCHES

TYPE 9 has not yet flourished in India, but because it is found in large numbers in the rest of the world, providing a substantial part of the Churches in other lands, and because it appears likely to develop in India too, I shall devote a chapter to such Churches. Their early beginnings throw further light on the relation of Christians to that most Indian of all cultural components: caste society. Indigenous Churches prosper, as we shall see in this connection from still another angle, when the convert does not leave the social structure in which he was born, but becomes a new creature in Christ Jesus while remaining part of it. Once more we shall observe that the relation of Christians and the congregations they form to the society in which they live is a factor of considerable importance in the growth of the Church.

Type 9 are *indigenous* congregations and denominations and must be sharply distinguished from the *indigenized*. But before we can discuss either one we need to note how the propagation of the Gospel inevitably results in forms of Christianity which are mixtures of foreign and native, and that indigeneity must be consciously sought.

STEADY ATTEMPT TO PLANT INDIGENOUS CHURCHES

From the beginning of the modern missionary movement, many missionaries have attempted to make the churches they founded indigenous. This policy was dictated both by necessity and by judgment as to what the Church is.

New congregations among illiterates living as subsistence farmers in a tight tribal society in a remote valley were of necessity very unlike congregations in London, Berlin, or New York. The language they spoke was different, their incomes were different, and their days were spent in quite different occupations. Their churches had, therefore, to be indigenous.

Moreover, since the Church is made up of men and women who have believed in the Lord Jesus Christ and accepted the Christian way of life as described in the Bible, and since the heart of the Christian religion is an inner righteousness and not obedience to external rules, congregations and denominations obviously had to assume the shape of the society in which people came to belief and salvation.

I say many missionaries "attempted" to make their churches indigenous. The attempt was always less than successful, and was set about with many pitfalls and snares. We have noted earlier that the only model of what the Church should be was the one the missionary knew from his homeland. The only hymns and tunes he knew were those he had sung. In restating this background I am only trying to keep it vividly in mind before us. The best way, it seemed, to build a gathering place for Christians was to follow the patterns of construction embodied in thousands of church buildings in Europe and America. So the models followed were always partly foreign. If hymns are to be sung, the only thing usually possible is to translate Western hymns and use Western tunes. If a gathering place of wood is to be built with a span of thirty feet, king-post or queen-post trusses must be used without further thought about it.

But the Western flavor is often temporary. As soon as Christians with a gift for music, a fervent love of the Lord, and thorough knowledge of the Bible appear in the new Church, the music can become indigenous. As soon as Christian poets who write in indigenous meter and rhythm find themselves overflowing with love for Christ and for God, then indigenous hymns begin to appear. The sole sway of temporary Westernisms can then be left behind. Any discussion of indigenous Churches must take into account the time sequence. Indigenous architecture, music, poetry, and the like come as the Church matures.

Shallow thinkers, fulminating against the lack of indigeneity of the Church, fail to realize that most aspects of Churches on new soil are by nature, language, economic capacity, and many other factors *already* essentially and ineradicably indigenous. Of the few aspects which are foreign, some will become indigenous with the passage of time. Others will of biblical necessity remain different. No one wishes indigenous congregations in Nagaland to ornament their place of worship with skulls taken from unwary enemies.

The steady attempt to plant indigenous churches focuses action on the few aspects of the new congregations and denominations which are indeed foreign. It asks *(a)* which of these ought to remain substantially different. Idolatry in India, though thoroughly indigenous, must not be brought into the Church. But shall Christians use or ban musical instruments employed in the temple to worship the idol? It also asks *(b)* whether the foreign components of Christian life which had to be adopted as a temporary measure are being replaced rapidly enough by native elements. Do we *now* seek to express in thoroughly Indian poetry the glorious truths of the Incarnation,

Atonement, and Resurrection, set to tunes commonly sung by the people of the land or to music that is really their own?

INDIGENIZED CHURCHES

We have already seen that, as the modern missionary movement streamed out across the world during the last two hundred years, it progressed in two ways. To sum up: a) in most places, as Christ was proclaimed, men and women by ones and twos against the current, often in the face of family opposition, commonly disowned by their peers, became responsible members of His Church. Each as he came in was in a minority, and the ways of earning, living, dressing, singing, and worshiping were set up by existing Christians. The missionary of necessity set the style for the first few converts, and they — again by necessity — for succeeding converts. Thus churches arose which, while no doubt indigenous as regarded a good deal of their life, had a foreign flavor so far as a remaining fraction was concerned. b) In a few places people movements to Christ developed and chains of families came to Christ, sometimes without seeing a missionary at all, and usually seeing him only a few times a year. Thus congregations arose which were much more indigenous (some would add: and much less Christian). However, even in these people movement congregations certain prominent parts of worship remained Western.

During the twentieth century, thousands of missionaries and national leaders have worked steadily ahead to purge the younger Churches of these lingering Westernisms and make them thoroughly indigenous. Forms of government and of support, too, have been indigenized. The missionary leader was replaced by the national. The missionary principal of the girls' school became the African or Asian educationalist. European bishops were replaced by Indian, Japanese, or African. Subsidy from North America was cut off and members trained in giving and stewardship. The goal was to make the young Church, which had started with varying degrees of dependence on foreign help, wholly independent, wholly at one with its surrounding culture.

This conscious attempt to diminish the foreign coloration of the Church and make all elements of its life thoroughly harmonious with its surroundings one may term, for lack of an easier word, *indigenization*. The world is full of *indigenized* Churches. The process goes on ceaselessly. It is a necessary part of reproduction, like weaning a baby or pushing an eaglet out of the nest.

INDIGENOUS CHURCHES

Indigenous Churches, on the other hand, are a different matter altogether. This is true on all six continents. The indigenized Churches originally planted by missionaries, facing great opposition but growing strong in the nest, inevitably imbibed some foreign ways. They needed to be *made* indigenous. But truly indigenous Churches begin out beyond the orbit of mission-related Churches. They are indigenous from the start.

Since these Churches are not to any large degree controlled or guided by already established Churches, but form their polity, doctrine, and ecclesiology according to their own ideas, they may easily become of doubtful orthodoxy, deviate from accepted Christian practice, or misinterpret some part of the Scriptures. Often the founder has elevated himself to a semidivine status. Or some component of the prior polytheism, animism, or other world view is maintained, contrary to the teaching of the Bible. Sometimes the very name adopted sounds strange to ears grown accustomed to the names of Western denominations. As a result, indigenous denominations all around the world have had a cool reception from mission-connected or indigenized denominations.

Sometimes this is unjust. The Type 9 Church may be soundly though somewhat unusually Christian. Thus the Church

established by Brother Bakht Singh in India sets standards of
Christian life and biblical obedience higher than those
maintained by the mainline Churches.

Sometimes the cool reception is warranted. The indigenous
denomination is perhaps only very slightly biblical and does not
throb with fervent loyalty to Jesus Christ. It may declare that its
authority is the Spirit rather than the Bible — and the Spirit it
obeys may cause it to say and do strange things. It is in fact a
syncretistic sect, not a Christian denomination.

In his book *Schism and Renewal in Africa* (1968), David Barrett
tells of six thousand new African denominations which have
arisen in the last fifty years. Of these, he counts five thousand as
reasonably orthodox Churches and a thousand as syncretistic
sects. In China between 1920 and 1947 a number of indigenous
Churches arose. The Little Flock, the True Jesus, and the Jesus
Family are the best known.

In Brazil, three indigenous Churches having no contact with or
indebtedness to foreign missions have achieved memberships of
200,000; 500,000; and 1,500,000. In Chile, the Pentecostal
movement numbering hundreds of thousands is really a series of
indigenous Type 9 Churches. In the Philippines, the largest and
most aggressive non-Roman Church is the famed "Iglesia ni
Christo," which numbers more than half a million members and
builds beautiful million-dollar churches in many cities.

India has seen a few indigenous Churches which claim or could
be awarded the designation "Christian." As I write, several come
to mind. Brother Bakht Singh's Jehovah Shammah is one. It has
congregations in Andhra Pradesh and Tamil Nadu, and others
thinly scattered across India. Since it does not keep membership
rolls, no one knows how many are involved. Some say 10,000,
some 20,000. The Gospel Association of India, founded by Shri
Rajaratnam, is another. Its small membership of 2,000 with
thirty-five pastor-evangelists in northeast Andhra affects a
population of 10,000 to 15,000. One-third of its members are
converts from the Shudra castes. Two-thirds are "converts" from

the Mala and Madiga Christian communities of Baptist, Lutheran, and Anglican origin.

The Ceylon Pentecostals are highly indigenous and are spreading in India vigorously among Christian and non-Christian populations. Dr. T.C. George has estimated that in 1974 they numbered about 25,000 in all India. Ceylon Pentecostal leaders wear a white garb closely related to the Hindu hermit's saffran dress. All believers are supposed to give a short testimony. The preaching always deals with separation, sanctification, and holiness. They teach that unless a person is baptized in the Holy Spirit, as evidenced by speaking in tongues, he has not been saved. They emphasize exorcism and divine healing. Their ministers live a celibate life *(The Growth of Pentecostal Churches in South India,* 1975:31-37). In a similar fashion other but smaller Pentecostal denominations have risen here and there, particularly in South India.

Bishop Neill writes me that "The 'Hindu Christians' of Tirunelveli have managed to maintain themselves for about a century, without growth."

Syncretistic groups, with mixtures of Christian and Hindu elements, are numerous. They vary all the way from polytheistic Hindu sects in whose temples pictures of the lords Ram, Buddha, Mohammed, and Jesus are hung on the wall, to the substantially monotheistic congregations of the Brahmo Samaj. In the city of Jubbulpore I visited a small congregation made up of twelve disciples of one man. Once a week he read the New Testament to them for an hour, then waved it before a shelf on which hung the pictures of Jesus Christ and Krishna, and dismissed the congregation. In 1832, W.J. Deerr, a German missionary of the Church Missionary Society working in Bengal, discovered a sect called Karta Bhoja. Half the adherents were Muslims and half Hindus. They said they were worshipers of "the Lord" and welcomed further information about Jesus Christ. By 1841, more than 2,000 had been baptized in the Anglican Church, and 3,000 more were waiting for baptism (Peter McNee, *Crucial Issues in Bangladesh,* 1975:106).

WHY SO SLOW IN APPEARING?

When other areas have such large numbers of thriving indigenous Churches (Africa with five thousand "reasonably orthodox" denominations), why have they been so slow in appearing in India? Why have so many died aborning — or been sucked back into Hinduism? Why does Type 9 not flourish on this subcontinent?

Before answering these questions one must step back and take into account once more that India is in fact a large federation of countries. Languages, different and complex cultures, and the ramifications of caste abound. Hesitant movements toward Christian faith have occurred in many places, but are known only to those who live in those parts. In my travels and investigations I have heard of many such beginnings and have had personal knowledge of several. No one has attempted to describe the all-India field. Consequently any attempt to answer the questions posed above runs the risk of speaking from only a small part of the total evidence. Nevertheless, the following factors appear to have something to do with the failure of indigenous denominations to do well in India. Readers may know of others.

The imperial presence is probably one reason why these spontaneous denominations did not at first flourish on the Indian scene. The strong central government, the well-organized missionary movement, and the highly educated ministry of the various sending denominations, all combined to present a picture of Christianity as very orderly, very educated, very imperial, and very much opposed to caste.

Christians in India had strong convictions as to what constituted the true Church. Anglicans, Syrians, and Roman Catholics held steadily that the true Church is found only where established by bishops properly ordained in apostolic succession. These denominations deny true churchhood — or the blessings of faith in Christ — to any but congregations whose pastors are in obedient relationship to the church hierarchy. Similarly, nonepiscopal Churches, staffed by men and women well versed in the Scriptures and dedicated to their own particular interpretations, have such a clear and final understanding of what the Church is that little room is left for the rise of new denominations which grope their way out of Animism or some form of Hinduism or other pre-Christian belief. The ecumenical mood also is very hostile to the emergence of any new denomination, whether indigenous or not.

The situation did not, and does not, encourage groping toward Christ. It opposed any understanding of scripture different from what existing denominations have reached. Yet our Lord's word to His disciples, recorded in Mark 9:39 and Luke 9:50, proposes another view: "Do not forbid him, for he that is not against you is for you." Again, Matthew (12:20) reminds his readers, as Isaiah foretold, that the Messiah would not "break the bruised reed or quench the smoking flax."

Another potent factor is that in Indian Christianity the social services have bulked very large. Education, medicine, and various forms of development have been the chief Christian activities in every section of the land. It is precisely the Church that pours out rivers of aid in leprosy homes, hospitals, dispensaries, schools, colleges, and agricultural demonstration centers. Christians are people who get educated and receive good salaries, rather than those who believe in the Saviour. Salvation by faith in Christ has been hidden by salvation through social amelioration. Indigenous Churches, not having the resources to carry on this degree of uplift, do not appear to the masses as really Christian.

What the masses seem to be saying is, "If you are going to be Christian, then go to the officially Christian denominations. They have money and can really help you. But insist that the Church give you schools and material help. Otherwise become Buddhist or put your faith in Ram. Do not be a Christian for nothing."

Still another element is the fact that pantheism and religious relativism tend to lead back into Hinduism movements which in Africa or China might have become indigenous Churches. The Brahmo Samaj and Prarthna Samaj of the nineteenth century are cases in point. Their leaders were tremendously attracted to Jesus

Christ but continued to regard Him as one among many. Subba Rao's movement — one fears — is more likely to develop into a form of Hinduism than into a form of Christianity. Also Hindu organizations such as the Arya Samaj carry on an aggressive program of reconversion to Hinduism.

Finally, the high value placed on caste, already considered in other connections, has largely blocked the emergence of indigenous Churches. As we have seen earlier, the fact that Christianity seemed to necessitate a complete break with caste, renunciation of endogamous marriage, mixing of the blood, and interdining with everyone has kept many movements toward Christ from coming to birth. Probably as Christianity starts to flow within each caste, we shall find indigenous Churches arising — for the spiritual discernment of Indians is high.

EVANGELISTIC POTENTIAL OF THE INDIGENOUS CHURCHES

The present indigenous Churches appear to have a low evangelistic potential. Jehovah Shammah wins adherents largely from existing Christians. One might better call it a renewal movement. The Gospel Association of India wins some hundreds of caste Hindus to full membership; each February it draws four or five thousand to its annual convention and perhaps half of these are caste people — Christians and inquirers. But so far no sweeping movement to Christ among the caste people has occurred.

The Ceylon Pentecostals are winning some from among non-Christians, but many more from nominal Christians.

All three of these small denominations (indigenous Churches) are multiethnic — made up of believers from many backgrounds. They are composed of the liberated. In fact, since they have not adjusted to the heart of Indian culture, one may reasonably say that these are not truly indigenous Churches.

Theoretically, multiethnic indigenous Churches ought to find great room to spread among the multitudes of Indians loosely affiliated with caste, out of caste for fault, moved to the new city or factory or mining town for work, or disenchanted with the whole caste system. However, so far such growth has not taken place. Probably this is because the number of those who sit loose to caste is not nearly as large as some have supposed. Possibly, also, because these indigenous Churches, being small, have not found the multitudes who sit loose to caste.

Suppose strictly endogamous Churches were to arise which proclaimed that one could worship the Lord Jesus, obey the Bible, and marry strictly within the caste. Could this kind of denomination propagate the Gospel in modern India? That is an essential question.

On the one hand, the power to propagate would be limited mostly to one's own caste. Christians coming from the Nair caste, for example, could effectively evangelize Nairs but would normally have no desire to evangelize outside that caste. When they came to the limits of their own people they would stop winning others, as did the Syrian Christians.

On the other hand, within the one caste Christian faith could spread like wildfire. It might become a way of life which "we Agharias" (or Narmadiyas, or Kayasths, or Suryavanshis) could adopt without "betraying our people." We have already seen how, when this idea concerning the Christian faith seized the minds of Velallas, Mizos, Chuhras, and Dherds, powerful movements to Christ developed within those castes.

The Subba Rao movement of Andhra Desh in the 1960s is a modern case in point. Subba Rao was the headmaster of a high school and a strong opponent of the Christian Church. He was led through dreams to pray to Jesus Christ to heal the sick. Christ miraculously answered his prayers. Subba Rao told his followers to throw away their idols and gathered them in groups to read the Bible, but he also continued his strong opposition to the Christian Church and especially to baptism. Did he desperately want to continue to be a Kamma in good standing in his caste? At any rate, his followers keep caste while becoming, to the degree indicated, disciples of the Lord Jesus. Were Subba Rao to carry the movement a step or two further, it might develop into an indigenous Christian Church, a Type 9 Church.

Examples of indigenous movements which did not quite reach Christian status could probably be compiled from all parts of India, but most of them have so far been swallowed up by Hinduism. They were opposed by the regular Christian Churches and missions. Most of them were not strong enough to develop independently. If they were friendly toward Christianity, they were taken in tow by the nearest Christian mission — see Karta Bhoja in Bengal in 1832. If they were hostile, they moved back into Hinduism.

However, in view of the worldwide example and the vast reaches of India in which the Churches are not evangelizing, it seems likely that as Christianity spreads into various castes we shall see many indigenous denominations. Some will be thoroughly orthodox and biblical; some will be heavily Hindu, even while worshiping Christ and throwing away their idols. I am well aware that this will seem an undesirable outcome to many Christians, but that will not keep it from happening. I do not advocate it; I am simply pointing out that it has happened on a considerable scale in Africa and may happen in India also. It is already taking place in many Asian countries.

CONCLUSION

The Coming
Great Growth of the
Church in India

In ORDER to understand the Church in any land we must see her in the right time perspective. In most nations of the Third World she now stands at the end of the third era of mission. It is a dangerous place to be, for she may move into a sealed-off, static condition like the Churches in Syria, Lebanon, and Iran. But it is also a place of great opportunity, for she is well poised for a breakout of enormous proportions.

Christian mission in most parts of the earth runs through four periods. First comes that of exploration. Missionaries are arriving, learning the language, being misunderstood, being banished, persecuted, or killed, establishing beachheads of one sort and another, commending themselves by good works and holy lives, winning the first converts, and founding the first few congregations. Long years elapse with scant results in terms of converts. Conglomerate congregations remain small and inevitably have a foreign flavor about them. They are allied with foreigners, and to some extent, despite the best efforts of missionaries, are more or less denationalized. The first translations of the Bible tend to be awkward, and often the Bible as a whole is not available for decades.

The second era of mission is that of strong and numerous mission stations. In a scattered but systematic way, the whole country is occupied. Central towns and cities are chosen as places of residence. Christian institutions which serve the public are established. Ground to stand on has been gained during the exploratory period. Now, during the mission-station era, good Christian work and much proclamation of the Gospel take place from the secure bases that have been established. But still "becoming a Christian" means "leaving our people and joining those foreigners." So converts are few and far between. Nevertheless, around the mission station Type 2 congregations do grow up and the number of Christians slowly increases.

In the third period, here and there in small measure responsive segments of the population, moved by cultural compulsion or other action of the Holy Spirit, begin to turn to Christ in a multi-individual way. Groups of men and women — sometimes a dozen, sometimes fifty — decide together to "become Christians." Congregations are formed out in the villages, or in the city wards away from the mission institutions and residences. Small people movements occur. Most of these are arrested at some point or die out. A very few spread like wildfire throughout some tribe or caste.

During this era three additional basic types of Church are founded in small numbers: people movements from tribes, people movements from caste, and modified conglomerates. In many parts of the land conglomerates (Type 2) remain the only kind of Church, and everywhere they are the typical form. In a few places where a people movement has flourished Types 3 and 4, monoethnics from caste or tribe, are found. Where people movement Christians, though living still in their villages, begin to cluster around and enter into the life of Type 2 centers, there the modified, Type 5 develops.

In this third era the Church grows strong. Schools and seminaries prepare leaders. Hymnbooks, prayer books, and good translations of Scripture are printed. Regular worship in well-built churches become an accepted habit of life. Christian ways of burying the dead, marrying, and celebrating religious festivals are developed and become precious to the Christian population. Pastors, elders, deacons, teachers, district superintendents, evangelists, and seminary professors are trained and function in an indigenous way. The institutional Church takes shape and fortifies the people of God.

The good lives of Christians, the good deeds they do and the transformation of life which faith in Christ brings, are noted by the neighbors. The intense persecution that accompanied the early stages of the spread of the Gospel tends to die down. The Church is small but strong. It appears likely to survive.

Transition to national leaders now takes place, in some cases in the latter years of the second era, and in some during the third. When the Church has grown strong enough, missionaries should move on to pioneer fields. Contrary to much common opinion, they are *not* sent primarily to help younger Churches. They are sent out by deed and word to communicate the Good News to those who have never heard. Failure to appreciate this basic fact and distinction often brings about a situation in which the mission stays on, "helping" the younger Church when it should be evangelizing sections of the population who have yet to hear. The word should never be "Missionary Go Home" but rather "Missionary, Go On Twenty Miles and Do It Again."

Some parts of India are at the end of the second stage or period, some at the end of the third. The transition to national leadership has taken place, and the whole Church is poised ready for the fourth era.

During this fourth stage in Christian mission, the Church ought to surge out in ceaseless, ardent evangelism, which will proceed on two tracks, bringing back two kinds of fruit. Along one line it will conduct *near-neighbor evangelism* (irrespective of caste), bringing individuals who awaken to the Gospel into already existing congregations and denominations. Because of the tight caste structure in India, this kind of evangelism inevitably implies "Leave your caste and come and join ours." Consequently it is strongly resented and rejected. The only people in India open to near-neighbor evangelism are, as we have seen, those who sit loose to caste or are actually out of caste. Newcomers in a strange city, men unable to get wives from their own caste, the elite who believe caste to be a source of great weakness to the country, persons under discipline by their castes or in a state of enmity with their caste fellows — these and others like them are the people who can be won by labors along that particular track. There are many such people in India, and most congregations, if they evangelize vigorously, will be increased by a constant trickle of them.

Along another line, evangelism will seek to bring those who believe *into congregations made up of their own kith and kin, their own caste fellows.* Among Nagas it will try to establish Naga congregations, among Nairs it will set up Nair, and among Kurmis, Kurmi congregations. This may sound impossible to Christians who have been reared in and know nothing but the conglomerate multiethnic pattern; but any India-wide view at once reveals that most of the growth of the Church there has occurred along these lines. This is the pattern that fits India, is culturally agreeable to the country, preserves Indian ways and customs best, and has most likelihood of surviving and spreading. It is both possible and highly desirable.

Evangelism on this second track will bring into the Church (not into the existing congregations but into new ones) groups of believers. As I write, a letter from one of my *chelas* (or students) in India tells of baptizing thirty believers from a total new Christian community of sixty-seven, thus establishing a third new congregation on the outskirts of a great city. He says, "The opportunities for the multiplication of churches here is enormous; but the laborers are few." Any survey of India as a whole will reveal literally scores, perhaps hundreds of chances to win groups to Christ. The Church in India — the eight great conglomerates and all the other Churches — face days of great opportunity. And as the Church grows, of great opposition. For growth usually arouses religious and political opposition, even when culturally agreeable.

There can be no doubt that India today is far more responsive than in the days of William Carey and the early pioneers. The strong Indian Church of 16 million, its ardent patriotism, its loyalty to India, its thousands of educated leaders serving the nation, and its multiplied good deeds — worked out in most cases with the help of Christians of other lands — commend Christ to the nation. Moreover, the rush to the cities, the tremendous educational program carried on by the Communists against the gods and the castes, the acids of modernity and growing secularization of all life, and the open-ended nature of the Churches almost everywhere — for they are ready to take in such as believe and want to join them — all bring it about that millions in India *talk* about becoming Christians.

Not many of them do it, but they consider it as an option. For more than twenty-five years the great Ambedkar talked about becoming Christian. This option is always before caste councils, particularly councils of the Depressed Classes and the tribes. In North East India the tribes, anxious to maintain their own identity, and observing that more than half of the Nagas, Khasis, Garos, Mizos, and Kukis are now Christians, frequently voice the opinion that "eventually we shall all become Christian."

Yet in the midst of this huge responsiveness it is alas quite possible for the Church to take the wrong turning and end up as a sealed-off community of perhaps 25 million which has little effect on the nation. It is popular among some leaders of Western Churches to renounce the biblical doctrines that Jesus Christ as revealed in the Scriptures is the only Saviour and that God commands the Church to open to all men the way of salvation through faith in Christ as revealed in the Bible. Many leaders of the Churches in India have followed this Western deviation. In consequence, great sections of the Church in India do very little evangelizing, and build heavy programs of social action into their seminary curricula. They turn away from evangelism in the very hour when hearing the Good News is ardently desired by many of India's sons and daughters.

The danger of getting sealed off is increased substantially by believing that the conglomerate Church is the only really Christian Church and consequently neither encouraging nor even permitting people movements to develop. The nub of the matter is that if the multiethnic Church is accepted as the norm, with its one-by-one-against-the-current mode of becoming Christian considered the best or even the only way, then the Church in India, no matter what they do, *are going to be sealed off.* The trickle of converts will continue but will not change matters much, and Christians will marry Christians and will come to be known ever more definitely as "one of India's castes."

Thus the history of the Syrian Churches will be duplicated in the last years of the twentieth century and the hundred years of the twenty-first. At present many Christians in India, when making application for entrance into a school, answer the question "Caste?" by writing the word "Christian." Instead of establishing that Christians are a supracaste community, all they are likely to accomplish in a society made up of over three thousand different castes and tribes is to add a new one. The Church will be sealed off. In modern Lebanon and Syria, the communities of sealed-off Christians live in what is known as the millet system. Though it differs in some details from the caste system, particularly in its theological justification, it effectively keeps communities of hereditary Christians detached from their neighbors. This will happen in India unless the people movement mode of church growth becomes well known and often practiced.

The people movement mode — taking the Church into each tribe or caste and letting it grow there — is the natural system for India. Men and women become Christian with no feeling of betraying their own people; instead they feel they are benefiting them. Multi-individual conversion will keep the Church growing in sufficient strength to affect sizable populations and bring the blessings of the Christian religion, active dependence on Christ, and guidance by His Holy Spirit, to tens of thousands of communities. Nothing more calculated to help India can be imagined. Nothing will so effectively release her great gifts and powers. The same release that America needs and has to a degree found will be experienced by India.

LOOSE THE CHURCHES
— LET THEM GO

What is called for today, then, is to break the chains of Western individualism so that ingathering that runs through caste becomes the normally expected outcome of evangelism. The goal is that each of the three thousand and more ethnic units should find flowing within it a strong movement to become disciples of the Lord Jesus and to feed on His revealed Word in the Bible. The Bible has broken the bonds of population after population and community after community through all the world. It has brought untold liberation to many peoples in the West. It has transformed* the Mizo people in Mizoram within the last seventy

---

*Chhangte Lal Hminga, a full blooded Mizo, devotes 17 pages of his doctoral dissertation on "The Life and Witness of the Churches in Mizoram" to a careful description of the revolutionary changes brought about by Christianization. He writes in detail about the *physical transformation* — village appearance, appearance of the people, social life, the place and manner of social gatherings, unification of the society, beneficent customs in regard to birth, marriage, death, and status of women and, perhaps most important of all, the way in which Christianity has transformed the traditional ethical code. He goes on to describe the *intellectual transformation* — from universal illiteracy to universal literacy, political insight, and the establishment of a sufficient number of primary, middle and high schools and colleges. He concludes by describing the *spiritual transformation*.

He quotes the first Chief Secretary of Mizoram, R.M. Agarwal, I.A.S., an eminent Hindu, as saying,

Thus the new religion became the single and central factor in the making of a new Mizo Society, and the Church as the most dominant institution. . . . The activities of the Church continue to have a strong influence over the individual's mind and his daily life at all levels and age groups. This is all very good. Everyone has reason to be proud of the all-round transformation of Mizo society which has taken place during the span of three quarters of a century. Religion has played the pivotal role. (1974:10 "Mizos at the Cross Roads" in *Mizoram Today, An Illustrated Quarterly,* published by the Government of Mizoram)

years. It enables men and women to live as sons and daughters of God, to see reality as it is (not *maya,* illusion), and to maintain those helpful and just relationships with their fellow human beings which are essential for any true progress.

The people movement to Christ is a thoroughly biblical way of coming to salvation. It was the way the Jews, the Samaritans, and the synagogue communities around the Great Sea came to Christian conviction. It should be systematically taught in all seminaries, so that every pastor, priest, and minister of the Gospel knows how these movements develop, has eyes open to discern responsive peoples, and knows how to shepherd a people movement when God gives him one.

People movements must be most carefully shepherded. Careless mass accessions, later neglected, are exactly what I am *not* suggesting. Nor do I advocate movements of castes or individuals toward some syncretistic faith. No! Loosing the Churches must give to the whole Christian population, and especially to their ardent leaders, such knowledge of the ways which God has blessed to the growth of His Church in India that they will cooperate with God — will joyfully march down Christ's way to India's heart.

E-ZERO, E-ONE, E-TWO, AND E-THREE

In Great India's enormously complex population of 620 million, soon to be 1,000,000,000 souls, the Church will grow in many different ways. Each of the nine types of Church described in this volume will increase in its own unique fashion. Growth possible to one type, as we have seen, is not possible to others; each has its peculiar and special evangelistic potential.

Against this background of extremely varied opportunity and potential let us distinguish four kinds of evangelism, already practiced in India to some extent, and which ought to be practiced much more. This is the other side of our coin — of our awareness of the various kinds of Churches — and it may be helpful, in thinking of evangelism, to clarify in a clear-cut way its major phases as we are concerned with them.

For convenience, by E-Zero one may denote evangelism directed toward existing Christians to encourage them to become better Christians. This is in reality renewal, not evangelism at all. It takes place in church buildings or at conventions where Christians gather, as well as privately. It constantly lifts up brokenness before God and increases personal dedication to Christ, personal holiness, a closer walk with God, more faithful Bible reading and prayer, and all the inwardness of a truly Christian life. These are, of course, highly desirable goals for all Christians. The true Church manifests every one of them; it requires these gifts of the human spirit. The Church is constantly in need of renewal and increased dedication.

Nevertheless, whoever would understand Christianity in India today must go on to observe that in a Church immersed in a caste-bound society, such dedication and renewal *seldom lead to effective evangelism outside the Church.* At the great Lausanne Congress on Evangelism, Dr. George Samuel of Kerala said to the two hundred delegates from India, "More than 98 percent of the evangelism of the Church in India is directed at existing Christians, and never reaches even a tiny fraction of India's 600 million souls who have not accepted Christ as Lord and Saviour."

The assumption that Evangelism Zero is a precondition for all other evangelism and is necessarily followed by more effective evangelization of the 600 million is untenable. Christians, quite rightly striving for the renewal of existing Churches, must abandon the naïve belief that evangelism of outsiders must wait until the Church is renewed. This is not the order we observe in the New Testament. The evangelism of the Gentiles did not wait until all the Christians in Jerusalem were perfect and loved all Gentiles as they loved their own kith and kin. No! While the Church in Jerusalem still had many problems, and the Church in Corinth many sins, the Holy Spirit sent forth missionaries from both congregations to carry the Gospel to the multitudes who had yet to believe. Renewal (E-Zero) *must not be substituted for the evangelism needed to win unbelievers to eternal life.*

Evangelism One (E-One) is real evangelism of non-Christians of our own language, culture, and social group. E-One takes place within the homogeneous unit in which the Christian finds himself. For instance, Christians in conglomerate congregations (Type 2) can carry on Evangelism One among non-Christians who sit loose to caste. These on conversion will not experience social dislocation and may readily become members of existing conglomerate congregations. Christians in Type 4 congregations (people movements from tribe) can carry on Evangelism One among the animist members of their own tribe, who can join existing congregations of tribals without social dislocation.

On the other hand, when Type 2, or conglomerate Church Christians, evangelize non-Christians of some caste (any caste), they are then carrying the Good News across a distinct ethnic barrier and usually educational, economic, and even linguistic barriers as well. This might be termed Evangelism Two. Please note that I am not at this point playing with words or classifying for the sake of classifying, but rather pointing out a most important condition for effective evangelism. They are evangelizing lost children of God who will find it difficult to join existing multiethnic congregations and will much more naturally join congregations of their own people. The Samaritans when they became Christians did not join congregations of Jews; they formed Samaritan congregations.

Similarly, when Kuki Christians in Manipur, North East India, evangelize Meiteis in the Manipur plain, they do not bring these into the Kuki congregations but into newly formed Meitei congregations, which as soon as possible are led by Meitei elders and pastors, and teachers and bishops as well. Kuki Christians engage in E-Two, not E-One. To set forth another example: when Syrian Christians of the Mar Thoma denomination evangelize Nairs or Iravas, their E-Two goal is to establish congregations made up largely of Nairs or Iravas. These would also be led by Nairs or Iravas as soon as possible.

Often Evangelism Two (E-Two) is conducted across an even greater economic, educational, or linguistic gulf. Thus when the Christians of Pakistan, who are overwhelmingly of the Chuhra caste, evangelize Muslims, they are operating not only across the Christian Muslim religious barrier, but across an ethnic and to some extent a linguistic one as well. For Mulsims are of many different ethnic origins. Pathan Muslims are quite different from Punjabi Muslims. The religious terms used by Urdu speaking Muslims differ considerably from those used by the Church which came in from a Hindu ethnic unit fifty to a hundred years ago. Further, most Muslims are economically better off than most Christians. The Blacks in the United States speak English and are American citizens, yet when they seek to evangelize Spanish-speaking or white Americans, they too must carry on Evangelism Two, not E-One.

Evangelism Three (E-Three) goes directly across still more formidable, including often geographic, barriers. For example, when Tamilian Christians of Nadar extraction go as missionaries to the hill castes of Himachal Pradesh they are carrying on E-Three: the ethnic, linguistic, geographic, and cultural gulfs are wide and deep. When Presbyterian Mizo missionaries by the dozen go to west Rajasthan to multiply churches among the Bhils, they are carrying on E-Three. While Mizos and Bhils are both tribals, the vast differences in language, economic condition, mode of agriculture, place in society, degree of permeation by Hinduism, and educational advancement are so great that we must term this evangelism to be not near-neighbor, and not E-Two, but E-Three.

It is a nice question whether, when Lutheran Christians around Guntur (98 percent from Mala and Madiga backgrounds) evangelize the Kammas and Reddis in their own backyards, they are engaging in E-Two or E-Three. The geographic distance is miniscule. They go only from their *palems* to villages a hundred yards away. They use the same language, Telegu. They often see these Kamma landowners, and work for them. Yet the caste system is so rigid that the social distance between the two peoples is enormous; overwhelming. I would not quarrel with any who termed such evangelism E-Three, though I prefer to call it E-Two. This mode of classifying is, of course, for convenience and clarity and can never be narrowly absolute.

With these distinctions in mind, however — for they touch upon vital differences which, in turn, involve difference in approach and also in results — we can now see that the Churches in India, great and small, should study their environment carefully to discover what kinds of evangelism each of their thousands of congregations can effectively engage in. There is no use in asking a congregation to carry out all kinds. Instead, each congregation, after a careful study of its peculiar and particular location and opportunities, should draw up a plan of evangelism that suits it and seems reasonably possible to it.

In a given plan, we may see much Evangelism One, a little Evangelism Two, and practically no Evangelism Three. On the other hand, a congregation of Syrian Christians in the St. Thomas Evangelical Church might find that it cannot carry on E-One, but has great opportunity to develop purposeful, effective E-Two. Ao Naga congregations in the land of their origin have no scope for E-One; all their near neighbors have become Christians. They may be carrying on some E-Two among the yet unconverted Naga tribes north and east of them, and a great deal of E-Three among the Saoras and Konds of Orissa or the Adis and Mishis of Arunachal. In Bombay, urban conglomerates (Type 6) have some E-One opportunity to win city dwellers who have broken caste by marriage or mode of living, and more E-Two opportunity to multiply congregations among receptive homogeneous units which have moved to Bombay from rural areas in which a people movement to Christ has flamed. On these two openings they should concentrate their prayers and programs.

In Shri Lanka, the Rev. Christopher J. Daniel's island-wide evangelism has demonstrated beyond the shadow of a doubt that the Tamil community of about a million, which arose from the indentured labor imported there in the nineteenth century, is responsive. Were any denomination in Shri Lanka to evangelize this segment of society intelligently and vigorously, it would plant many new congregations. And that in a country which has for years borne the name of being resistant.

THE UNTAPPED RESOURCE
— INDIAN MISSIONARIES

To understand the Church in India one must realize that to date the enormous reservoir of potential missionaries in the 16-million-member Church of that country lies largely untapped, like the vast pools of oil beneath Saudi Arabia. So far, Indian Christian conscience has been satisfied with "evangelism" of existing Christians. But times are changing. The Indian Evangelical Mission, the National Missionary Society, the Friends Missionary Prayer Bands, the Zoram Baptist Mission, the Church Growth Missionary Movement, and other missionary societies funded from the Churches of India hold out rich promise of things to come.

The Churches in Asia are listening to the command of Christ to disciple *ta ethne* — the thousands of ethnic units in Asia — and are beginning to experience the joy and blessing that come to faithful Christians and congregations.

Throughout two thousand years of history, the evangelization of the tribes, clans, and segments of society has been carried out, not by the Church as a whole, but very largely by bands of the warmhearted, by apostolic teams in the New Testament, by monastic orders in the Middle Ages, and in the last two hundred years by missionary societies. Sometimes small new denominations full of devout people have carried on ten times as much mission as the colder large denominations. The Methodists, for example, in their early days in proportion to their size, achieved many times more evangelization and church multiplying than the Anglicans from whom they sprang. The Assemblies of God have missions in more than fifty countries, while many "mainline" denominations five times their size evangelize in only a few lands. Societies of the warmhearted — "sodalities," to use Ralph Winter's term — will spring up in India with or without the blessing of the Church to which they belong, and propagate the Gospel among the myriads who have not yet heard, *and* among the multitudes who *have* heard but have not responded, and are thus in grave danger of perdition (2 Thess. 1:8, 9 and 2:10, 12).

To recapitulate some part of our thinking, it is highly desirable for such Indian missionaries to divest themselves of the trappings of Western missions. It is not necessary for missionaries to be college graduates or to live in seeming affluence. It is not necessary for them to have cars and hospitals. It *is* necessary that they be full of zeal, know their Bible from cover to cover, and be sent out by the Holy Spirit to the work to which He has called them (Acts 13:2-4). It is essential for Indian missionaries to be thoroughly trained in cross-cultural evangelism. For example, the Garo missionaries sent from Meghalaya to evangelize the Garas of Orissa ought to be on probation until they have learned Oriya thoroughly well and surveyed intensively how God has raised up a Gara Church of about 25,000 souls in the Baptist and Mennonite denominations. Or, if they are sent to Tripura to evangelize the Jamatias, they must learn Tripuri thoroughly well and study carefully how the fifteen tribes in Tripura (both the Zo group and the Tripuri group) have or have not become Christians. Missionaries of the St. Thomas Evangelical Church might well go to the Reddis of Andhra Pradesh with the deliberate purpose of starting Reddi congregations. In so doing, the Syrian missionaries would need to learn Telegu thoroughly and survey with great care the way in which God has raised up a Church of more than 2 million from among the Malas and Madigas, and has already led more than 50,000 middle-caste individuals to Christ in Andhra Pradesh. The Syrians ought also to learn thoroughly the many ways in which Churches grow in India and other lands — for they do not know which way the Reddis will turn.

To compress what I said in my address at the Lausanne

Congress on Evangelism, major advance will become possible as soon as some workable scheme is discovered whereby the affluent denominations of other lands can contribute money to Third World missionary societies engaged in discipling receptive *ethne*. Thus the manpower of the Asian Churches would be reinforced by the financial power of Christians in other lands.

Such a scheme, agreeable to Churches and missions, is not easy to devise. Money should *not* be given without strings; it must be given specifically to evangelize those who have yet to believe. The plan must involve truthful, regular membership accounting, so that the degree to which evangelization does plant churches is immediately known. Cooperation means that both partners share the common goal, both give an honest accounting of money and growth statistics. Both have a say in direction. The day-to-day management will be largely that of Asians, but the Asians must not say, "You give us money and we shall do with it what we please." No responsible Christian in any land should give on that basis. The money from outside India, furthermore, must always be in proportion to money raised in India. To be a blessing to Indian Churches the enterprise must be primarily theirs, yet at the same time it should be recognized that others are legitimately concerned with the manner of mission and the outcome.

As missionary societies — sodalities of the warmhearted, apostolic teams — multiply in India, missionaries should be deliberately sent to segments of Indian society which have proven receptive and responsive. Then great harvest may confidently be expected. To date, many Indian missionaries have been sent to the most resistant fields. Instead of obeying the biblical injunction to thrust laborers into fields white with harvest, Indian missionary societies have sent them to where, before any harvest at all is in sight, they must cut down the forest, clear off the stones, build the fences, plow the fields, sow the seed, and wait fifty years for the harvest to ripen. This curious policy has been defended in various ways. Statements like the following have been made: "Indian missionaries must not compete with old, established congregations." "It will confuse non-Christians for two organizations to be evangelizing within the same district." "We have already occupied this *taluq* or *tahsil*. In its population of 300,000 we have two congregations of a hundred members each and three paid workers. Don't come in here." Such bankrupt thinking must now be abandoned.

Responsive populations need Christian missionaries—Indian, Korean, Canadian, American, European — at the rate of one missionary to ten thousand or sometimes as few as two thousand souls. The congregations that arise should be within walking distance of each other. Only so will each congregation give social encouragement to other new congregations. Only so will enough people become Christian within a small enough geographical area and a short enough time for a normal Christian community to arise. By normal, I mean one large enough to provide suitable young men for young women and young women for young men, and enough Christians so that on annual occasions when they all come together, they will have some sense of weight and numbers. After all, when the Lord began the Church, He arranged for three thousand to be added in one day.

A New Welcome to Foreign Missionaries

If maximum propagation of the Gospel is the end sought then there should be a new welcome to foreign missionaries. The possibility of domination no longer exists. Freedom from the fathering missions has now been gained. There was a time when the mission establishment outweighed the small weak congregations and dominated. It was no doubt in the providence of God that the mighty missions have been dismantled. Perhaps it has been done too fast and too emotionally. Perhaps some of the losses could have been avoided by more skillful devolution. Be that as it may, the process has now been completed. In 1977 the evangelization of India does not suffer from too many missionaries. It suffers from too few.

The riches of Korean, Japanese, and Philippine Christians and the Norwegian, Australian, and American congregations and denominations ought to be harnessed for the further evangelization of India's 600 million, soon to be 1,000,000,000, who do not know Christ as God and Saviour.

True, some doors are closed, and missionaries cannot come in; but Christians have never been finally defeated by closed doors. They fall on their knees and pray them open. They petition, demonstrate, marshal public opinion, and in a thousand other ways influence government to open doors to the telling and explanation of their faith to whoever cares to listen. They point out that Indian missionaries by the hundreds, proclaiming the Hindu religion, are allowed to go into the United States and are even helped by American government money in some cases. Hindu missionaries to North America amass great wealth from America and send it back to India. Great India, manifesting the fairness for which she has been famous, can scarcely do less than open her doors to missionaries from other lands. I am not thinking primarily of North America. Apostolic bands from Korea, Japan, Burma, Sweden, Germany, New Zealand, Fiji — as well as those from the United Kingdom — ought to be telling the Good News and baptizing into eternal life such as believe.

THE HEART OF THE MATTER

Churches in every land throughout the earth stand at a parting of the ways. Either they will surge forward to growth or they will be sealed off and remain as ghettos in the general population. For instance, in post-Christian Sweden, either the Churches will win hundreds of thousands to devout obedient Christian life, or they will become small enclaves of less and less importance. In Korea, either the Churches will evangelize the ninety percent of the population which has yet to believe, or they will become a frozen minority of about a tenth of the population. The future in every land is full of promise — and of danger. The Church of Jesus Christ in any given population may be one percent of the population or forty percent, it may be strong or weak, it may be standing on the biblical certainties or on a quicksand of doubt. It may be most cordially regarded by the rest of the people, or disliked if not hated. Ethnic realities vary from place to place, but are of tremendous importance if the Churches are to communicate Christ.

Bearing this universal situation in mind, we are now ready to observe that the situation in India illustrates it beautifully. What is true in India is true in many lands. The ethnic realities which India so vividly portrays are powerful influences in every segment of every nation.

As the Church of 16 million souls in India presses forward, no question is more important than this: Will she go on now to the greatest era of Gospel propagation, or to hundreds of years of sealed-off encirclement? Both outcomes are possible. This volume has put before the reader the steps which must be taken if the result is to be growth, and is a warning as to those that appear likely to lead to ingrown encirclement. There may be ways of advance hidden from us. If any disagree with the convictions here expressed, I cordially invite him — or her — to set forth the conditions he or she thinks must be fulfilled for the Church in India, grateful to the Saviour, to carry out the Great Commission.

As Christians in many ways and many lands obey that command, God will create the hundreds of millions of new creatures needed to enable nations everywhere to solve their problems and to be the blessing to the world He intends them to be.

APPENDICES
AND
BIBLIOGRAPHY

Appendix A
An Ecclesiological
Point of View

Anyone describing the Church inevitably does so from a particular ecclesiological point of view, usually that of his own tradition. Observing the actual forms of the Church today, the churches described in the New Testament, and the essential nature of the Church according to the Bible, I have perforce developed an ecclesiology which I myself believe to be both realistic and biblical. It fits the many contemporary Churches and is faithful to the Scriptures.

I know that other Christians have other views, and readily grant that the flesh-and-blood Churches all over India may be described from several angles of perspective. But I would like to ask readers holding other ecclesiologies to remember my primary objective here: to describe the existing Churches — the Khasi-, Bengali-, Tamil-, and English-speaking clusters of congregations, and so on — rather than to set forth and defend any particular ecclesiology or policy. One may grant, for instance, that congregations and denominations might be described from the point of view that the only true Church is in obedient relation to the Supreme Pontiff at Rome. But that is not the conviction of this writer, who must write from his own beliefs. The reader should rest comfortably in the knowledge that good Christians, on solid biblical grounds, do have different theoretical frameworks or ecclesiologies. One hopes that he will not waste his time complaining about the "weak ecclesiology" of this volume (by which he means one different from his own), but rather let it show him the many kinds of congregations and denominations now composing the Christian scene in India.

The Church is made up of the redeemed who believe in Jesus Christ, live in Him, adore Him, and trust Him. It is not merely a gathering of good men and women engaged in moral pursuits. It is Christ's Body in conscious relationship to its Head. "As there is only one Christ and one Body, so there is only one ministry, that of Christ in His Body."

Some congregations have become so *un*conscious of a living relationship that it is an open question whether they are truly of the Church or not; and few, moreover, live continuously at a high level of obedience and adoration. Persecuted churches may include believers who have quite literally not had the chance formally to confess faith in Jesus and be baptized. Some congregations include many persons who have not yet come to belief at all. Hence the Church, particularly as it forms on new ground, includes some congregations which may or may not be wholly within the true Church, and some members who may or may not be practicing Christians. While comparisons are odious, the widespread nominal church membership in the West may well give us pause and a moment of humility in this regard.

While in extraordinary circumstances it may be that our sovereign God saves men and women who have not heard of Christ, it is clear from the Bible that His plan of salvation, sealed in the blood of the Cross, is that men should be saved through faith in Jesus Christ. The Word is clear that there is "no other Name." Our Lord said plainly, "No one comes to the Father but by me." Saving faith in Christ means living in Him, in His Body, in His Church. The writer, therefore, holds that membership in a Church which confesses Christ before men and follows the Bible as the one sufficient and final rule of faith and practice is an essential completing step to saving faith.

I hold that the Church of Jesus Christ is essentially, intentionally, and constitutionally One. Its three dominant symbols are: the Bride of Christ, the Body of Christ, and the Temple of Christ. It has one Lord, one faith, one baptism, one God and Father of us all, one Book, one goal, and one Judge. Since the Churches that compose the One Church are made up of very different races and kinds and conditions of men and women, these embodied Churches take many different forms. As within the supreme authority of the Bible many interpretations seem reasonable to Christians facing different conditions, so a variety of somewhat different doctrines and polities are espoused. This diversity is abundantly allowable within the overarching unity of the Church represented by biblical symbols. Yet Christ is not divided; neither in the mind of God are His people.

If one may use an analogy, there is one granite rock in the world. Granite is granite wherever found. Yet there are many different kinds — pink, white, grey, green, and black; coarse-grained and fine-grained; New England granite, Canadian granite, Zairean granite, Mongolian granite, and so on.

The unity of Christians is that demanded by the biblical revelation. The diversity is that required by local conditions and conditioned by historical background, language spoken, cultural peculiarities, economic situation, and the like. The diversity must always be strictly within biblical limits; but these must neither be defined by the Church of any one nation, country, or part of the world, nor appropriate to it only. The unity of the Church is unity *in Christ.* He is Head of the Church — the only Head she has. He calls and appoints leaders of each Church, gives them power and authority, and requires that their understanding of the Church, in their circumstances, be determined strictly according to *His revelation in the Bible.*

The One Church appears in the twentieth century as an amazing company of Churches — literally hundreds or, counting linguistic segments, thousands of separate ones. I state here not what ought to be, but what *is.* This company is rich beyond description, and all its constituent parts are true Church, so long as they live filled with the Holy Spirit and ruled by the written Word and the Word of God who is the risen and reigning Lord Jesus Christ.

Both the ecumenical movement and the evangelical movement stress the validity of Churches other than the speaker's own. Provided other Churches are following the Bible as the rule of faith and practice, and Jesus Christ as God and Saviour, they are all *valid* Church, though perhaps not as correct a Church as each speaker believes his own to be! Thus the twentieth century (whatever the ecclesiology of the speaker) displays a marvelous unity in the Church, together with rich and fruitful discussion, debate, and controversy as to church union, doctrinal purity, the historic episcopate, freedom of conscience, the indwelling of the Holy Spirit, the nature of God and man, and the evangelization of the world.

Great India is a company of substantial nations each speaking a different language and some having distinct scripts of their own. The Church in Great India is therefore necessarily a very complex form of the Body of Christ. For example, Christians who speak Khasi and read the *Roman* Khasi script are quite helpless to read the Hindi Bible in the Devanagari script, even though Hindi is the national language. Christians who read the Hindi Bible fluently cannot read a word in the Malayalam Bible. The tribal cultures of North East India are leagues removed from the Depressed Classes cultures of the Churches of Andhra Pradesh. One can speak of "the Church in India," but it is much more exact and realistic to speak of "the Churches of India." The fact of the matter is that the embodied Church on every continent is not one; it is many. Its unity consists entirely in an internal loyalty and obedience to Jesus Christ as God and Saviour according to the Bible.

Appendix B
Caste and Brotherhood

IN THIS book I have thought it unnecessary to present in detail the abundant existing evidence that, despite some interdining among the educated, and integration in education and travel, and despite high and low castes working at the same factory or in the same office, *caste feeling remains strong.*

Particularly among Christians who belong to conglomerate congregations and denominations, the word *caste* is repellent. They do not like it. Some of them have indeed risen above it. Many Indians react violently against racism in the West, which discriminates against dark-skinned peoples, and strongly maintain that what traces of caste there may be in India are rapidly disappearing. All across America, visiting Indians tell their audiences that because caste is now outlawed in India, caste feeling is no problem.

This is "conglomerate" thinking. In conglomerate

congregations and denominations (Type 2) there is universal interdining and intermarriage between all sections of the community. It is natural that educated Type 2 leaders should believe that what they so deeply desire and practice is true of all the other types.

Unfortunately the supracaste mind-set is not characteristic of seven out of the nine types of Church I have noted, nor of eighty out of every hundred Christians in India. And it is not true of the Hindu population generally. Since the proof will be painful reading for many Christians, I have confined it to this Appendix, believing that as readers work their way through the volume, the enormous hold that caste has on the general population and upon many good Christians will become apparent, and that by the end of the book they must find themselves squarely facing the reality in which all Indian Christians live and in the midst of which the Christian faith has to be propagated.

This Appendix is added lest there be any whose thinking on the disappearance of caste is not so easily shaken, and who will disagree with the main findings of the book on the grounds that the caste system is not there at all! Some early readers of the manuscript have faulted *Ethnic Realities and the Church* on the ground that, while there may be some communal feeling here and there among backward sections of the Church, it is happily a thing of the past for most Christians. Such persons say things like: "You are thinking of an India which existed a hundred years ago." "We have made much progress in India and caste is almost nonexistent. Interdining and intermarriage are common." "It would be a great mistake, when both Church and government are winning the battle against caste, for the Church to adopt any position other than that caste is an unmitigated evil, is happily on the way out, and must be completely renounced by anyone becoming a Christian." "Your passion for numbers has led you to a sadly unnecessary compromise on the all-important matter of caste." "It has to be brought home to the Church in India by its own leaders that any church which directly or indirectly permits any degree of separateness on race, caste, or class lines repudiates the Gospel of reconciliation between man and God and man and man."

I wish these statements were true, but as the following pages will show — at least briefly — caste feeling, caste prejudice, the awareness of profound difference, and strong ethnic pride are quite common. It is of no use, I believe, simply to ignore these things. They will not go away through mere denial that they exist.

I believe the solution is to permit, and indeed in suitable circumstances to encourage, each homogeneous unit (an elastic term which might include half a dozen economic classes, or one section of one subcaste only) to form a cluster of congregations within itself. Thus when Backward Class Christians of the Church of South India in Kerala in 1966 split off to form an "independent CMS Church" [Church Missionary Society] they did so because they felt: (1) they were not taken seriously but were despised and humiliated; (2) they were underrepresented in diocesan councils and boards; (3) the pastoral care provided by the CSI failed to look after them; and (4) at the social level, nothing was being done for them. This regrettable incident well illustrates the difficulties and tensions.

I have noted in my text the pertinent little book by Mr. Ninan Koshy, *Caste in the Kerala Churches,* published by the Christian Institute for the Study of Religion and Society of Bangalore. In the preface M.M. Thomas says,

> Caste has been an integral part of the traditional social order of India. Today, as we seek to modernize society and build a new national community, we find ourselves hampered at many levels by the spirit and structure of caste which obstruct the emergence of the new society. The Christians of India, as citizens, are called to participate in the struggle for a new society. They have in the idea of Fellowship in Christ a moral and religious reason and resource to build up new patterns of society which reflect more nearly the new humanity created in Jesus Christ, a society free from the natural or historical barriers between man and man and conducive to the full fellowship of persons. . . . The Church is called to be the foretaste of the Kingdom of God and His Christ on earth. (p. iii)

The study on which the book was based was carried out by Mr. Koshy under the auspices of the Kerala Christian Council and the Bangalore Institute. The following paragraphs show some of his findings in regard to the degree to which caste is a real factor in Christian life.

There are separate places of worship, separate congregations, separate cemeteries, etc. for the different caste sections of the same denomination within the Church in various parts of Kerala. . . . The South Kerala Diocese of the Church South India . . . has a membership consisting of groups of three backgrounds — the Syrian Christians, the Nadars, and the Backward Classes. (p. 23)

In the Mar Thoma Church, converts from the Backward Classes were organized into Sabhas, a name for Backward Class Christians as against Idavakas, which is the name for the parishes of upper-class Christians, the latter being invariably Syrian Christians. Very recently one or two Sabhas have been up-graded into Idavakas. . . . In the Church councils, the Sabhas are represented by a small number of members named by the Metropolitan. As a result of this and the general backwardness of the community, their share in the administration of the Church is very limited. The situation has brought about a sense of grievance in the members of the Backward Classes against the Church administration, as well as against the upper classes of the Christian community (invariably the Syrians). . . . These converts are very backward and do not have membership in the ordinary sense of the word." (pp. 24-25)

Mr. Koshy presented an extensive questionnaire to hundreds of Syrian Christians. The following are a few of the more vivid and revealing replies.

Q. What is your attitude toward the convert [from the Backward Classes]? The answers show that there are mainly two attitudes among Syrian Christians: the old social service attitude of giving a helping hand to the inferior, and a hostile attitude. Example of the first: "I am proud of them and am glad we could do at least something for them" — given by about 30 percent of the CSI and Mar Thoma Syrians. Example of the second: "It is nonsense to have converts" — given by 40 and 56 percent of the CSI and MT respondents respectively. "They are trying to assert their rights and I cannot tolerate it" — given by 27 and 30 percent of CSI and MT respondents respectively. (p. 28-30)

Q. Are they good Christians? The majority of Syrian Christians who responded to this question believe that Christians from the Backward Classes are not good Christians. Many said: "How can a Pulaya be a good Christian? He will always be a Pulaya." (p. 31)

Q. Under what circumstances can you think of your son or daughter marrying one from a converted Christian family? "This cannot be thought of for a very long time to come," is a typical answer. Ninan Koshy says, "These two groups very rarely intermarry and thus in practice form endogamous groups, irrespective of common religious bonds. They mix freely in all walks of life except intermarriage. . . . The union of Churches [resulting in Church of South India] has not affected the endogamy of the Syrians. Mai Thoma and Orthodox Churches are exclusively Syrian." (p. 37)

Q. How will you address them? Koshy gives the exact answers and summarizes by saying, "It is generally admitted that when addressing or referring to Backward Class Christians, caste appellations such as Chacko Pulayan or Nathai Pulayan, are used. . . . this form of address is most resented by the Backward Class Christians." (p. 39)

Q. Do you like to have them eat with you? Koshy summarizes the data by saying, "The vast majority are totally opposed to the very idea of eating with members of Backward Class community . . . and expect the members from the Backward Class community to wash their own dishes after taking a meal in Syrian houses."* (pp. 40-41)

Q. How would you like them to address you? Summarizing the data,

*I have myself been asked to wash the dishes from which I had eaten in the home of Hindu friends in Madhya Pradesh. It is common practice, frequently camouflaged by having a servant wash the dishes. The idea back of it is that food touched by a lower-caste person conveys pollution. So he washes his own dishes, and having cleaned them, hands them back to the owner. — D.M.

Koshy says, "There is uniform agreement that when Backward Class Christians address persons belonging to the Syrian community, they should always show respect due their superiors." (p. 43)

Q. Would you feel offended if a converted Christian took the freedom to move very freely with you, without any usual formalities and gestures of respect? Out of 615 persons who answered this question, 576 replied yes. (pp. 42-43)

Q. Would you like a priest from the converted group to baptize your child? No, by 72 percent of the CSI, 81 percent of the MT and 87 percent of the Orthodox. (p. 47)

Much more evidence could easily be adduced, and not from Kerala only. The fact that similar proofs of persisting prejudice could readily be obtained from the Caucasian Christian community in the United States about Black Christians, in Japan about Etta Christians, in Ruanda about Bahutu Christians, and among Latin American mestizos about Amerindian Christians, simply illustrates the widespread nature of the problem.

In India the problem is keen because the Hindu religious books (Vedas, Gita, and most others) give separation into superior and inferior castes *religious sanction.* In America, by way of contrast, ethnic feelings exist *in direct contradiction* to the basic equalitarianism of the Bible. In India the more devout a Hindu is the more likely he is to say, "The castes are different and will always be different. It is *right* that we should recognize this." In any society which has become substantially Christian, the more devout a person is the more likely he is to say, "God has made all peoples of one blood. All are equally sons of Adam and all equally sinners saved by grace. It is *wrong* to think of some as superior by birth. We expect that as men and women become Christian these wrong attitudes will be abandoned; but for the time being, looking at the actual economic, educational, and spiritual condition, we do, alas, make distinctions."

Critics will probably ask, "Have you picked your illustrations from Kerala — the one place in all India where caste distinctions are still made — and thus given all India a bad name?" I plead innocent of the charge. One of my readers from North India, an eminent leader of the Church in India who knows the situation well, after going over this book in manuscript wrote me as follows: "I must say you describe the general situation well. I myself do not like a Christian from the Depressed Classes to come to my table or even into my kitchen. I ought not to feel this way, but I do." Similar evidence is abundant in practical experience.

AGAINST THE FACTS OF CASTE, WHAT IS RIGHT CHRISTIAN STRATEGY?

Down underneath superficial judgments that caste is nothing, India has no race prejudice, the problem is being solved, and a new casteless national community is in the making, the hard fact is that *the Church in India faces a Hindu social order which believes that men and women are made in different molds by God Himself, and that some are forever superior and other forever inferior.* Even while some sectors of society (such as the Dravida Munata Kalagam party in Tamil Nadu, or the elite of the Congress party) carry on extensive anti-Brahman or anticaste activities, their members practice caste and feel superior to castes lower in the social scale. What is right Christian strategy in this matter?

The position I have consistently argued is in full harmony with that expressed by M.M. Thomas in the passage from *Caste in the Kerala Churches* quoted on p. 252. Christians are indeed called to participate in the struggle for a new society. They should indeed remember that God has created us all (of whatever language, color, economic condition, or education) "of one blood." Before the Throne we all stand equal. All have equal access to God's presence, forgiveness, and power, and will be judged impartially. All ought to have equal opportunity, for all are brothers and sisters. Christians who believe that the Bible is the only Word of God and that Jesus Christ is the only Way to God have no other option.

However, this is not to say that the practice of full brotherhood, the realization of every aspect of equality and justice, ought to be made a condition for a person becoming a Christian. There is no warrant in Scripture for any such position. As I have argued at length *(Missiology,* April 1973 and April 1974), while the Bible says clearly that in Christ all are one (Jew and Greek, slave and free, male and female), it also presents indubitable proof that Jewish Christians continued thoroughly Jewish and Gentile Christians thoroughly Gentile. The overarching unity had plenty of room for diversity. Gentiles were not forced to give up eating pork. They did not have to be circumcised. Culturally, they did not have to become Jews. And Jews did not have to eat pork or cease to circumcise their boy babies.

I hold that when one becomes a Christian, the *religious* justification for believing that various ethnic groupings of men are inherently superior and others inferior is abandoned. The Bible must be believed that in Christ we are all one, have equal access to God, are equally forgiven for our sins. In this, all cultural distinctions whatever of education or position are, to use Paul's word, rubbish.

However, as a matter of convenience to the "yet to believe" — as a means of holding the door to salvation open to those whom we are calling from death to life — homogeneous-unit congregations may be started. Since the Church is a place to feel at home, a family of like-minded people, speaking the same language, eating the same food, and sharing the same culture, *separate congregations when advisable and feasible may be encouraged.*

Christ will indeed break down the middle wall of partition between Jews and Gentiles, but he will do it for those who through faith become parts of His Body. The longest stride any Hindu population can possibly take toward the new national ideal is to become Bible-believing and Bible-obeying Christians. Becoming Christian in the ethnic unit in which he was born and the community in which he has married, far from reinforcing caste is the most effective step one can take to achieving a citizenship in which caste distinctions play little part.

Compared to the excellence of knowing Christ Jesus, the racial inheritance of the Christian is small dust in the balance; though for the sake of his kindred, and in the hope of their salvation, the Christian may do as Paul did in conforming in minute detail to Jewish culture (Acts 21:26).

What I propose is not mere theory. It is actually happening all over India. The real situation is described in this volume. Together with the supracaste society which Type 2 congregations and denominations have to a considerable extent achieved, there goes the somewhat castelike society of monoethnic congregations and denominations: Syrian, Naga, Vellala, Nadar, European, Chinese, and many others. All types of Churches constantly stress brotherhood, equality, fellowship, and justice. They do this because the Bible and the Holy Spirit require it. Theological training at all levels builds brotherhood. Literature builds brotherhood. The international Church insists on it. *There is an irreversible trend to brotherhood.* It is impossible to believe that humanity will proceed toward more and more caste, more and more discrimination, less and less brotherhood, and that eventually one-tenth will enslave the nine-tenths.

The real issue therefore is: *How can the Church adapt to de facto while renouncing de jure caste?* How can men and women in large numbers become Christians, accept the Bible as sole revelation and the ultimate authority in faith and morals, accept the lordship of Christ in all matters of conduct and worship, and form natural congregations and small denominations of likeminded men and women? How can these continue for years or decades to practice endogamy, and thus keep open the door to salvation to the rest of their caste fellows?

The issue may be stated simply: Can a truly Christian congregation and denomination practice endogamy? I believe the answer is yes. The dangers of racial pride which endogamy easily generates can be avoided. Brotherhood can be built. The grace of God, sufficient to make all within the sacramental Body truly One, is available. The power of the Bible to break all chains is mighty. An endogamous Christianity which comfortably coexists with a truly supracaste Christianity already prevails in India in two groups of congregations and denominations. In the first are Types 1, 3, 4, and 7; in the second group are Types 2, 5, 6, and 8.

Nor need any feel that if we allow this point there will be a sudden rush to create caste denominations. Many are called, but few are chosen. The way of the Cross is never easy. But in the midst of the 500 million souls whose culture is essentially caste-conditioned, I believe the people movement way of coming to Christian faith ought to be consciously opened to men and women of all communities, high or low. Some will hear and follow and come to eternal life.

BIBLIOGRAPHY

Barrett, David. *Schism and Renewal in Africa*. New York: Oxford University Press, 1968.

Boyd, Robin H.S. *India and the Latin Captivity of the Church: The Cultural Context of the Gospel*. New York: Cambridge University Press, 1974.

Dyck, Paul Irvin. "Emergence of New Castes in India." Master's thesis for the University of Manitoba, 1970.

George, T.C. "The Growth of Pentecostal Churches in South India." Master's thesis, School of Missions, Fuller Theological Seminary, 1975.

"The Life and Growth of Churches in Bangalore." D. Miss. dissertation, School of Missions, Fuller Theological Seminary, 1976.

Hedlund, Roger E. *Church Growth in the Third World*. Bombay: Gospel Literature Service, 1977.

Hutton, J.H. *Caste in India*. New York: Oxford University Press, 1961.

Keay, F.E. *A History of the Syrian Church in India*. Delhi: I.S.P.C.K. (Revised edition, 1960; originally published 1930, available from P.O. Box 1585, Kashmere Gate, Delhi)

Koshy, Ninan. *Caste in the Kerala Churches*. Bangalore: Christian Institute for the Study of Religion and Society, 1968.

Kumar, S. Vasantha. "Image of Christians in Non-Christian Novels."
International Review of Missions (January 1976).

Manikam, Rajah B. *Christianity and the Asian Revolution.* New York:
Friendship Press, 1955.

McGavran, Donald A. *Founders of the Indian Church.* Jubbulpore: Mission
Press, 1939.

———. *Bridges of God.* New York:Friendship Press, 1955.

———. *Understanding Church Growth.* Grand Rapids: Eerdmans Publishing Co., 1970.

———. "Loose the Churches. Let Them Go!" *Missiology* (April 1973).

———. "Without Crossing Barriers? One in Christ vs. Discipling Diverse
Cultures." *Missiology* (April 1974).

McNee, Peter. *Crucial Issues in Bangladesh.* Pasadena, Calif.: William
Carey Library, 1975.

Majumdar and Madan. *Introduction to Social Anthropology.* New York: Asia
Publishing House, 1976.

Nelson, Amirtharaj. *A New Day in Madras.* Pasadena, Calif.: William
Carey Library, 1975.

Pickett, J. Waskom. *Christian Mass Movements in India.* New York: Abing-
don Press, 1933.

———. *Christ's Way to India's Heart.* New York: Friendship Press, 1936.

Pickett, Singh, and McGavran. *Christian Missions in Mid-India.*
Jubbulpore: Mission Press, 1938.

Pickett, Warnshuis, Singh and McGavran. *Church Growth and Group Conversion.* Pasadena Calif.: William Carey Library, Fifth Edition
1975.

Pothen, S.G. *The Syrian Christians of Kerala.* New York: Asia Publishing
House, 1963.

Raju, C.N. *Are the CSI Churches Growing? A Study of Trends and Growth.*
Madras: privately printed, 1965.

Samuel, George. "Growth Potential of Urban Churches: A Study in
Bombay." Master's Thesis, School of Missions, Fuller Theological
Seminary, 1973.

Sargunam, M. Ezra. *Multiplying Churches in Modern India.* Madras: privately printed, 1974. Available from William Carey Library, 1705
N. Sierra Bonita Ave., Pasadena, Calif.

Shrinivas, M.N. *Caste in Modern India.* New York: Asia Publishing House,
1962.

Soddy, Gordon. Quoted in preface of Peter McNee, *Crucial Issues in Bangladesh.* (cf. above.)

Thomas, M.M. Preface to Ninan Koshy, *Caste in the Kerala Churches* (cf. above).

    Some Theological Dialogues. Madras: Christian Literature Society, 1977.

Womack, David A. *Breaking the Stained Glass Barrier.* New York: Harper & Row, 1973.

Printed in the United States
44623LVS0000

3 4711 00177 4142

9 780878 081684